LOOKING BACK

HOWARD OBERST

PREFACE

In the ancient parable *The Blind Men and the Elephant* a group of blind men each touches a different part of an elephant and then describes to others what they believe the elephant looks like. This results in widely different descriptions of the same elephant. The parable teaches how people can perceive the world differently based on their firsthand experiences. The parable applies perfectly to DEA agents who rarely saw the whole story in real time.

Agents will have vastly different experiences depending on when and where they worked, what they were involved in, and the grade they held. There are commonalities among agents, but when their careers are over each one will have a collection of experiences uniquely their own. There are several books written about famous investigations and legendary agents like Kiki Camarena, Michael Levine, Louie Diaz, and others. However, there is a treasure trove of untold stories from the lives of everyday agents. Agents are some of the most humorous and engaging individuals you could ever work with. With that in mind, I tried to tell my stories with the humor fellow agents would appreciate.

Most of my stories are lighthearted. But law enforcement is a dangerous and serious business. I had friends injured and killed. Out of respect for their sacrifices, I felt compelled to include some of the serious realities of the job.

My oldest grandson Brady has always been fascinated with my stories and escapades. Ever since he was a little boy, he loved to sit and listen to my friends and me tell stories and laugh. Aware that one day I'd no longer be able to tell those stories, I decided to write some down. I started with a few short, humorous stories from my time as a street agent in Indianapolis. Then when my daughter, Sarah, read them, she was surprised and said, "Jeez dad, I never realized that's what you actually did." Her response puzzled me at first. Did she really not know?

Noel, another agent I worked with in Indianapolis, has a daughter, Monica. Monica and Sarah are friends and work together. Sarah told Monica about some of the crazy things their fathers had done. To my surprise, our daughters never really knew what their dads had been up to all those years. Even my wife, while editing for me, was surprised at what actually happened in South America. I responded with, "Well, you knew I was down there." To which she replied, "Yes, but I didn't know what you were actually doing!" Only then did I realize how much my own family didn't know. As unbelievable as that may sound, it was true. Now, compressing all those years into paragraphs and chapters describing the nitty gritty has brought it all back to life, even for me.

I shared my stories with some non-agent friends and their responses were unanimous, "You should write a book." Inspired by the interest and questions, I decided to go back to the beginning and tell the whole story. Thankfully, I had boxes of photographs, newspaper articles, letters, certificates, awards, travel logs, performance reviews and other documents that helped refresh my memories. What I did not have access to were my official DEA-6 investigative reports.

As I continued to write, I realized the best part of my story wasn't actually me. The best part came from all the amazing people I had the privilege of working with. Three years later the ramblings of an old man became a book.

DISCLAIMER

These writings are based on actual events that took place, in some cases decades ago. Memories do fade, but there are some things I'll never forget. I have done my best to tell the stories as accurately as I remember them.

The people in this book are real. They will certainly recognize themselves. Hopefully they will find my portrayals to be reasonably accurate and fair. Out of respect for their privacy, I've mostly used their first names. There are, however, some agents and people I've kept anonymous. In some cases where agents and officers have died, I used their last names to honor their memory. I have changed the names of all my defendants except for those who had already gained notoriety.

This is not a history book or a textbook. It's meant to be entertaining coupled with a few life lessons, and some interesting trivia. The opinions and observations expressed in this book are mine. They do not necessarily reflect those of the Drug Enforcement Administration or other special agents.

I used dialog to help color the mood and tone of the stories. Much of the dialog is close to verbatim. But these conversations were never recorded, so I can't swear to the absolute accuracy of every single word. It would be unrealistic to expect that.

Dedication

I am profoundly grateful for the support and encouragement I have received from so many people throughout my life. While it is not possible to recognize everyone, there are a few to whom I must extend my sincere appreciation. First, I express my deepest gratitude to my late parents, Roger and Betty, to whom I owe my very existence. To my deputy sheriff father who opened the door for me to start my law enforcement career.

To the late Don Hoppe the Darien police chief who gave this 20 year old kid a chance. To to the late Walworth County Deputy Sheriff Don Swart who spent years tutoring me in the fine art of interrogation. To Special Agent Bucky Beavers for his help and encouragement during difficult days at the DEA academy. To DEA Special Agent Tom Casey who was instrumental in transforming me into a DEA street agent. To Jon and Troy for guiding me through the complex world of covert tracking and satellites. To DEA Special Agent Rick who did his best to try and keep me out of trouble in Chicago. To Special Agent Dale for recovering my 'lost' badge. To DEA Special Agent Claud Davidson for giving me a new beginning after DEA.

And to my children Sarah and Jacob, along with my wife who made significant sacrifices due to my dedication to DEA. A special thanks to my wife Luanne for her endless hours of editing my writing in an effort to make me appear literate. And to Bob and Dianne Miskelly for helping in the final push.

COPYRIGHT

paperback ISBN 979-8-218-54088-3 *
e-book ISBN 979-8-218-55079-0

LOOKING BACK

CONTENTS

~ 1 ~

HOW IT BEGAN

The Call

I walked into the house just in time to answer the phone. The woman identified herself as Maria from the Drug Enforcement Administration's recruiting office. She asked me if I was still interested in accepting a position as a DEA Special Agent. I felt a rush of emotion as if I had won the lottery, while at the same time, a wave of ominous anxiety passed through me.

The next few words out of my mouth would decide the fate of the rest of my life. If I said yes, my life would change in ways I couldn't imagine. If I said no, I would spend the rest of my life wondering what might have been. My wife Luanne and I had spent a great deal of time discussing what to do if this call ever came. I knew I had her support, so there was no reason to hesitate. I told Maria yes. I would accept the position.

On May 16, 1985, I received the Offer of Employment letter instructing me to report at 9 AM, Monday, June 10, 1985, to the Milwaukee, Wisconsin DEA Resident Office. On that day I would be appointed a Drug Enforcement Administration Special Agent.

I was scheduled to start Basic Agent Training in BA Class number 38, beginning June 17 and ending September 13, 1985, at the Federal Law Enforcement Training Center in Glynco, Georgia. The last sentence in the second paragraph of the letter read, "Continued employment with the DEA is contingent upon successful completion of training..." I didn't grasp the significance of that sentence until later when some of my classmates were dismissed from the academy for failing to meet the required minimum standards. In fact, the academy was the final stage of the selection process. Accompanying the letter were several other forms including a Mobility Agreement. Signing it meant I agreed to be relocated anywhere within the United States.

It all seemed to be happening quickly. In reality, it was anything but. I initially applied for the position 20 months earlier on September 21, 1983. By submitting a five-page application called a Personal Qualification Statement Standard Form SF-171. This is the government's version of a basic employment application detailing background, education, employment history and references.

Within a few weeks, I received a letter informing me I met the basic requirements, and my application would begin processing. A medical examination was required including vision and hearing tests. In addition, an in-person interview was scheduled at the Chicago Division Office located in the Everett M. Dirksen Federal Building on North Dearborn Street.

When I arrived for my interview, a receptionist led me to an impressive conference room furnished with a large table surrounded by a dozen black leather chairs. I stood as the interview panel arrived. There were four senior Special Agents, all of them slightly older than me. They had a swagger about them, laughing and talking with each other as they introduced themselves. The interview started with the usual introductions and pleasantries. I noticed they had a copy of my SF-171 employment application. They knew everything about me, while I knew nothing about them.

For the first half hour, they took turns inquiring into various aspects of my past and the investigations I conducted. I sensed they pegged me, and rightly so, as a small-town cop with no experience in narcotics, no experience with complex conspiracy investigations and not well-traveled. I felt they were unimpressed with me.

In the next half hour, the tone changed. They started pressing me about whether or not I understood what I was getting into. One of them made a point of telling me that my first assignment could be New York City.

I explained that I had put a lot of effort into preparing for this job. I had gone to night school for years to finish my college degree. One of them responded, "This is not a job, it's not even a career. It's a lifestyle. Are you prepared to live the lifestyle of an agent?" In truth, I didn't know what he meant.

They continued driving home the point that an agent's work was different from police work. "You will work in dangerous environments, will be in and out of bars and nightclubs, put in long days and travel often. Is your wife going to be OK with that? You will be working undercover and dealing with some dangerous people. Can you handle that?"

It was clear they were challenging my conviction. I questioned myself, was I getting in over my head? Then I thought, wait a minute... I had over 10 years' experience as a cop. I had solved many crimes including home invasions, robberies, arson, and child abuse cases. I dealt with the aftereffects of suicides. I removed the bullet from the brain of a murder victim during his autopsy. I had investigated dozens of serious and fatal car crashes. I worked on a police boat where I rescued people from boating accidents and recovered the bodies of those who drowned. The job would require a huge commitment from me and my family. I understood their point, but I knew I could learn to do this job.

One of the agents rhetorically asked me if I could drive drunk, chuckling a little as he said it. I knew he was messing with me just to see how I would respond to an off the wall, awkward question. I shot back, "Well I've never done that, but I'd be willing to learn."

They laughed and one of them said, "I like this kid." I was 29 at the time.

For the rest of the interview, they took turns telling me how to prepare for Glynco. I guessed I had passed. As I was walking out, one guy said, "Hey, Howard, think about this: Divorce is common among DEA agents. This job will take a toll on you, your wife, and your kids. If you're not careful, it will consume you. I recommend you start a running regiment. Run at least every other day and build up your endurance. If you don't prepare, you'll never finish the academy."

I took his advice and started running. At first it was painful. I'd have to alternate running and walking. Eventually I could run several miles at a time. To combat the boredom, I would run as far as I could, ending up in a neighboring town where I would find a payphone and call my wife to pick me up. The agent was not exaggerating. The running part of the training was brutal, especially in Georgia's summer heat.

Top Secret Security Clearance

All DEA Special Agents hold a Top-Secret Security Clearance, which requires a comprehensive background investigation. Agents must disclose every detail of their lives including every residence, school attended, and all jobs. That information was entered into a Standard Form 86 Security Investigation disclosure form. In my case, the document totaled 18 pages that I submitted November 25, 1983.

In 1983 the FBI conducted my DEA Background Investigation. They investigated every item on the application, including a paper route when I was 12 years old. They also used my information to develop other people to interview, all in an effort to determine my worthiness to possess the clearance. I knew the FBI was investigating me after several people called to tell me an FBI Agent was asking questions about me. Later in my career, the DEA began conducting their own clearance investigations. I participated in several applicant clearances and learned how thorough those investigations are.

One objective was to identify anything in the applicant's past that could be used to extort them. The applicant's financial status and their ability to manage their finances are both crucial factors. The DEA had learned from experience that employees with poor personal finances are often more prone to corruption and internal theft.

On July 20, 1984, I received a letter confirming that my background investigation was complete, and I was suitable for employment. The letter noted that "many thousands of applicants apply for agent positions, and very few successfully pass all the hurdles..."

When I received my offer of employment I was living in Delavan, Wisconsin with my wife and two young children. I was serving as the Police Chief for the Town of Delavan. My wife and I shared a car, but we would now need a second car. A friend of mine owned a local gas station and sold used cars. I bought a $400 puke yellow Ford Pinto station wagon with faux wood paneling and rust spots that no one else wanted. My friend priced it cheap.

I notified the town board chairman, Wayne, that I had accepted a position as a DEA Special Agent and had to report in two weeks. I offered him my resignation to take effect on June 10, 1985. He told me he would not accept my resignation until I completed the academy. Then, if I still wanted to resign, he would accept it.

Years earlier Wayne had served as a part-time police officer under my dad, who was then the Police Chief for the village of Walworth. Later my dad left the police department to join the Walworth County Sheriff's Department where he rose to the rank of sergeant.

Twenty years later, I was the Police Chief for Delavan Township and Wayne was the elected Town Chairman and my boss. Wayne owned a TV and appliance store but retained his passion for police work. He was an advocate of our police department as well as supporting my appointment with the DEA.

I Will Support and Defend the Constitution

I woke early on Monday, June 10, 1985, and put on my black suit, white shirt and tie, the same outfit I had worn for my initial interview. I got into my ugly yellow Ford Pinto and headed east on I-43 to Milwaukee. I arrived early and waited in the hall for the staff to arrive. The office support women arrived first. I soon learned agents rarely arrived first. The women were friendly, welcoming me and introducing themselves. One of them told me Lee, the Resident Agent in Charge, RAC, would be in soon. In the meantime, I should make myself at home.

The office had a bullpen layout in one large open room. The desks were next to six large windows overlooking the Milwaukee skyline. Within a few minutes, Lee arrived and welcomed me to the DEA family. Lee told me I couldn't do much until I completed the academy. The first week was considered a dead week. I completed and signed several forms including health insurance, life insurance, and tax deduction forms.

The next agent to arrive was Bob. He was a few years older than me. He told me that he'd started with DEA two years ago. He was a police officer in Iowa before joining DEA. Prior to that he had been an Army infantry squad leader while serving in Vietnam.

The boss asked Bob to schedule a time with a magistrate to swear me in. Soon the other agents arrived, two men and a woman. The female's name was Jeannie. Like me, she had grown up in Walworth County. She was a couple of years younger than me, tall with long dark hair, attractive, gregarious, and intelligent. Bob said she was perfect for undercover assignments and did a lot of them.

Bill was the next agent I met. He was 10-12 years older than me, tall with an athletic build. He seemed more aloof than the others. Once I learned how the DEA hierarchy worked, I understood his aloofness. A GS-13 is the highest grade a street agent can achieve before becoming a GS-14 supervisor. Grade13 agents are a bit like army sergeants. They take charge when the GS-14 supervisor is absent.

Bill was the only agent other than the boss with a private office. He showed me to his office where he told me he was the designated Security Officer. He presented me with a one-page typed document with no title on it. The first sentence said, 'Welcome to the Drug Enforcement Administration.' The document detailed rules and regulations related to security matters. Most of it addressed prohibited disclosures of classified and sensitive information which included everything I saw, heard, or knew about within the confines of the DEA. This non-disclosure rule applied to everyone outside DEA and specifically noted spouses, family, and friends. He instructed me to read and sign the document, asking if I had questions. I told him, "No, I understand."

About 4 PM Bob said, "We have to go. We're due in Magistrate Court in 15 minutes." I followed him through the building to a federal courtroom where the judge was finishing a hearing. After the courtroom cleared, the judge called Bob and told us to approach the bench.

The judge congratulated me, saying this was no small achievement. He added that being an agent of the government brought with it enormous responsibilities. He asked me if I understood the significance of the oath I was about to take. He went on, "You understand you are about to swear to defend the Constitution of the United States, including the amendments known as the Bill of Rights. In the course of your duties as an agent of the government, you must never overstep your bounds and violate anyone's civil liberties as defined by the Bill of Rights." I nodded and said, "Yes sir, I understand."

Judge: "Raise your right hand and repeat after me, I will support and defend the Constitution of the United States against all enemies, foreign and domestic, that I will bear true faith and allegiance to the same, that I take this obligation freely, with no mental reservation or purpose of evasion, and that I will faithfully discharge the duties of the office on which I am about to enter. So, help me God."

With that, I was a sworn Special Agent of the Drug Enforcement Administration. Bob and I returned to the office where everyone shook my hand and congratulated me. Bob announced it was time to adjourn and reconvene at the Hilton Hotel bar down the street from the office. Bob bought me my first official drink as a DEA agent. As staff began leaving, they wished me good luck at Glynco. It was just Bob and me. I confessed to him I was getting nervous. He said, "The drinks here are expensive and watered down. Let's go. I know a better place." We got into his vehicle and drove to a small neighborhood bar where we took a table in the back. While we were drinking whiskey and cokes, he began telling me about his investigations, all of which were interesting.

The building had a back door three feet from the end of the bar that opened to an alley. Patrons had been coming in and out that door all night long. I looked up to see the door open and a uniformed police officer stepped inside. The bartender walked over and poured him a shot. He slammed it down, turned and walked back out. I was still that small town cop and drinking on duty was something I wasn't used to seeing.

Without thinking, I blurted out to Bob in a whisper, "Whoa, did you see that?" Bob looked at me, tilted his head slightly forward, raised his eyebrows and said, "I didn't see anything and neither did you." I knew how Dorothy felt when she realized she wasn't in Kansas anymore.

When we got back to my car, Bob said, "When you get to the academy, remember everything you do is evaluated, measured, and scored. Don't be the guy in first place and, above all, don't fall into last place. Stay in the middle and don't draw attention to yourself. One more thing, they're going to mess with you. Don't whine or lose your temper. If they start to dog you, stay focused. The one thing they can't do is stop the clock. You will get through as long as you don't quit."

Thursday Lee gave me my orders with the instructions I would need to report to the academy. The boss told me to go home, spend time with my family and get my affairs in order. He wished me luck and said he would see me when I got back.

~ 2 ~

GLYNCO

Finding Glynco

I went home and packed a suitcase with everything I thought I might need. My head was spinning, but I tried to stay focused and pay as much attention as I could to my wife and kids. Family and friends stopped by, knowing I was leaving soon. Our ugly yellow Ford Pinto got a lot of laughs, but my canned answer was, "It starts every time."

My wife finally said she didn't want me to drive the Pinto to Georgia. I told her I didn't care what it looked like. She replied, "It's not how it looks. I'm not sure it will make it that far. You take the Mercury, and I'll drive the Pinto."

This was 1985, a time before cellphones, computers and Google maps. I looked in a Rand McNally Road Atlas to locate the town of Glynco where the Federal Law Enforcement Training Center, FLETC, was located. I couldn't find Glynco. Then I remembered someone had told me Glynco was near Brunswick, Georgia. I found Brunswick, it was about 1,100 miles from our house. I estimated it would be a two day drive, so I would need to leave on Saturday morning.

What a heartbreaking morning that turned out to be. My daughter, Sarah, was six and was daddy's girl. She had never been away from me for longer than an overnight with her grandparents. My son, Jacob, was two, old enough to know something big was happening. The kids were crying, holding on to my legs. I was trying to keep it together. My wife was the strong one. She told me they would be fine once I left. As I backed out of the driveway, I saw Sarah standing inside the glass front door with her hands holding her head, crying her eyes out.

I drove all day Saturday, stopping north of Atlanta where I got the cheapest motel I could find. Sunday morning, I filled the gas tank and headed for Brunswick on the Georgia coast, halfway between Savannah, Georgia and Jacksonville, Florida. When I finally saw the Welcome to Brunswick sign, I stopped at a gas station to get directions to Glynco.

This was June 16, 1985, about 6:30 PM in the southeast corner of Georgia. When I got out of the air-conditioned car, the heat and humidity smacked me in the face. Then it hit me, the most gawd-awful, foul smell of rotten eggs I'd ever encountered! I thought, what could smell that bad?

I went inside and asked the guy behind the counter if he could tell me how to get to Glynco. In a heavy southern accent he said, "Where?" I repeated myself, speaking slower and clearer. "G L Y N C O."

"I heard you the first time. I don't know where G L Y N C O is."

"It's a town somewhere close to here. Do you live around here?"

"Yep, all my life. Look, buddy, where are you trying to go?"

"I'm trying to find the Federal Law Enforcement Training Center."

"Then why didn't you just say that?"

I was about 20 minutes away. I'm not sure if he was messing with me because of my Wisconsin plate or if 'Glynco' isn't used by the locals. My guess was he was messing with me. As I was leaving, I asked, "By the way, what the hell is that smell?" He laughed. "That's the paper mill. I'm used to it. I don't even smell it anymore."

As I pulled up to the front gate, I saw a 'Welcome to the Federal Law Enforcement Training Center' sign. A guard came out of the security shack to greet me. I identified myself. He checked the clipboard and said, "OK, D E A," like it was my name. "You're scheduled for a 7 PM meeting in the Welcome Center," and pointed to a building and parking lot inside the gate. There weren't many cars in the lot.

When I entered the building, it was buzzing with the basic agent trainees of the BA-38 class. A distinguished-looking man in a dark suit greeted me and identified himself as Rudy. He asked for my name. I told him and he said, "Great, you're with me. I'm your class counselor. We're the Red Team. Come over and introduce yourself to the rest of the guys." The names came too fast to remember any of them. There were eleven of us on the Red Team.

I did a quick assessment. Everyone in the room was about my age, 28-32. I was thirty-one, in the middle of the pack. Bob would be proud. Rudy told us to hang out for a bit. The Class Coordinator, Robert, was on his way to welcome us. I learned that most of the students had flown into Jacksonville Airport and the academy transported them by bus. That explained the empty parking lot.

I noticed everyone was dressed in either a suit or a sport coat. I'd been in the car all day and was wearing a Milwaukee Brewers T-shirt and sweatpants, clearly under-dressed. I told Rudy I needed to change clothes. He said not to worry about it, "Tonight is informal." The room was humming as the four counselors sorted out and rounded up their respective teams before Robert arrived.

About 7:00 PM Robert walked in like a man on a mission. He wore a dark suit and wire-rim glasses. After introducing himself, he welcomed us to the academy. He said our counselors would give us our housing assignments. Then he told us to get settled and classes would start in the morning. As he started toward the door to leave, he walked by me, stopped, looked me up and down and asked, "Where the hell do you think you are? This is not a damn ballpark. You show up on your first day at the academy dressed like that. Who are you?" He looked at Rudy, shook his head as if to say, you better straighten this guy out. All I could hear in my head was Bob's last words to me: "Do not draw attention."

Rudy gave us a 15-page booklet with a blue cover titled *DEA Office of Training - Class Schedule*. The first page had the trainees' names broken into four teams: Blue, Gold, Red and Green. The book also showed the class divided in half with Group A comprised of Gold and Blue Teams, and Group B comprised of Rudy's Red Team and the Green Team. The groups and teams would make sense later when we began training and doing breakouts.

There were two numbers behind each name. Mine was 381/210. This meant I was in building 381 and my room number was 210. Rudy motioned us to follow him to the parking lot. He pointed down the main road and told us to walk in that direction until we found our building. "Inside you'll find your assigned rooms." It was still hotter than hell and someone asked how far it was. Rudy said, "Not far."

I was already a little suspicious of Rudy so I told the guys on my Red Team that I had a car and would shuttle them. It ended up being about a ½ mile, not far by car. It was 90 degrees with 90% humidity and, dressed in a suit, dragging suitcases, it was more than 'not far.' As I shuttled back and forth, the column of nicely dressed trainees plodded along. One by one, they peeled off their suit coats exposing sweat-soaked shirts. For the next 13 weeks, my car made me a popular guy.

My room

There were eight guys assigned to my building. We each had our own bedroom. Those were the guys that became my closest friends. We shared a communal living room that became headquarters for our study groups.

We dropped off our stuff and six of us set out to find the lecture hall where we were to report in the morning. We found a path behind our townhouse that went past a pond through a wooded area and came out near the lecture hall. It was a 10-minute walk. The cafeteria was a 5-minute walk from the lecture hall. The gym was a little farther, maybe a 20-minute walk from the townhouse. The academy had the vibe of a college campus.

After I returned to my room, I began unpacking and found a framed picture of my wife and kids under my clothes. I smiled and put it on my dresser. I stuffed my Brewers T-shirt in the side pocket of my suitcase vowing never to wear it again. I hoped Robert would forget my name and maybe even my face, but I knew he wouldn't forget that shirt.

There was a knock on my door. It was Hector from Puerto Rico. While talking, he noticed my Milwaukee Brewers baseball hat on the dresser. "Whoa, I love the Brewers, and I really like that hat."

"You like the hat? It's yours. I have a T-shirt too if you want it." I figured after being publicly chastised, he would decline.

"Are you sure?" He must not have seen my ass-chewing.

"Yeah, I have a ton of that stuff at home. You can have it, just don't wear it around here."

Week One

I was too nervous to eat so I showered, put on my black suit and walked to the lecture hall building. Inside was a big lobby with a bank of doors that opened into the lecture hall. To the left was a glass-enclosed office where I could see staff moving about. The lecture hall had a stage with theater-style tiered desks fitted neatly together in three rows divided by a center aisle. On each desk there was a cardboard nameplate, a stack of books and miscellaneous course material.

Seated on my right was Brian from Chicago and on my left was William from Phoenix. William lived in a different townhouse and was assigned to group A. I was in Group B, so I never got to know William well. We talked a little in the classroom and he told me he was an attorney. About three months after we graduated, I learned William was killed during an undercover operation. He was shot in the back seat of a car when a drug buy turned into a robbery.

The booklet we received Sunday night included a schedule detailing activities we would be doing hour by hour, day by day, for the next 13 weeks. Today, 8:30 to 12:30, was orientation and staff introductions, lunch, and from 1:30 to 5:30, student introductions. During staff introductions I learned the counselors were not permanent staff. They were field agents on temporary assignment to mentor students through training.

Robert took the stage and told us there were several recreational activities available on campus, such as softball and basketball. He strongly recommended that we, "don't participate." If we were injured, the academy would dismiss us. Next, he told us to examine the nine-page *REQUIREMENTS FOR SUCCESSFUL COMPLETION OF THE DEA SPECIAL AGENT TRAINING PROGRAM* booklet. The document outlined the requirements for passing the training program. There would be two exams every Monday morning, one covering law and the other general knowledge. Failing either of these would put us on permanent academic probation. Failing a second test would result in dismissal from the academy. In addition, failing to meet the required physical fitness tests, firearms qualifications, practical applications skills and driving skills would result in dismissal.

The Basic Agent Review Board, BARB, was the procedure used to dismiss someone from the academy for anything deemed unsatisfactory. Robert then took off his glasses, set them on the podium, panned slowly across the room and said, "I want to make one thing perfectly clear. You are not Special Agents. You are Basic Agent Trainees, BATS. If, and I mean if, you finish this academy and graduate, only then will you be a DEA Special Agent. One more thing, unless you can prove you are a direct descendant of Captain Kidd, get rid of the earrings."

The Offer of Employment letter I received clearly stated, "Continued employment with the DEA is contingent upon the successful completion of training..." The reality of what that meant began to sink in. Robert dismissed us for lunch. When we returned, there were a dozen staff members and instructors sitting in the front row. Robert came to the podium and said it was time for us to introduce ourselves. He began calling us up one at a time in no particular order.

The staff had copies of our SF-171 personal history form. The exercise turned into a chaotic, probing, prodding, taunting, no holds barred circus. One of the staff members spoke six or seven languages. He would stand up and converse in whatever language a student claimed to speak. It was impressive and intimidating. The afternoon was a non-stop exercise in stress-overload. Considering our ages and backgrounds, it should not have been that difficult, but the staff's tactics were strategic.

Most of the trainees had successful backgrounds and accomplishments and DEA was a second career. As the introductions progressed, no one stood out, except for one man. When San Diego

Jeff took the stage, he got the usual first question: "Why do you want to be a DEA agent?"

"For the same reason I joined the military. I want to be where the action is. I volunteered for Vietnam but missed out. I stayed in the military until I heard about DEA. I knew that's what I wanted to do. In fact, I'd like to volunteer for Mexico."

Robert: "You know if you graduate, your first office will be a domestic office. Nobody is assigned to a foreign office after graduation." His point may have been taken into consideration because he drew San Diego as his first assignment.

On April 28, 1988 the television program *48 Hours* aired an episode titled *"In the Cocaine War"* a documentary featuring *Operation Snowcap*. They interviewed a couple of DEA agents in the jungles of South America, one of which was my classmate San Diego Jeff who on day one had volunteered for Mexico. He had successfully made his way to the front lines in the "War on Drugs."

I found out later why he referenced Mexico. In February 1985, a drug cartel kidnapped DEA Special Agent Kiki Camarena in Guadalajara, Mexico. Cartel members horribly tortured and murdered him. This incident gained national attention and outrage. Initially, the Mexican government didn't cooperate with DEA's investigation. That changed when US Customs Agents unofficially shut down entrance into the US for Mexican commercial trucks. Agents began thoroughly inspecting every truck, which created a back-up extending for miles. This show of solidarity with DEA crushed the Mexican economy. Once the DEA got the cooperation they needed from the Mexican government, Customs Agents began allowing trucks to move across the border again.

It was my turn. I expected some kind of comment about my Milwaukee Brewers T-shirt from the first day. But I got the same generic question: "Why do you want to be a DEA Agent?" I answered, "I've been a police officer for 10 years. I loved the job, but this opportunity could take me to the next level." Fortunately, I was the last interview of the day. Robert joined me on the stage and announced the session was over. I left the stage, feeling euphoric, and thinking, "Boy, did I luck out?" As I was leaving the lecture hall, the Green Team counselor made eye contact with me and slightly flipped his head to motion me over. When I got close, he said in a muffled voice, "Get rid of those shoes." I was wearing new shoes. I must have had a puzzled look. He repeated it, "Get rid of the shoes. This place is not a friggin' country club." Apparently, brown shoes with beige soles made them look casual.

My wife and I did not have extra money. I emptied our savings account, $400, hoping to make it stretch for the duration of the academy. Buying new shoes wasn't part of the plan.

Fast forward the time machine 39 years to 2024. I had recently finished the first draft of this book which my wife had been reading/editing with me. Together we attended the retired agents convention in Charleston, South Carolina. Aware of the infamous brown shoes with beige trimmed soles story, she began pointing out all the retired agents sporting the formerly felonious shoes. She was like a mosquito in my ear as she continuously leaned over and whispered, "There's another pair." Everybody's a comedian. Back to Glynco.

When I got back to the townhouse, Mike was there. Mike was a police officer from Dallas, Texas, but he fit my image of a Texas Ranger. Mike was grumbling about one counselor, who he called Bullet. Bullet told Mike to, "Get rid of the cowboy boots. This isn't a frigging rodeo." I asked him what he was going to do. He said, "Ah, it's no big deal. I brought a regular pair of shoes." I told him about my shoes and that I didn't have a second pair. Mike was baffled. "I understand him not liking my cowboy boots, but there is nothing wrong with your shoes. Maybe he thinks they look too casual." Mike had an idea. We walked to the convenience store down the street, where I bought a round tin of black shoe paste. The two of us worked the paste into the edge of the soles, giving them a black finish.

Later that night we returned to the academy where we were issued four white shirts and four pairs of brown pants and ugly brown baseball caps with big yellow DEA letters. They were the same shade of yellow as my puke yellow Pinto I'd left in Wisconsin.

My range group

Next we had photos taken for our laminated student ID badges. Two more copies went to a print shop for our official DEA credentials. The last copy was made into a projector slide. The staff conducted weekly progress reviews where our pictures were displayed on a screen as they discussed us. The photograph ensured the instructors and counselors were talking about the same trainee.

In 1992 I was a counselor at Quantico for BA-89 and participated in those weekly reviews. The process was the same. The reviews are necessary and productive. The process could also result in a bandwagon effect. Counselors and instructors opinions can influence other instructors. Negative comments in particular could take on a life of their own and follow a student throughout the duration of their training. I witnessed this with one of my trainees. In my opinion, an instructor had assessed him unfairly. This forced me to disagree with the instructor. As it turned out, I was right. The trainee developed into an excellent agent.

The next day we reported to the lecture hall. Robert walked to the podium. He looked angry and said, "This will never happen again. Do we understand each other?" None of us had a clue as to what had happened or what we had done. "When anyone takes this stage, be it an instructor or janitor, you will stand in unison and greet them with a 'Good morning, sir' or 'Good afternoon, sir.' I need a volunteer to call the class to attention." When our first instructor took the stage, he was greeted with a loud 'Good Morning, Sir,' as we stood tall. Thus began our first official class lecture on DEA's organizational structure and its mission.

For the next three days we had non-stop lectures on all things drugs: stimulants, crank, cocaine, opiates, depressants, heroin, cannabis, hash, LSD, MDMA, Ecstasy, meth, designer drugs, crack, hallucinogens, plus the legal drugs that were commonly abused. The sheer volume of information coming at us was staggering. It was like trying to drink from a fire hose. As the lectures droned on, my mind wandered back to the interview in Chicago when the agent remarked that I knew nothing about drugs. Now I understood what he meant.

Philadelphia Bob had the room next to mine in the townhouse. Before joining DEA, he was a narcotics detective on the Philadelphia Police Department. All week I asked him a ton of questions. He answered all my questions, no matter how dumb they were. We all liked Bob. He was a class-act.

We learned DEA's primary weapon is information and it must be managed correctly. Our job as agents was to collect it and use it in a way that would make a mission possible. Much time was devoted to interviewing and interrogation, something I was good at. Classes included lots of Practical Exercises, PEs, comprised of role players acting as drug suspects. Everything was done under the watchful eye of the instructors and counselors.

To cap off the first week, we had a medical exam and blood draw. The blood draw predetermined our blood type in case an emergency blood transfusion was ever needed. I am sure it also included a complete drug screen. Like President Ronald Reagan famously said, "Trust but verify."

The weekends were long prompting me to study a lot. I did my laundry every Sunday. The washers and dryers were free. I also gathered my change and called Lu and the kids from the payphone in front of our townhouse. Talking to them gave me peace of mind that all was well at home. The guys relied on me and my station wagon to take them into town for shopping trips. I enjoyed driving them and it helped fill my time.

Gym Class

The class was split into two groups. The groups alternated between firearms training and gym class. Friday of the first week Group A reported to the firearms range for orientation, while Group B reported to the gym. When we arrived, we met our primary PT instructor, Darrell. Next to him was a canvas cart filled with gym shirts and shorts, he told us to take two shirts and two pairs of shorts. He led us to a weight room where he told us, "This is where we'll start every class. We'll be using these 10 machines working in pairs. The first 30 minutes of class are three minutes at each station, rotating every one and a half minutes on my whistle. I've got some good workout music to keep you pumping."

He showed us to the back door of the gym where a barrel of body grease was kept. "Before we go out to run, you're going to want to stop here and grease your nipples and inner thighs to protect yourself from chafing. You will go out this door and form two columns in the parking lot. The two people at the front of the column will be the road guards. When the column approaches an intersection, the guards will sprint ahead and block the intersection by raising their arms up. I need a volunteer to be the cadence caller." Brian raised his hand and said he'd done that in the Marine

Corps. He gave Brian a sheet of paper with cadence songs and told him to memorize them.

We went back inside and he led us to the laundry area. "When we come back in from our run, you're gonna need a dry shirt. Throw your wet one in the bin and these nice ladies will give you a new one."

He then led us to a smaller gym with cushioned mats covering the floor. "This is where our self-defense training will take place including boxing, judo and everyone's favorite, Aikido. I'll warn you now it's going to get physical and rough." DEA doesn't train agents to become black belts in martial arts. They train them to survive violent altercations. We learned specific moves and dynamic techniques to effectively end a fight quickly. We drilled these techniques repeatedly until they became instinctive and embedded in our muscle memory.

He showed us the indoor swimming pool. "Y'all know how to swim, right? This pool is 10 feet deep, so if you can't, tell me now. OK boys, that's it, the tour's over. Your schedule shows PT starting at 7:30 AM and ending at 9:30 AM. Because this is summer in Georgia, we're going to start at 6:00 AM instead of 7:30. We have to finish our run before the sun comes up because the temperature will skyrocket. The academy shuts down all outdoor exercise with a black flag after 90 degrees."

Sunday Morning Calls

I promised my wife I would call her every Sunday morning. There was a coin payphone in front of our townhouse. I had been saving my change, leaving it loose on top of my dresser. I scooped it up and took it to the phone booth and spread it out on top of the pedestal.

As soon as Luanne answered, a recording came on telling me to, "Please deposit $1.60 for the first three minutes." When I got down to 30 seconds left, the recording came on again and said, "Please deposit 90 cents for an additional three minutes."

I gave her an emergency contact number. She told me everything was fine and asked if I had any problems getting there. I told her the drive was easy, and I made it in time for the 7 PM meeting which I hadn't known about until I got there. She asked how that went, and I told her it was great, no problems. I left out the part about the Brewers T-shirt.

She put Sarah on the phone. "Hi Daddy!" I said hi and asked what she had been doing? She said they had been going to the beach and great-grandma's house. I could tell she was getting a little weepy. "Mommy says you can't come home. Why? I really want you to come home."

"Don't worry. I'll be home soon. You have fun and take care of your little brother." Lu came back on, and I told her I was about to run out of change, so I'd call next week. My wife was so supportive. She held things together and sent me cards, letters, and drawings from the kids almost every day. We received our mail in an old-fashioned mail call every day in the lecture hall. Within days I got this letter from my daughter "How was your trip...I wish you could come back...I like you."

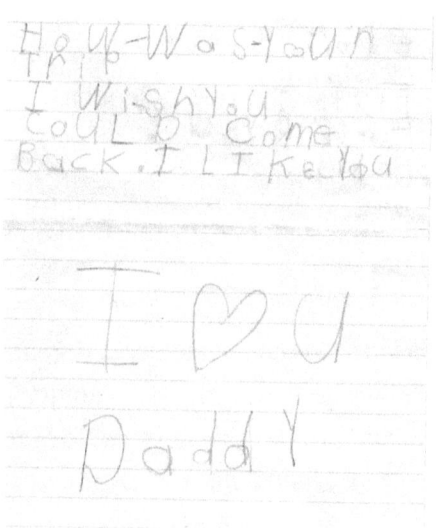

Sarah's note to Daddy

Bucky

After I got off the phone, I walked behind the townhouse to check out the pond we'd been walking by every day. I was standing next to the water, admiring the blue sky. It was a gorgeous day except for the ever-present smell from the paper mill. The pond was like a sheet of glass. Out of nowhere, an alligator appeared inches from my feet. I could've slapped him on the head with a stick if I'd had one. I did a fast high-step backwards and watched his head slowly drop under the water.

I hightailed it back to the townhouse and found David sitting at the kitchen table doing a crossword puzzle. "Dave, Dave, there's an alligator in the pond behind our townhouse." Without even looking up, he replied, "Call me Rusty. Nobody calls me David."

"OK, but I'm serious. The thing was only a foot away from my feet."

"Bud, every pond in Florida and Georgia has gators. Somebody's been feeding him."

"Is he dangerous?"

"Probably not to us, but he'll snatch a dog or a kid in a New York second."

Brian soon changed Rusty's nickname to Bucky, a nickname he kept for the rest of his career and beyond. Bucky Beavers was a character created by Disney in the 1950s to promote Ipana toothpaste. Brian began calling him Bucky because his last name was coincidentally Beavers.

Bucky said, "I'm bored. Do you want to get out of here for a while? Let's go somewhere and get some actual food." I wanted to explore the area anyway. As we walked outside, I offered to drive. He looked at my Mercury station wagon and said, "You're kidding, right?" We walked a short distance to another lot. Parked under a shade tree was a beautiful gold Nissan 300ZX. In amazement, I asked if that was his car. He replied "No, I'm gonna steal it! Of course it's mine. Let's go."

We ended up at a waterfront restaurant on St. Simons Island. When we walked in, Bucky told the hostess he wanted a table on the balcony with a view of the water, not in the direct sun. A server soon came over. I ordered a Diet Coke. She turned to Bucky to get his order. He was staring at me, "A Diet Coke, seriously?" He shook his head and said, "I'll start with a beer and a dozen oysters on the half shell with lots of extra hot sauce." I hadn't looked at the menu, so I ordered a cheeseburger and fries.

I became aware of the smell of the ocean. It smelled great! Evidently, the steady breeze coming off the water pushed the stench of the paper mill inland where it hovered over the academy.

Bucky had a witty smack-talking sense of humor that made me laugh. Yet he still had the cool confidence of a Mel Gibson in *Lethal Weapon*. He asked if I'd ever had oysters on the half shell. I said no, but I'd had oyster stew. He laughed. Being a farm boy from Wisconsin, raw oysters didn't appeal to me. "I ordered enough so you can try some. They're delicious." He asked what I did before DEA, and I told him I had been on a small police department in Wisconsin for 11 years.

"What was your rank?" I told him I was the chief.

"Whoa, you were the Chief?"

"Yeah, but it was a small department."

"Chief, that's what I'm going to call you from now on."

He told me he had been an Seminole County deputy sheriff assigned to the Orlando DEA Task Force. "I know how all this DEA stuff works in the real world. A task force officer does everything the agents do. Walking into a task force office, you wouldn't know the difference between a cop and an agent. Plus, I'm a pilot so most of my time was spent flying. Did you know DEA has an air wing with over one hundred different aircraft? There is currently a shortage of pilots, which is why I was recruited."

I asked him why the place was called Glynco. He told me it dated back to WWII when it was a Navy airbase named Naval Air Station Glynco. "The government took it over and turned it into the Federal Law Enforcement Training Center, FLETC. Customs is the lead agency. DEA is one of 30 agencies that train here. The place is huge. There's even an abandoned airport on the backside. There are entire neighborhoods of empty ranch houses left over from the military. DEA uses some of them for practical exercises."

I asked him what he meant by practical exercises. "You know, mock drug deals, arrests and raids. It's all pretend. DEA hires role players and the exercises follow a script. The exercises start out simple then get progressively longer and more complex. Some go all night."

Bucky asked, "How did you manage to get here without knowing any of this?" I answered, "To be honest, the first DEA agent I ever met was at my interview."

"Now that is impressive. If you don't have someone pulling strings, it's extremely difficult to get selected by DEA. There are hundreds of applicants for every opening. There are only about 2,000 agents worldwide, which is about the same number of SEALs the Navy has."

The server brought our food and Bucky's platter of oysters was a sight to behold. To me they looked like cow snot on a seashell. Watching him eat them was even more mesmerizing. He doused each one with a huge amount of red sauce and sucked them into his mouth with a slurp. Watching him slam beers and slurp oysters was all Rodney Dangerfield. I knew then we were going to be friends. The server brought our bills. Bucky took both and said, "Don't worry, Chief. I got you covered."

As we were walking back to his car, he asked me if I wanted to go anywhere else. I told him no. I was ready to go back. I suggested maybe he could keep the speedometer in double digits. He said, "Oh, sorry Chief, no can do. I'll be blasting past that in third gear."

After a heart-stopping ride back, he dropped me off in front of the town house. With that, he shot out of sight toward the front gate. Bucky was already living the agent's lifestyle my interviewers had alluded to. Monday morning, we woke up to find Bucky passed out on the couch face down, smelling like a bad hangover. Mike said he heard him come in about 4 AM. When I woke him he said, "Hold on, I'll be ready in 10 minutes." Ten minutes later he came bouncing down, showered, looking sharp and talking a mile a minute about what a fun time he had last night. The six of us, Bucky, Mike, Bob, Hector, Brian, and I headed to class.

Firearms

On the first day of firearms the Unit Chief welcomed us as six firearms instructors gave us a handbook explaining the safety rules and range commands. The chief made no bones about it. Any kind of flagrant safety violation would be grounds for dismissal. He told us we would be given three chances to qualify. Failure to do so would result in dismissal from the academy.

The indoor shooting range had thirty lanes each equipped with a remote-controlled overhead target rail. The rails carried targets to specific distances and rotated them. Timed exercises ended when the target turned sideways.

The outdoor range had the same number of lanes. The lanes had designated shooting stations at fixed distances ranging from 50 yards down to seven feet. Most of our training drills took place at the 7-foot and 21-foot mark. These were the distances in which historically most DEA shootings occurred. Examples include motel rooms, inside houses or in close quarters around a vehicle. The drills were designed to develop our ability to shoot fast without giving up accuracy.

The other half of the outdoor range was a tactical course furnished with shot-up cars, metal desks and mock-up door frames.

Here we practiced tactical maneuvers like shooting and moving between cover positions.

BULLET HOLES ARE PROMINENT IN THE REAR of this late model car which was involved in a high speed chase through the city of Delavan early Sunday morning. The rear window was a victim of a Delavan police shotgun blast, after the fugitive, wanted in connection with an armed robbery in Janesville Saturday night, tried to get away from Delavan police. After abandoning his car in a field near Walworth, and a subsequent man hunt, the suspect was arrested near Bailey road and County Trunk F. (Delavan Enterprise photo)

Bullet holes in the suspect's vehicle

During one of the drills, I found myself shooting over the hood of a car which brought back a memory. When I was on the police department, an armed robbery took place at a K-Mart store in Janesville, Wisconsin. While escaping, the two robbery suspects got separated. One fled on foot, broke into a house and took the family hostage. The second one escaped in their car. The fleeing suspect was spotted by Delavan officers driving through town, heading toward Milwaukee. The officers chased the vehicle. I heard them report over the radio they had been shot at.

We set up a roadblock using two patrol cars. As the suspect approached us at a high rate of speed, it appeared he was going to smash into us. With no other choice, we opened fire at his car causing him to veer off the road, down an embankment, through a fence and into a cornfield. For the next three hours, twenty police officers from six different departments continued to pursue him on foot in sub-zero weather. When we finally caught him, his ears and fingers were severely frostbitten.

Our tactical training would be taken to a new level. DEA uniformly trains agents to work cohesively in a technique known as the 'snake.' The snake provides a coordinated tactical approach to high-risk entries. When executed correctly, it is speed combined with overwhelming force that makes it effective.

When preparing to breach a door, four or five agents line up at a 90 degree angle to the doorway. First in line is the Breacher. His only job is to bust the door open then step aside. Behind him is the Number One position. He enters first, followed by Two and Three. The Breacher rejoins at the end of the line. The 'snake' moves quickly, securing each room, overwhelming the suspects with the speed of action. If the leader, One, is shot, number Two takes the lead, providing cover as Three and Four extract the injured agent. The agents withdraw in an orderly manner, providing cover for one another as they systematically rotate out. Executing this technique at full speed requires a lot of practice especially with instructors providing obstructions.

DEA also used the newest technology at that time called FATS, Firearms Training System. This was an audio-visual shoot/don't shoot simulator. A video played on a six-foot-by-six-foot screen that immersed us in the action as seen through the camera lens. The FATS system presented us with a series of scenarios as they unfolded. The challenge was to decide if or when it was necessary to fire our weapon. The time we had to make decisions was measured in milliseconds.

The simulator trained or rather forced us to focus on the suspect's hands rather than their eyes. Humans are programmed to look each other in the eyes. But the real threat is the hands, not the eyes. The simulator's programming made each exercise progressively more difficult and frustrating. The scenarios eventually became impossible to survive, which was the point. It prepared us to accept the fact that we may encounter a situation that is simply not survivable.

We were issued a six-shot revolver. We fired at least one hundred rounds per session, mostly dedicated to close-quarters, combat-style shooting. We also shot from the 50-yard line. Shooting from that distance required a much steadier hand and a smooth trigger pull. That was when I noticed my gun had a slight catch on one of the cylinders. It only affected one cylinder, but it was causing me to miss every sixth shot at the 50-yard line. It wouldn't prevent me from qualifying, but it would ruin any chance of winning Top Gun. I was a good shot and had won first place in tactical shooting at the basic police academy in Wisconsin.

After I discovered the flaw, I told the armorer when I turned my gun in. I made the mistake of suggesting he smooth it out with an emery cloth. He looked me straight in the eyes for a full five seconds. That's a long time! He sarcastically said, "Sure, let me

Cleaning my gun

get right on that for you," as he turned and placed my gun back in the rack. I knew I had overstepped, thinking, "What an idiot!" I just told a gunsmith how to fix a gun." I couldn't take the words back. I had to tolerate the burr for the rest of the training.

On the last range day in week twelve, we started our routine at the 50-yard line. Immediately I could feel the trigger action was smooth as silk on all six cylinders. When I turned the gun in for the last time, I looked at the armorer and said, "Thank you." He knew exactly why and replied, "You're welcome, Agent. Be careful out there." I left the academy with the smoothest shooting revolver I'd ever had.

Physical Training - PT

On the first day of PT, we arrived at the gym at 6:00 AM. Darrell told us to choose a partner and pick a workstation. Philadelphia Bob and I partnered up and started at the pull-up bar. The music was blasting and the whistle blowing. The workouts became a rhythmic routine so much so that every session ended with the same song Bryan Adams' *Summer of 69*. To this day, that song takes me back to Glynco.

After the last whistle, Darrell would shout, "Form up." On our way outside, there was always a small crowd of guys gathered, pulling down their shorts and smearing body grease in their privates while others were pulling up their shirts, greasing their nipples. There was always the one guy doing exaggerated circular motions triggering childish laughter.

We ran four to five miles per day at a pace of a nine-minute mile. The road guard duty was ridiculous. We were on the back roads of a secure facility. But at every intersection, the guards sprinted ahead to protect the column from the non-existent vehicular traffic. This was summertime in the lowlands of Georgia so snakes were not uncommon. We saw more snakes on the road than vehicles.

A police officer got bit while I was there. He was attending a seminar and went for a run alone at dusk. He saw what he thought was a stick in the road. As he stepped over it, the 'stick' bit him in the back of the leg. Luckily, he made it back to get medical attention. I never heard what kind it was, but there were plenty to choose from: rattle snakes, copperheads and water moccasins.

With Darrell up front on the left and Brian on the right, Brian called out: Left - Left - Left Right - Left, as he listened for our steps to synchronize. Then Darrell would give him the command to pick it up and we would break into a jog. Brian always started out with this song, calling out one line at a time in cadence, triggering us to repeat his words and match his cadence.

> Brian: *C-130, rollin down the strip*
> Us: *C-130 ROLLIN DOWN THE STRIP*
> Brian: *DEA daddy gonna take a little trip*
> Us: *DEA DADDY GONNA TAKE A LITTLE TRIP*

Brian had a dozen songs to choose from, though we didn't sing all the time. He would use the songs for motivation or to force us to control our breathing. Occasionally, we would meet another column coming toward us. Most often, it was a Border Patrol platoon. Brian would tweak them as we passed with this song:

> Brian: *I don't know but I've been told*
> Us: *I DON'T KNOW BUT I'VE BEEN TOLD*
> Brian: *DEA's badge is made of gold*
> Us: *DEA's BADGE IS MADE OF GOLD*
> Brian: *I don't know but it's been said*
> Us: *I DON'T KNOW BUT IT'S BEEN SAID*
> Brian: *All the others are made of lead*
> Us: *ALL THE OTHERS ARE MADE OF LEAD*

Later that particular morning I found myself in the lunch line with some of the Border Patrol guys. When they saw me, they started laughing and I asked them what they were laughing about. One of them said, "Because you boys smelled like a brewery when we passed by you this morning." It must have been a Monday because there was a lot of beer consumed over the weekends.

Bullet ran with us every morning at the rear of the column. There were usually a few students unable to keep up with the column and would fall behind. When that happened, he would slow down and run with them to offer 'encouragement.' I heard his motivation style was mostly ranting.

To break up the monotony, Darrell had some running games. His favorite was the front two people would step out and do 25 push ups while the column continued. After completing the push ups, they would have to sprint to catch the column. Once they caught up, they would take the rear positions and the next two people in the front dropped out and did the same drill. It broke the monotony, and anything was better than those constant damn group wind sprints. Our shirts were soaked when we returned to the parking lot. Even after changing into dry shirts, the fresh ones would fill with sweat as we cooled down. Once I weighed myself before and after a run and I had lost seven pounds, nearly a gallon of sweat.

At the end of week two, we walked into the padded gym to find a rolling canvas cart full of boxing gloves. Darrell told us to get a pair of gloves. The gloves were well-used like they'd kissed a lot of faces. He had us form a circle. Yep, a blind man could see what was coming next. Every time he blew his whistle and called a name, that person entered the circle and boxed the reigning champion until one of them got knocked down. The champion kept boxing until they were defeated. To everyone's surprise, Hector dominated the circle. He had been a Golden Gloves boxer growing up in Puerto Rico. His reign ended when Philadelphia Bob dropped him like a bad habit. Bob told us later he didn't mean to hit Hector that hard, but he was just so quick. It was a lot of fun with cheering and laughing and a whole lot of "Ooh, that had to hurt" and "That's going to leave a mark." Darrell told us, "Getting punched in the face is DEA's way of preparing you for what's to come." The defensive tactics they taught us were no-nonsense stuff. If you're fighting for your life, nothing is considered unfair.

Philadelphia Bob was unassuming and could fit in anywhere, a talent acquired from years of undercover work in Philadelphia.

But he was full of surprises. One day before gym class some of the muscle guys got into a bench-pressing contest. Three of them were going at it while the rest of us watched and cheered. The weight had gone to somewhere north of 400 pounds. Bob whispered to me, "Watch this." The contest was almost over when he stepped up and asked if he could try. They said, "Sure, where do you want to start?" He replied, "Let's make this quick and add another 20 pounds." Bob benched it like it was nothing. When no one else could do the lift, he was declared the winner with one lift. He told me later he had waited until their muscles were fatigued. He knew with fresh muscles he could lift that amount, but only once. He didn't just out lift them, he outplayed them.

One morning we woke up to a thunderstorm. It was raining hard as we ran to the gym. After finishing in the weight room, Darrell announced, "Because of a lightning alert, no running today. Change into your suits and meet me at the pool." We swam laps, making sure everyone knew how to swim. By nature, agents tend to turn everything into a competition and the races began. I'd been a Red Cross Certified Lifeguard from my time on the Delavan Lake police boat and was a good swimmer. But these guys were the best of the best at everything. As usual I finished in the middle of the pack. Milwaukee Bob would have been satisfied.

I noticed the counselors rolling a pair of car tires into the deep end of the pool. Darrell said he had one more challenge for us. "I want you to dive, bring the tire to the surface and keep it there. Red Team against the Green Team."

We dove in after the tire. When I grabbed the tire, I saw hardened concrete inside it. It took a coordinated effort of five guys treading water to hold it up. Four couldn't do it. If someone let go before being replaced, the tire would sink. Then we'd have to dive down and restart the process. It took several attempts to coordinate as a team.

I was reminded of a time on the Delavan Lake Police Department when I had recovered bodies from the lake. One memorable night a car had careened off a bridge into the lake. Being the first patrol car on the scene, I could see the fading glow from the headlights underwater. I took off my shoes, stripped to my waist and went in. The water was about eight feet deep and pitch black. I dove and found the car upside down with the driver's door jammed. I could stand on one of the car's tires to get my head above water to catch my breath between dives.

The next car to arrive was a Walworth County Deputy Sheriff who joined me in the water. We took turns pulling on the door until we got it partially open. The deputy cut the seat belt, freeing the deceased driver and pushed the body to the surface. I was standing on the tire with my head barely

Delavan Lake police boat

out of the water when the body popped up. We were face-to-face inches apart. He could have kissed me had he been alive. I let out a little kid scream! We pulled him to shore and handed him off to the rescue squad, who transported him to the hospital. Doctors pronounced him dead on arrival. I went home, took a shower, put on a clean uniform and finished my shift.

On average, our lake had about one drowning accident a year. There was one miraculous moment when we came upon a horrific boating accident while on a boat patrol. A young girl brushed a rotating boat propeller while climbing into their boat. The propeller seriously cut her back open. Keep in mind, the lake was about 2,000 acres with 13 miles of shoreline. On that day, at that exact moment, we were within sight of the accident just as it happened.

We saw girls frantically waving their arms at us. We pulled up within seconds and saw blood in the water. My partner jumped in and pulled her *to the surface. We got her into our boat, stuffed a towel into her cut and radioed for the rescue squad to meet us at the dock. With the boat wide open, we raced across the lake to a waiting Delavan Lake Rescue Squad that transported her to Lakeland Hospital in Elkhorn. I heard the surgeons saved her life.*

Rescuing a weighted tire from a swimming pool wasn't particularly stressful. It was, however, exhausting.

Academic Shock

Monday morning of the second week Robert greeted us from the stage saying he hoped we had prepared for the weekly tests. As we put our books on the floor, the counselors handed out the one-hour legal test. Next was the general knowledge test, again one hour. After the tests were turned in, the counselors dismissed us for an early lunch. The cafeteria was like a *Golden Corral* on steroids and could seat 300 people. All the food you could ever want, and it was free.

After lunch, I walked into the lecture hall to find a group of guys gathered around the back wall in front of a cork board. The test results were posted on the board. I looked for my name and was relieved to see I had passed both tests. There were two men that failed the law test and another two that failed the general knowledge. All my roommates passed, even Bucky who I didn't think had studied much.

Robert came to the podium. "You've seen your scores. Some of you are not taking this academy seriously. For those of you who failed either test, you are now on academic probation. If you fail another test, I will dismiss you from this academy. Your respective counselors will meet with you after class to sign formal written probation notifications."

Back at the townhouse, Mike gathered us in the living room. "Look guys, I passed today, but not by much. If we're gonna get through this, we need to work together. I want to hold regular study groups." We all agreed. I was a regular attendee and I believe it was those sessions that got me through. Texas Mike was a natural leader. His confidence was contagious and the guys, including me, were comfortable following his lead.

The rest of the week was more of the same: drugs, report writing and law classes. Thursday was the 4th of July. We had the day off, which was a total bust for me because all I did was study. As the day wore on, I realized I should have gone somewhere because I began to ruminate about Lu and the kids. Their pictures made me homesick. I had to put them in the bottom drawer of my dresser so I could stay focused.

Another week went by, and it was test day again. We knew the drill, everything on the floor. The counselors handed out the first test and then the second. After we finished the second test, we left for lunch.

This time when I returned, the test results weren't posted. I thought, well crap, they must not have been scored yet. As we took our seats, I noticed Rudy come in and tap the guy in front of me on his shoulder. He leaned down and whispered something.

Me and Texas Mike

The guy got up and they both walked out the back of the room. This was not unusual.

A few minutes later, the doors in the back of the room burst open. Robert and all four of the counselors rushed in, yelling for us to get out, get out now. Either the building was on fire or there was a bomb threat. They yelled, "Don't stop, go all the way outside!" We stood outside for about 20 minutes before we were summonsed. Right away I noticed my desk was one spot closer to the aisle. They rearranged our desks while we were outside. How bizarre! Then I saw the mess on the floor in front of the stage. There was an overturned desk, books and papers strewn across the floor. On top of the mess was the student's paper name card torn in half, facing our direction and clearly readable. Robert took the stage. "I told you from day one. I warned you. If you fail two tests, you're out. This trainee didn't take me seriously and now he's gone. I don't enjoy doing this. Frankly, it pisses me off. This guy deprived someone else from coming here. DEA invested a lot of time and money in each one of you and now he's wasted it. That Top Secret background investigation costs DEA $100,000 apiece. If any of you think for one second I won't dismiss you, remember what happened here today." Over the coming weeks, there were other recruits dismissed. Their dismissals were handled in a more discreet manner. Robert's show of force only had to be done once. We got the message loud and clear.

Driving Class

The driving class took place on a Saturday. It started with the academy bus taking us to the airfield. The first thing I saw as we pulled onto the tarmac was 10 Ford Mustang 5.0s lined up. Four driving instructors greeted us. There was a table full of helmets behind them. Our primary instructor informed us we would need to qualify on two driving courses that day. The first course was a timed serpentine course. The second was a skid control pan where we had to demonstrate our ability to control a vehicle during a power slide.

The lead instructor told us to get a helmet. "Red Team, take five cars and follow those instructors for skid control. Green Team, you stay with me." It was a full-on race to get to the driver's seat. Losers got shotgun seats. The instructors took off and we floored the Mustangs to keep up. This was going to be a fun day. As we slowed, there was another instructor standing near the skid pan who signaled us to line up the cars. In the middle of the blacktop runway was a large white foam patch. We watched as Mike went first. He got in the driver's seat with the instructor in the shotgun seat. Suddenly black smoke was rolling off the rear tires as they launched down the runway. I'm guessing they were going about 70 mph when they hit the foam. The car instantly went into a wild series of 360-degree spins. As soon as the car hit the dry pavement, it let out a monster screech and rocked to a stop. I thought, wow, Mike lost it. Maybe he didn't know how to drive on ice, being from Texas. I grew up in Wisconsin and knew how slippery black ice was.

I was second in line and had watched Mike from my car. Now I knew what to expect and prepared myself to hit a patch of black ice. As soon as they cleared, my instructor said, "Hit it and don't let off the gas until I tell you." I was doing 70 mph and when I hit that foam, friction ceased to exist. I knew if I made only the slightest steering adjustments, I could maybe float through to the other side. Well, that plan went to shit when the instructor pulled the emergency brake handle between the seats, locking the rear wheels. This sent the car into the same insane 360-degree donuts that I saw Mike do. I never saw that coming. My stomach lodged in my throat as we spun our way down the landing strip. My whole theory of Mike being from Texas proved to be inconsequential. When we hit the dry pavement and stopped, the instructor said, "Get back in line and don't tell anyone about the brake. It'll spoil the surprise."

After three hours of high-speed heart-stopping insanity, they slowed it down. To pass the course, we had to slip slide around a series of orange cones and recover from a few power slides. At noon, we took the bus back to the cafeteria for a quick lunch and returned to the airfield. The groups switched places and now we had the serpentine road course. That course was a mile long with big arching turns coupled with mixed hairpin turns. The course was defined using dozens of orange cones. We took turns practicing the course, driving as fast as we could.

The helmets had built-in radio speakers so the instructors could talk to us as we were driving. Sounds logical, right? The problem was all the speakers were on the same radio frequency. With two or three cars running the course simultaneously, we couldn't tell who the instructor was talking to. This created a total state of confusion. I think it was done to amplify the stress level. All afternoon there was the sound of squealing tires, the smell of burning rubber and fishtailing cars sending cones flying, an amazing sight.

The first guy to qualify was Ben from Tennessee. Ben passed on his first try. I'd failed several attempts, so I asked him if there was a trick to it. In a heavy southern accent, he said, "I don't know. I just floored it and drove like hell." I thought, OK, no real secret, just drive faster. I could do that. I used the Ben principal and just floored it. I qualified on my next attempt. By the time we boarded the bus to go home, I was mentally and physically exhausted. Even my butt muscles ached.

I felt bad for one of the female BATs on the other team. She was from New York City. All her life she had used the city's mass transit system, never having a car or a driver's license. Upon her selection by the DEA, she needed to get a driver's license. The total of her driving experience was the behind the wheel driver's course and a BMV driver's examination. I can only imagine what her day must have been like.

We Get Our Assignments

At the end of the first month the Chief of Agent Assignments arrived from headquarters to announce our assignments. As he walked to the podium, he was greeted with, "Good afternoon, sir" as we stood at attention. He reminded us that we had previously signed a mobility agreement. Reading each of our names from a prepared list, he continued.

David (Bucky) Orlando to Chicago
Michael El Paso to McAllen
Brian Chicago to Detroit
Hector San Juan to Miami
Robert Philadelphia to Philadelphia
Howard Milwaukee to Indianapolis

The week prior we had filled out a 'wish list.' I got my second choice. There were a few guys who weren't so lucky. Theodore, a cop from Memphis, was assigned to San Francisco. For me, Indianapolis meant money would be tight for a while. But for Teddy, San Francisco was the highest cost-of-living city in America. He faced a serious financial crunch. Like me, he had a wife and two small children. Both he and his wife worked to make ends meet in Memphis.

I saw Teddy years later. He told me he had to leave his family in Memphis when he moved to San Francisco. All he could afford to rent was a bedroom in an elderly woman's home. Six months after arriving in San Francisco his father died, and he couldn't afford a plane ticket back to Memphis. The agents in the office pitched in and bought a round-trip ticket so he could attend his father's funeral. He hadn't seen his wife and children in six months. After the funeral, he called his Group Supervisor and told him he wasn't returning. His GS flew to Memphis and convinced him things would eventually work out and they did. It took another year before he could reunite his family in San Francisco. His story made me realize how lucky I was to be assigned Indianapolis.

While sitting in class one day, I felt a tap on my shoulder. It was Rudy and he asked me to come with him. Oh shit, my heart sank.

We walked into the office, and he told me I needed to call my Milwaukee office while pointing to a phone on a desk. I looked at the phone, puzzled. I didn't know how to use an FTS phone, Federal Telephone System. He explained how to use it and handed me a phone number. A secretary in the Milwaukee office answered. After I told her who I was, she said, "I have two pay checks here for you. What do you want me to do with them?" I asked her to mail them to my wife, and I went back to the classroom enormously relieved.

The following Sunday it was time to call home. As I scooped up my change off the dresser, I did a double take. There was a lot more change than I had put there. Somebody was adding coins to my pile. I never knew who it was, but someone had figured out my system and was graciously giving me more time to talk to my wife and kids.

I told Lu about our Indianapolis assignment then asked about the kids. They were doing fine adjusting to my absence, which was bittersweet. I asked Lu if she had gotten my pay checks from DEA and thankfully, she had. She asked me if I knew how much my pay checks were. I didn't know. She told me the amount and added, "If that's your salary, you're making $100 less per week than you were on the police department. That won't cover our bills." She also told me the Delavan Town Clerk said my vacation time had run out. That meant no more paychecks from the police department. I told her I'd figure it out and call her back. As soon as I hung up, I went looking for Bucky. I went up to his room. He was reading a *Sports Illustrated* magazine swimsuit edition. Bucky asked me, "Have you seen this? These girls are amazing. You have to check it out."

"No, Bucky, I haven't seen it."

I told Bucky about the call with my wife and that I might have made a huge mistake because of the pay difference. Bucky told me to, "Calm down, Chief, take a breath. You'll be fine. After we graduate, our AUO will kick in. Agents get paid an additional 25% of their base pay to compensate for all the mandatory overtime. That alone will make up the hundred bucks. Trust me, you didn't make a mistake. In three years, you'll double your old police salary." AUO stands for Administratively Uncontrolled Overtime.

As I was pacing around his room, I noticed the open closet door. He had about six uniform sets on hangers, half covered with plastic dry-cleaning bags. We were only issued four sets. I asked him, "How did you get extra uniforms?" He laughed and said, "It's all about who you know, Chief." That was Bucky, living large. With an equal amount of bewilderment, I asked, "You take your clothes to a dry cleaner?"

"Seriously, Chief, do you really think I wash my own clothes?"

The Raid House

Surveillance is one of DEA's primary tools and agents must learn to do it well. Basic vehicle surveillance sounds simple but it's the coordination and smooth transitions that complicate it. A simplified explanation is agents follow a suspect vehicle in a line, like an invisible parade. The lead car, eyes on, will call out over the radio what they're seeing. At some point, the lead car pulls off and the second car in line becomes the lead car. The former lead car maneuvers around and rejoins the parade at the back of the line.

That's covert surveillance in its simplest form. There are countless twists that can complicate a surveillance. Success depends on coordinating agents' moves. Much time is spent teaching students the tricks of the trade including endless hours of practice and preparation. Most agents keep a change of clothes in their vehicle. They also have cover stories and props such as a magnetic real estate sign for a slow drive through a neighborhood, a dog leash and a lost dog story for a walk through someone's backyard. Agents may end up in a bar or nightclub where blending in requires the consumption of alcohol. Agents are permitted two drinks per hour, which is reimbursable. Not only is drinking permitted, but it is also partially funded. Agents never run a bar tab in case it's necessary to leave quickly. Skipping out on a tab is not permitted and would draw unwanted attention.

We did several practical exercises on the academy grounds using the residential neighborhood of abandoned houses. DEA reclaimed and furnished some of the houses for mock drug deals and raids. Later we would go off-base to St. Simons Island and Jekyll Island for more complex exercises. Some surveillance operations lasted a few hours while others went on all night. Typically exercises would start with a briefing to explain the objective including descriptions of suspects and vehicles. There was always missing information that needed to be gathered through surveillance to complete the assignment. Some exercises included the use of an undercover agent or a confidential informant, CI. A trainee was designated as the team leader.

Most exercises ended with an arrest inside one of the raid houses at the academy. The houses were set up with several hidden cameras allowing instructors to remotely monitor the students. The 'arrests' were very intense and often involved arresting armed suspects, played by DEA instructors. The exercises concluded with a review session. We sat on the floor as they critiqued our performance, better described as rantings about our mistakes and missteps. Following people without being detected is not easy.

To put this in perspective, fast forward 26 years to 2011, five years after my retirement from DEA. I was working as a contract instructor for the State Department's Anti-Terrorism Assistance program. I was in Bangladesh training an elite counter terrorism unit in advanced surveillance tactics. The lead instructor was a former CIA Case Officer, and the course channeled the CIA's methods and practices. The course included two weeks of extensive field training exercises. I learned the differences between a DEA surveillance and those of the CIA. The primary difference was that the CIA used three times as many people as DEA. That differ-

ence meant the CIA's surveillance operations were almost always success-
ful and nearly impossible to detect.

One review session turned particularly ugly. During the exercise, our team 'arrested' and handcuffed several role-playing instructors who had been putting up physical resistance. Philadelphia Bob handcuffed one of the role players who then claimed the cuffs were too tight. As a result, the role player/instructor was pissed. Remember, these exercises simulated real life. Sometimes we couldn't tell acting from reality. Bob was a seasoned Philadelphia narcotics investigator. He knew how to apply handcuffs. I don't believe for a second that he did it wrong. However, during the critique the angry instructor called Bob to the front of the class, berated him and then handcuffed him. The instructor intentionally cranked the cuffs extremely tight as he said, "Now, how do you like it?" The instructors left Bob standing off to the side to both punish and humiliate him while they continued their rant.

A few minutes later, the instructor asked Bob if the cuffs were hurting. He replied calmly that they were but displayed no sign of pain or discomfort. Bob was strong both physically and mentally. He wasn't going to give them any satisfaction. With that the instructor said, "Well then, let's just let 'em bake for a while." I think we all felt this was unnecessary and wrong on more than one level. Bob was the only Black man in the room. I admired Bob's courage as he stood tall and refused to surrender his dignity.

As soon as the instructor finished telling Bob, "We'll let 'em bake," Texas Mike stood up without saying a word, walked in front of the instructor who was still in full rant and removed the cuffs from Bob. Together they walked back and as they passed the instructor, Mike handed him the cuffs without looking at him. This left the instructor speechless, and the session abruptly ended. That night Mike showed us what it meant to be a stand-up guy. It takes a special kind of courage to do something like that, and I've never forgotten it.

Throughout Mike's career, he earned multiple promotions, reaching the position of SAC, Special Agent in Charge, which put him in command of a field division. He proved himself to be the leader we all knew he was. Sadly, while drafting this book, I received a notification from our Retired Agent's Association that Mike had passed away in 2024. I hope his family knows what he did that night.

On Monday of the following week, I walked into the weight room and saw the attention was focused on Bob and Bullet. They were engaged in a verbal confrontation. I heard Bob telling Bullet he'd had enough of his bullshit. "You're all mouth, little man. You want to go, let's go."

Bullet was walking backwards, weaving his way through the weight machines. He'd witnessed Bob inside the boxing circle and bench pressing over 400 pounds. I'm sure he didn't want any part of that. As he was fast walking out of gym he yelled back at Bob, "You're done. You're out of here. It's over for you, buddy." With that Bullet was gone. Darrell got the class back in order and we continued on.

When we got to the classroom, everything appeared normal. Mid-afternoon in the middle of a lecture, Robert came in. The instructor stopped talking as Robert tapped Bob on the shoulder. All eyes in the room watched as Robert walked Bob out the door. Standing outside in the hall were three of the four counselors, absent Bullet.

After class, we went straight to Bob's room. The door was locked. We never locked our rooms. One of the guys picked the lock. The room was trashed. Papers, books, folders covered the floor. The realization set in that our friend Bob was gone. Hector found a piece of paper with a scribbled message, 'meet me at gas station at 8.' The gas station was located off the academy grounds on a dead-end street about one hundred yards from our town house. We used a hole in the security fence to gain access to the gas station where beer was sold. Brian, Bucky, Hector, Mike and I went to meet him. In reality we were helpless to do anything for him other than offer our support.

He said, "I appreciate your concerns but don't worry about me. My SAC in Philadelphia told me I'd be back in the next class." He told us that after he left the classroom, they took him straight to a BARB, Basic Agent Review Board, hearing. "It was a done deal before it started. Bullet testified I threatened him. I countered that he was the one who provoked me. It only took 10 minutes for them to rule and dismiss me from the academy. They took me to my room and watched me the whole time making sure I didn't take anything that belonged to DEA, not even a pencil. When I finished packing, they drove me to the front gate and left me. The guard came out and let me use his phone to call a taxi. I got a motel room in town, and I fly back to Philadelphia in the morning." We shook hands and told him he didn't deserve any of it.

I heard he graduated in BA39, the first class to graduate from the new academy in Quantico, Virginia. The last thing I heard was he had been promoted to a Group Supervisor.

At about week 8, my wife and children visited for the weekend. I drove to Jacksonville airport Saturday morning to pick them up. We spent Saturday night in a motel on Jekyll Island. On Sunday I showed them where I was living, our townhouse and the alligator in the pond. The guys were super nice to my wife and kids. Sunday was my laundry day, and my wife and kids wanted to help. It was then that my wife discovered I'd been washing my clothes with Downy fabric softener instead of detergent. I guess I hadn't read the label very well and thought it was soap. My clothes may not have been as clean as they could have been, but they were soft! As the weekend ended, my wife took our car and drove to Clearwater, where she stayed with my sister. She returned the following weekend and flew home on Sunday night. The visit reinvigorated me to push to the end.

Last of the Best

We were told the Deputy Administrator was flying in from Washington to give a talk to our class. He also wanted to run PT with us. This was a big deal. All the counselors and several instructors ran with us too.

On Monday we ran our usual five-mile route with the Deputy along with the new faces. Why Bucky chose that day to release his song, I don't know. But he did. Midway through our run, Bucky broke out in cadence singing his song. We're a team so everyone followed his words.

Bucky: *"This job is the best excuse, for getting out and cutting loose"*
US: *"THIS JOB IS THE BEST EXCUSE, FOR GETTING OUT AND CUTTING LOOSE"*
Bucky: *"Tell your spouse you're working late"*
US: *"TELL YOUR SPOUSE YOU'RE WORKING LATE"*
Bucky: *"Meet your honey for a date"*
US: *"MEET YOUR HONEY FOR A DATE"*

On any other day he would have gotten a big laugh. But today all the staff had their jocks in a twist. Later that morning in the lecture hall, the Deputy looked directly at Brian, our lead singer, and announced the purpose of his visit. He was here to talk to us about ethics and integrity. "Considering the nature of one of your songs this morning, I think you all better pay close attention." The Deputy didn't realize it was actually Bucky who had momentarily hijacked the class. While Brian was taking the heat for Bucky, the rest of us could hardly keep from laughing. That was Bucky.

Later that night I saw Bucky coming back to the townhouse and he was pissed. They had jumped his ass for embarrassing the training staff in front of the Deputy. He was ready to pack up and leave. "I wouldn't have to put up with any of this petty bullshit back at the sheriff's department." I panicked. This place would not be the same without him. I tried to give him a pep talk and ended up saying, "Hey. I'm getting bored with this place. Do you want to get out of here for a while and get some real food?" He laughed and said, "Yeah, that sounds good, but where have I heard that before?"

We jumped in his car and headed for Brogen's Bar on St. Simons Island. The bar had a rustic atmosphere, wraparound porch and wooden rocking chairs overlooking the water. It had speakers all around playing a mix of oldies and country music. We had used this place in a few of our practical exercises, and it became our go to place for hanging out. I told Bucky this time it was my treat. We ordered beer and two dozen oysters on the half shell. I told the server we needed lots of extra red sauce. For me, it was a waste of money because I ended up in the bathroom throwing up my share of the oysters. But I didn't come for the oysters. I wanted to make sure Bucky didn't quit.

I repeated back what Bucky had told me weeks earlier. "You know it's all a game, just play along." I parroted Milwaukee Bob with, "They can't stop the clock." Eventually we laughed more than cursed and left when the bar closed.

The next thing I remembered was Hector waking me up. "Come on, man. We got gym class." Oh, my lord, I felt awful.

I don't know if we were being punished for Bucky's song or not. This was by far the most grueling workout we ever had. It was the end of August, and the heat and humidity were awful. After we finished in the weight room, we ran our usual route out to the airport then on to the tarmac. Darrell had us doing wind sprints and push-ups. Up and down the runway a hundred yards at a time followed by twenty-five push-ups. While doing push-ups, sweat was running off my nose, creating a puddle. All the counselors were with us making sure we did every push-up.

When we finally made it back to the parking lot, our normal stopping point, Darrell, led us across the parking lot and back out onto the road. Mentally I had already shut down, believing the run was over. It was crushing. Brian told me later that it was an old Marine Corps game intended to prove you're capable of doing more than you think.

Off we went. But Darrell miscalculated the time. When the sun broke over the tree line, the temperature shot to a hundred degrees. Still a mile from the parking lot, some of the guys started falling out of formation from leg cramps. Darrell slowed us to a walk and sent Brian ahead to get help and water. Soon golf carts and 4-wheelers arrived to pick up the guys that couldn't walk. We were all badly dehydrated and fending off leg cramps. Once we got back, Darrell apologized, ended the class and sent us to the showers.

Our next gym class was equally interesting. Once again I can't say if this was an unofficial punishment. But it was coincidental that during our Aikido session, the instructor called Bucky to the front of the class for a demonstration. The lesson was how to incapacitate a person with a kick to the lateral femoral cutaneous nerve. That translates to a powerful kick to a specific location on the outside of the thigh. When executed correctly, the kick will temporarily paralyze the affected leg.

In demonstrating the technique, the instructor kicked Bucky so hard he instantly collapsed. It was obvious he was in serious pain and unable to stand because of the aforementioned paralysis. Bucky limped around the academy for the rest of the week, though happy because the doctor gave him a medical release from PT class. The release was rescinded after one of the academy staff members saw him dancing over the weekend at his favorite bar. Bucky told me, "Oh well, I'd been milking it anyway."

Bucky graduated and eventually made it to the air wing where he was certified to fly all of DEA's aircraft including helicopters. Besides flying all over the U.S., he flew many dangerous missions in South America in support of Operation Snowcap. It didn't surprise me when I heard he'd crashed a helicopter but walked away unscathed. That could only happen to Bucky.

We took our final PT qualifications. I ran the mile and a half in 11 minutes and 17 seconds. I exceeded all strength requirements, and my body fat came in at 12%. I weighed 190 pounds when I arrived, and I weighed 190 pounds when I graduated. I hadn't worn my suit in three months, and when I put it on, it was too big. I had to use safety pins to create a fold in the waistband and tighten my belt. The suit jacket made me look like a teenager wearing his dad's clothes. I was in the best shape of my life. Sadly, I never maintained it in the real world.

BA 38
"LAST OF THE BEST"

Our class logo

It was a DEA tradition that every class establish a motto and design a logo. We had our logo screen-printed on polo shirts. Traditionally students buy a shirt for themselves and donate money to buy a shirt for the staff and counselors. We learned our class was the last class to graduate from Glynco. DEA was moving its training program to Quantico VA where a new building would be built specifically for DEA. Our class motto was 'Last of the Best,' and our logo was a sketch of a plane crashing into the ocean and a ship sinking titled, 'Smugglers Blues.' After 40 years, that shirt continues to hang in my closet. Looking back, we were not the last of best we were just part of the best of the best.

A week before graduation, we had our class party. Robert, all the counselors and staff members attended. The party was a blast. Bullet ended up being the star of the show. We were surprised by his entertaining nature. He prepared gag gifts for several of us. He found an old pair of boots at a garage sale and glued rhinestones all over them along with a big tinfoil star glued on the front and presented them to Texas Mike.

From a piece of foam-core poster board, he made a colorful hand-painted mock plaque with my name and titled it, 'The First Annual Uncle Bud Award for being a really great guy.' I think the award should have gone to my Mercury Station wagon taxi. The next day we had our formal class picture taken and we turned in our uniforms.

Graduation

Our graduation took place in the auditorium building at 12:30 PM with a reception following from 2:00 PM to 4:00 PM. On the morning of graduation, we went to the range and the armorer issued us our weapon and a box of ammunition. We would leave the academy fully armed. I had my car packed. After graduation I planned to drive home non-stop.

About noon, Mike, Hector, Brian, Bucky and I headed over to the auditorium. This was the first time we had been in the building since attending the BA 37 graduation. There was a small crowd, mostly family, gathering outside the building.

Suddenly, I saw my wife, Wayne, the town chairperson, and his wife, along with my brother Bob and my sister Cindy. I could not believe my eyes. I did not expect anyone to be there. Wayne and his wife drove my wife from Wisconsin and my siblings drove from Clearwater, Florida. After a quick hug from my wife, I told them I had to go, but we would gather after the ceremony.

The organizers had planned every detail of the ceremony. The Deputy Administrator came from headquarters and was the keynote speaker. An award and their choice of assignment went to the trainee with the highest overall academic score. The Top Gun award was given to the best shooter. One at a time we crossed the stage, shook hands with the Deputy Administrator and Robert awarded us our graduation certificate. As we left the stage, our designated counselor presented us with a black leather ID case containing our gold DEA badge and our Special Agent Credentials.

At the reception, I thanked Wayne for bringing my wife and taking the time to attend the graduation. He said he would not have missed it for anything and added he only wished my dad could have witnessed it. He then pulled an envelope out of his breast pocket and asked me, "What do you want me to do with this?" It

My wife Lu and I on graduation day

was my letter of resignation. I told him how much I appreciated everything he had done for me, but he would have to accept it. Wayne replied, "I thought you would say that, but I was hoping you might take it back."

Many of my classmates came to our table to introduce themselves, talking and telling a few stories. The counselors came and talked for a few minutes. Robert visited with us for 10 minutes.

Soon it was time to leave. Lu and I said goodbye to Wayne, his wife, my siblings and we all left in different directions. Lu and I walked to our car and drove out the front gate. It was over. My mom had given Lu a graduation card for me with a $100 in it. We drove to Atlanta and spent the night at the top of the Hyatt

Regency hotel, taking in the impressive view of the city's night lights. Saturday, we drove to Wisconsin, picked the kids up from their great-grandmother's house and went home to Delavan. Our new normal was about to begin.

~ 3 ~

MILWAUKEE

Indeed It Is a Lifestyle

After graduating on Friday, I reported for work in the Milwaukee office on Monday. The boss, Lee, stated the office had a lot of things going on and could use help. He reminded me I was there temporarily and not to open any cases. He wanted me to support the other agents with their investigations.

Lee told Bob to assign me a car. Bob and I went to the garage where he handed me keys to a late model silver Chevrolet Monte Carlo SS and told me this was my car and parking space. He said one of the women in the office would issue me a gas credit card. He said, "Let's take your car home and I'll bring you back." When I pointed to my puke yellow Pinto, Bob laughed. "Is that your car?"

Now that I had an assigned government vehicle, we didn't need the Pinto. I sold it for $200 more than I paid for it. That was the one and only time I made a profit on a car.

DEA agents operate and function collaboratively in groups. A typical group is comprised of 7-12 agents. Agents initiate their own investigations and support the other agents in their group. The Milwaukee office had four street agents which meant their group was understaffed. Two of the agents were divorced and one had never been married. They were free to work crazy long hours.

For the first week, I jumped from one investigation to another. The agents were juggling more investigations than they probably should have. I spent a considerable amount of time doing surveillance, much of it in the ethnic neighborhoods of Milwaukee. Our instructors taught us several tricks for blending in. One trick I used was a hooded sweatshirt. It helped conceal my police appearance.

We learned how to identify counter surveillance. In my 21 years with DEA, I encountered only a handful of situations where traffickers used sophisticated countermeasures. In Milwaukee, whenever our surveillance were compromised, it was because kids in the neighborhood spotted us and hollered, "Five-0" to their friends in the vicinity. The term 'Five-0' originated from the popular TV series *Hawaii Five-0*. The kids assumed we were local cops never realizing who we really were.

Every night for the first week, we were doing undercover deals, night surveillance or meeting with informants. I never got home before 10 PM the entire week and left my house by 7:30 AM. I didn't see my kids awake for the first four days. The unwritten rule in the office was Friday night was off-limits for work, at least most of the time.

At the end of my first week, I got home on Friday at 6:00 PM to find my wife upset. She asked me, "Is this what our life is going to be like?" I honestly didn't know. The only thing I could hope for was that the Indianapolis office would be more family friendly.

DEA culture requires an agent to pitch in and help fellow agents as needed. Working overtime is not an option, it's expected. Agents receive a 25% salary bonus called AUO, Administratively Uncontrolled Overtime, for the overtime they work. The DEA requires this commitment, and it's part of our job. There are no excuses. You're either all in, or you're not in at all. It's part of the lifestyle that my interviewers had forewarned me of and has resulted in many divorces.

Teamwork

DEA investigations have a life cycle. They start when an agent selects a target and begins gathering and analyzing background intelligence. Success as an agent begins with choosing worthwhile targets. Agents often use a confidential informant, CI, who must be managed under strict guidelines. Introducing an undercover DEA agent is often a useful investigative tactic.

The case agent manages and controls the investigation. His job is demanding and time-consuming. The case agent has the option to manage the CI, or he can select a co-case agent and have them manage the informant. Likewise, the case agent can do the undercover role himself or have another agent do it. Surveillance is labor intensive and usually requires support from several agents in the group.

As the investigation develops, it can involve drug purchases for evidence, undercover operations and could lead to a telephone wiretap. Most investigations will conclude with the execution of search warrants and arrest warrants, followed by an assortment of court hearings. It becomes somewhat of an assembly line in that the agent starts the case, builds the case, and finishes it with the help of his fellow agents.

Imagine 7-12 agents in a group, all generating and managing investigations, while providing support for other agents doing the same. The time demands on all agents increase exponentially.

Making use of available resources and maximizing the confidential informant's potential is essential to being a successful case agent. It sounds easy but it's far more difficult than one can imagine. Every day agents navigate through a myriad of pitfalls and landmines coming at them from every direction.

Apple Pie and Ice Cream

One day Bob asked me to go with him to Whitewater, Wisconsin to meet with one of his informants. I told him I wanted to drive separately so I could stop to see an old friend at the Walworth County Sheriff's Department. The friend I was referring to was Deputy Don, one of my dad's old friends . He was one of the most skilled and successful investigators I'd ever encountered.

After meeting with the informant, I met Don at his office. He was now a lieutenant in charge of the detective bureau. Don was thrilled that I had graduated from the academy and was now a DEA Special Agent. I said to him, "Not bad for a small-town kid from Walworth." I thanked him for all he had done for me. Aside from my dad, he was the first of many career mentors. We talked about my dad and laughed about the first time he had met me.

The first police department I worked for was the village of Darien. Dad was friends with the Police Chief, Donald Hoppe. As a favor to my dad, he hired me as a part-time night shift officer beginning on August 3, 1973. Darien was a sleepy village with a population of about six hundred. It had one lone blinking stoplight.

In 1973 in Wisconsin, a newly sworn police officer had one year to complete the six-week police academy. The state permitted new officers to work in the interim. I attended the basic police academy in La Crosse, Wisconsin, and finished second academically in my class of eighteen on June 28, 1974. I was the number one gun in the tactical shooting portion. Incidentally, Luanne and I got married on August 17, 1974.

I'd only worked a few nights when I got my first call to a domestic disturbance. I arrived at the house and a woman greeted me, inviting me into the kitchen. She was visibly upset but holding herself together. There were two children in the living room watching TV. She told me that, yes, she and her husband had a terrible argument, some yelling, but no physical contact and he left in his truck to cool off.

I was so new to police work. I had no idea what I was supposed to do. My racing mind was not well-organized. I intended to ask if her husband would be calmed down when he got home. What came out of my mouth was, "Well, um, what were you arguing about?" What I said wasn't even close to what I meant to ask. She assumed she had to answer my awkward and intrusive question. She was embarrassed, lost her composure and burst into tears. To make matters worse, the kids came running in, grabbed her legs and cried too. In an instant, I'd turned a perfectly calm situation into a full-blown disaster. I would later learn in a police academy class that many domestic arguments between spouses are over money or sex. Looking back, I'm guessing money wasn't the reason for that argument.

In the middle of the disaster, Walworth County Deputy Sheriff Don Swart arrived, flying through the door like Kramer often did on Seinfeld. In seconds he assessed the situation, realized there was no danger and simply defused it. He was an expert in reading humans. The first words out of his mouth were, "Ah, ma'am, is that an apple pie on your stove?" She stopped crying, perked up, and said, "Yes, it just came out of the oven. Do you want a slice?" "Only if you have vanilla ice cream." We all ended up sitting at the kitchen table eating apple pie and ice cream.

While sitting with her, Don reassured her that arguments between husbands and wives happen. He said he and his wife argued all the time. I later learned that wasn't true. Don and his wife rarely, if ever, argued. Don treated untruthfulness as a tool to be used sparingly. I later learned from him that untruthfulness can be an essential tool for interrogating suspects. I watched him obtain confessions from difficult suspects when other detectives had given up.

Over the next 10 years, Don and I became great friends. He taught me the delicate art of interviewing and interrogating people. Don and I shared an obsession with learning and understanding human behavior, a key element to successfully interrogating people.

In December 1980, Don and I attended a 4-day Criminal Psychology seminar in Milwaukee, Wisconsin. The instructors were two FBI agents, John Douglas and Robert Ressler. These men initiated the study of serial killers, which led to the creation of the FBI's Behavioral Science Unit. They authored several books which I have read. Their course included several case studies demonstrating how important it was to understand the human mind and motivations. Their story was featured in the 2017 Netflix mini-series *Mindhunter*. The knowledge I gained from those two FBI agents influenced me for the remainder of my career. Sadly, Don passed away after I moved to Indianapolis. I didn't learn of his passing in time to attend his funeral, one of my regrets.

"Life is Like a Box of Chocolates. You Never Know What You're Gonna Get." Forest Gump

In the fall of 1974, I left the Darien Police Department and took a police officer position in the neighboring community of Delavan Lake. It was a larger and more active department, providing more opportunities to gain experience. A friend of mine named Pete took my place in Darien. Three months after Pete started in Darien he was dispatched to a domestic violence call. I got hot apple pie and ice cream. Pete got shot. When he arrived, the suspect, Jose, opened fire from inside the house with a high-powered 30/30 caliber rifle, hitting the police car several times. One round struck the door frame sending metal fragments into Pete's forehead. Fortunately, his injuries were non-life threatening.

I was one of the first back-up cars to arrive. I saw Jose coming out of the house with his hands in the air, surrendering to a deputy sheriff. Then I saw Pete sitting leaning against the tire of his patrol car, his face covered in blood. I thought for sure he'd been shot in the head and was probably dying. The rescue vehicles had just arrived and began treating

BULLETS FROM A HIGH POWERED RIFLE damaged the Darien police squad car, in a shooting incident early Sunday morning. Officer Peter Labbe sustained a forehead flesh wound as he knelt beside the open left door of the vehicle, reaching for the radio microphone to summon assistance. Jose Herrera, 26, Darien, has been charged with Labbe's attempted murder and his bond has been set at $50,000. (Freddie Kaehler photo)

Darien police car

Pete. As they loaded him into the ambulance, he saw me and gave me a thumb's up which was a great relief. After the ambulance left, I looked at my old patrol car with a bullet hole in the window and Pete's blood splattered all over the door frame. This was an example of the unpredictable risks that police officers face daily.

Pete later told me that he'd been in several firefights as a Marine in Vietnam, but this was more terrifying because he did not expect it and wasn't mentally prepared for it.

There's no question narcotics enforcement is a dangerous business, but most of the time we knew where the danger zone was. We could anticipate it, even plan for it. Police officers work in a 360-degree threat zone, never knowing where or when a threat will appear.

On the day Jose made his initial appearance in court for the attempted murder charge, my dad was the court bailiff. In a stupid attempt to escape, Jose wheeled around and kicked my dad in the groin so hard it caused him to pass blood for a day.

Milwaukee John

John, one of the senior agents in the office, graduated from the first DEA class BA-1 in 1973. He was an accomplished agent with excellent instincts. My last week in Milwaukee John asked me to go with him to a local police department. Their narcotics unit had seized a considerable sum of cash and wanted the DEA to initiate a federal forfeiture action against the currency. After discussing the case with the detectives, John made the decision to accept the currency and do the forfeiture. We took the cash back to our office and recounted it to verify their count. We took the cash to a local bank and exchanged it for a cashier's check.

John told me to never view the cash as anything other than worthless monopoly money. He said, "If you even start to fantasize about it that's when it can begin to seduce you. It can take you down a path you can never come back from." Throughout my career I participated in numerous cash seizures collectively exceeding several million dollars. His words of wisdom remained embedded in my brain. All I ever saw was worthless monopoly money and never gave it a chance to tempt me, not for a second.

House Hunting

When agents are transferred, the agency supports them with paid moving costs and five paid days to find suitable housing. After six weeks in Milwaukee, I scheduled my house hunting trip to Indianapolis. My wife and I drove to Indy and went directly to the DEA office to introduce ourselves.

We were welcomed by the administrative assistant, Darleen, who was outgoing and friendly. She took me to meet the Resident Agent in Charge, RAC. The boss took us to meet the group. There were nine agents working in a bullpen style office. The introductions came fast, and a few guys gave me advice about which side of town to live on.

Gary offered to drive us around to look at apartments. He took us to the east-side of Indianapolis and showed us an apartment complex he had lived in for a few years. We talked to the rental agent as we walked through an empty unit and signed a one-year lease. This apartment had more square footage than our house in Wisconsin and, for the first time, we had central heat and air-conditioning. Our Wisconsin house was a winterized lake cottage. The only source of heat came from an old-fashioned gas stove in the living room and a wall heater in the kitchen. The air conditioning was an open window with a one-size-fits-all screen.

For most of us, there are four major stages in life. The order in which you place them will determine how complicated your life could be. The easiest route is education, job, marriage, and children. The more you mix them up, the harder it gets. I chose job, marriage, children and education

Sarah and Jacob's last Halloween in Wisconsin

which meant working two jobs to make ends meet, raising children, taking college classes whenever I could fit them in and sharing a car with my wife. I was 31 years old before I finished my degree.

When I got back to Milwaukee, I worked a few more weeks. We celebrated our last Halloween with family in Walworth and moved to Indianapolis the first week in November 1985. Our living room window in the apartment overlooked the city interstate bypass I-465. Coming from a small rural town, we were mesmerized by all the non-stop traffic 24/7.

~ 4 ~

INTRODUCING THE PLAYERS

The Users

The illegal drug industry, like any other commodity, is driven by supply and demand. We'll start with demand. If everyone stopped using illegal drugs, the problem would no longer exist. As the saying goes, 'Rarely is there a simple solution to a complex problem.' People use illegal drugs because they provide a powerful chemically induced euphoria. A defendant informant, a cocaine user, told me that, for him, cocaine's euphoria was better than an orgasm. His life would have been far less difficult had he followed Nancy Reagan's advice to 'Just Say No.' Ask any tobacco smoker who's quit smoking. Most will tell you, 'It would have been easier to have never started.'

It's not surprising that the path to addiction begins with that first exposure and ironically it will likely be a trusted person, relative, friend, classmate, co-worker, girlfriend, or boyfriend who will set them on that path. Don't believe me? Ask an addict or recreational user what their relationship was to the person who first introduced them to drugs. The urban legend claiming an unknown stranger in a trench coat is supplying people with drugs is a fallacy. This old wives' tale originated from a picture depicting such a character in a 1968 *Life Magazine* advertisement.

Drug deterrence should be the first line of defense and that begins with education. Unfortunately, society's record for accurate anti-drug campaigns isn't good, beginning with the inaccurate portrayal of marijuana addiction in the 1936 movie *Reefer Madness*. More recently was the Len Bias tragedy of 1986. Bias, a basketball superstar from the University of Maryland, was signed to play with the Boston Celtics. While celebrating his draft selection, he died from cocaine-induced heart failure. His death launched a nationwide awareness campaign as proof that cocaine could be lethal. In 1986, experienced cocaine users knew dying from a cocaine overdose was an anomaly and the campaign was viewed as a scare tactic. It did scare the segment of society that wasn't using cocaine. I'm not cynical but scare tactics are generally ineffective.

Having said that, the introduction and spread of fentanyl and its derivatives has changed the landscape in today's world. Fentanyl is an extremely powerful and dangerous drug and has the real potential to kill without warning. That's not a scare tactic. Cocaine related deaths have risen since 2000, particularly in the male population. One possible explanation may be the practice of mixing cocaine and fentanyl.

Marijuana has been referred to as a 'gateway drug.' In the 1960s as a child, I was taught that marijuana users develop a tolerance, leading them to need stronger drugs to get high. In my years as a DEA agent, no marijuana user ever told me they developed a tolerance and moved on to stronger drugs. I believe the term 'gateway drug' in some instances has been incorrectly defined. Perhaps a better explanation of the term 'gateway' is that marijuana may contribute to a more complacent attitude toward illicit drug use, potentially leading to experimentation with other drugs. Prevention is our best line of defense because rescuing those who have crossed over into addiction, is far more difficult and costly.

Several states have legalized marijuana in varying degrees. What is concerning about legalizing marijuana is that it fosters the belief that because it's sanctioned, it must be safe. This may prompt curious people to experiment, potentially leading to adverse consequences. Legalization might well be society's next failed strategy. Time will tell.

Researchers have studied drug addiction and have extensive knowledge on the subject. What seems to be lacking is a simple and practical understanding of drug abuse. I recall a distraught mother of a teenage girl who was addicted to crystal methamphetamine, meth. The mother, desperate to help her daughter, told me, "I don't understand it. She's killing herself with this drug." I saw the girl. Sores covered her arms, and several teeth were missing. The mother said, "I need to understand. I don't know how to help her. I would never use drugs, but if only I could put my hand on her forehead and feel what she's feeling, maybe I could understand it."

The woman, obsessed with blaming the drug, failed to realize that her daughter was actually addicted to the euphoria meth produced. The drug was the means for her to reach that euphoric state. I explained to her, "Your daughter is not addicted to meth. She is addicted to the euphoria that meth produces. If it were possible for you to put your hand on her forehead and feel what she feels, you may end up addicted to touching her forehead."

Helplessly witnessing the destruction of her daughters health was so devastating, she placed the blame on the existence of illicit drugs. Her story is a microcosm of society's decades long 'War on Drugs.' The 'war on drugs' must include a plan to reduce demand.

The Dealers

Cocaine in the 80s and 90s sold for $100 a gram. A packet of Sweet and Low contains a gram of powder, a fair representation of what a gram of cocaine looks like. A gram is a personal use quantity easily consumed by one or two people. Some users may eventually consume thousands of dollars worth of cocaine weekly, likely spending money that should be used for rent, food, and clothing.

Drug use may also result in the user losing their ability to hold a job. Many users learn to sell cocaine to support their habit. This is how a user can turn into a dealer: 3 ½ grams of cocaine is called an '8 ball.' It's called that because dividing an ounce, 28 grams, by 8 equals 3 ½ grams. An 8 ball was usually wrapped in a transparent plastic baggie shaped into a ball. Remember, this is equivalent to 3 ½ packets of *Sweet and Low*. The average price for an 8 ball was around $300. A user quickly learned that buying an 8 ball, 3 ½ grams, for $300 was cheaper than buying three single grams at $100 apiece. If he sold the 3 grams, he could keep a ½ gram free. That's how to become a small drug dealer. But the criminal charges jump from simple possession to possession with intent to distribute.

One gram Sweet'N Low packet

The volume and profits also grew exponentially. The price for an ounce, 28 grams, sold for about $2,000 in Indiana. Reselling the 28 grams individually at $100 would net the dealer an $800 profit or eight free grams. The wholesale price of a kilogram of cocaine in Miami during the 1990s was about $25,000. A kilo contains 1,000 grams. At $100 per gram, it had a street value of $100,000 in the Midwest. The profit from a single kilo imported from Miami to Indianapolis could net a dealer a whopping $75,000.

One round trip to Miami transporting and distributing ten kilograms of cocaine, could put $750,000 in a dealer's pocket. In actuality, distribution networks are far more complex. This illustrates how profitable the drug trade can be. These figures don't include the practice of diluting cocaine, known as cutting. Adding filler to cocaine reduces its purity but increases the volume, thus increasing the profit margin for the seller.

Some small dealers grow their business to levels that can set them on a collision course with law enforcement. Many can encounter other problems. The illegal and clandestine nature of the business creates opportunities for robberies where neither the buyer nor the seller can call the police. One can quickly be killed over a business dispute. Not all dealers are addicts. Some entrepreneurs viewed it as a profitable business and amassed vast fortunes. Our mission was to take those fortunes away and send them to prison.

What does DEA do with the millions of dollars and assets that are seized? After the forfeiture action is completed in court, the money is deposited into the U.S. Treasury's general fund. The Treasury is referred to as 'America's checkbook,' because it's used to pay the government's bills. The DEA is permitted to press into service certain high-value assets such as cars and boats used to provide the bling in undercover operations. In 1986 the U.S. Government began an Asset Sharing program, which allowed DEA to share seized drug proceeds with state and local police departments who participated in the investigation.

If all this money entices you, remember: this business is not for a person with a conscience. The anxiety will be relentless. Nor is it easy. A brick of cocaine is worthless unless it can be sold. Pray the person you're selling it to isn't an undercover agent or a cop, or a 'trusted' friend setting you up. Someone could be planning to take it from you at gunpoint and there's no guarantee you won't be killed anyway. Buying drugs can be even more dangerous. Imagine roaming Miami with $25,000 or more in cash to purchase illegal drugs. That's a potential death sentence even if you know what you're doing.

The Informants

Hollywood makes movies. Agents work in the real world. Managing informants, referred to by DEA as Confidential Informants, CIs, is a no-nonsense business. The FBI refers to them as CSs, or Confidential Sources. Some intelligence agencies and military refer to them as HUMITs, Human Intelligence. Regardless of what they are called, the controlling agent must ensure that the CI's actions don't cause injuries or death. I cannot emphasize enough how challenging it is to manage and control CIs. Every agency, federal or otherwise, has fallen prey to double dealing CIs.

One of the most tragic examples of an informant going bad happened to the CIA. In December 2009, a group of CIA's top terrorist hunters gathered at a location in Afghanistan. They were hoping for an opportunity to meet with a Jordanian informant who could infiltrate the highest levels of al-Qaeda. The Jordanian intelligence officer managing the CI brought him to the meeting. As the CI stepped from the car, he detonated a bomb strapped to his body. The explosion killed seven of the CIA's most valuable terrorist experts. This tragedy was the agency's worst loss of life in decades. If you'd like to read the whole story Google 'Humam Khalil Al-Balawia.'

Managing and controlling CIs is an art not a science. Intimidating them physically is not effective nor is it permitted. I found the most effective means was to establish a working relationship, coupled with a healthy degree of psychological control. Simply put, they must fear the consequences of their crime more than the fear of informing on their associates. Regardless of your profession, be wary of anyone who's too comfortable tattling. Their motive is as important as their information.

Someone walking into a DEA office offering to become an informant must be evaluated by an agent. The first thing the agent must figure out is their reason. Agents are trained to ferret out hidden agendas. Failure to expose hidden agendas made our job treacherous. Most importantly, an informant's information must be independently corroborated. It's a quandary. The better their information, the deeper their criminal involvement, with few exceptions. *Swans don't swim in the sewer. If they know what's happening in the sewer, they are not swans.*

Occasionally good people will have useful information. But for DEA agents, that wasn't our arena. We dealt with criminals. Most were attempting to negotiate a deal on pending drug charges. Once I even worked with a convicted murderer.

A common misconception is that agents cut deals with criminals. In fact, it's the prosecutors who negotiate the deals. Agents work with offenders to give them an opportunity to prove their willingness to sever ties with their criminal associates and expand the investigation. The extent of their cooperation is taken into consideration by the prosecutor when making the deal. Charges are rarely dismissed. At issue is how long the defendant cooperator will spend in prison for their crime. One should think long and hard before getting involved in the illegal drug business, because the retirement plan sucks.

Some aspiring informants claim they are doing it for money. We refer to them as profiteers. Profiteers usually have ulterior motives. They may be trying to use the police to exact some measure of revenge or eliminate their competition by helping the police to arrest the competition. They may attempt to outsmart law enforcement by giving just enough information to gain their trust and protection. Some are clever enough to work as informants to learn our techniques and equipment capabilities.

While I was working with another agency and their informant, I suspected their CI was more interested in studying us than working for us. We had a new body wire transmitter disguised as a pager. I didn't want him to know that. I gave him the pager and told him we would be sending him messages. I then put a BIC pen with a plastic cap in his pocket and told him it was the transmitter. He messed up the deal so badly that the suspects were chasing him. We could hear him running and shouting as he guided us to a pickup point. As he emerged from an alley, I could see him holding the BIC pen like a stage mic. We rescued him and promptly fired him. At least he didn't learn about the pager. With profiteers, it's especially critical for the agent to determine their true motive. I learned to never underestimate how deceptive and manipulative people could be. It was the game we all played. I preferred to work with defendant informants. Their motive was clear, and our relationship was symbiotic.

Having said that, defendant informants still try to outplay the agent, usually by holding back information, giving up only enough to get their deal. They always know more, usually trying to protect a loved one or someone they fear. The challenge is to get all their information and not settle for only what they want to give.

It takes an experienced and talented agent to manage and control CIs. Some agents are better at it than others. The biggest mistake by police and agents is giving too much control to the CI. I'll tell more about my senior partner, Tom, in the next chapter but one of his favorite maxims was, "Who's running this investigation, you or your informant?" Looking back, I'm convinced a seasoned drug dealer could spot an inexperienced agent faster than a hungry kid could eat a piece of cake.

The Agents

Because a significant percentage of my investigations began with state and local law enforcement, I include them in this category. I never tried to hijack an investigation. The investigators I worked with trusted that I'd include them. This is one aspect of my career of which I'm most proud.

The primary challenge for narcotics agents is understanding the illegal drug trade. The Top-Secret Security investigation that agents undergo assures DEA that the applicants have a clean background. It also means that most applicants may have had little exposure to drug dealers. They will lack an understanding of how a drug dealer thinks and how the business works. No matter how good the training is, it's not possible to teach a new agent all the things a drug dealer has spent a lifetime learning. The exception to this may be a former police officer with extensive narcotics experience.

Inexperienced agents are at a disadvantage going up against seasoned drug traffickers. It takes time and experience to level the playing field. The academy training and senior agents can impart a wealth of knowledge. But the best way to learn the behaviors, habits, idiosyncrasies, and nuances of a drug dealer is from a drug dealer.

Most of DEA's best informants are former drug dealers. Working with them, while at the same time learning from them, is a like high-wire act. Any mistake can result in catastrophic consequences. In the long history of DEA, there are countless examples of informant disasters. At the same time, many of DEA's biggest and most successful cases result from informants.

The 'war on drugs' is actually thousands of individual battles being fought by law enforcement across America and beyond. In the coming chapters I'll tell you some of my battle stories. My stories don't scratch the surface. There are thousands more happening everyday by the men and women who have chosen to enter the arena.

~ 5 ~

INDIANAPOLIS

Let the Games Begin!

The first week in the Indianapolis office I spent getting acquainted with the staff and adjusting to the city. The office consisted of five GS-13 Senior Agents, Jim, Larry, Tony, Tom and Steve, two GS-12 Journeyman Agents, Gary and NY Thom, and three new agents Paul, Noel, and I. An agent's radio call sign is a number based on their seniority in the group. When I first arrived, I was number 10 on the radio.

Unlike most police departments, federal agencies such as the FBI, ATF and DEA denote rank by the Government Schedule, GS, pay grade system. New agents start at a GS-7. Promotions occur yearly for three years until reaching Journeyman grade GS-12. Attaining the GS-13 senior grade requires a supervisor's recommendation along with specific accomplishments. A GS-14 is DEA's first line supervisor. GS-15 is the second-line supervisor referred to as an Assistant Special Agent in Charge, ASAC. At the head of a field division is the Special Agent in Charge, SAC.

Our office was fortunate to have an incredibly efficient group secretary, Starr, who somehow managed paperwork for 10 agents. She was like a little sister, always in a good mood. The agents knew and appreciated how hard she worked. On top of everything she was thoughtful. She loved to bring in donuts and then tell us months later we were gaining weight.

The administrative assistant, Darleen, started with DEA following high school and grew up around agents. Ten years later, with a fresh crop of new agents arriving, there wasn't anything she hadn't heard or seen before. She could run the office in her sleep, so she took on the more important role as the lunch coordinator. Both she and Starr delighted in keeping our egos under control by roasting us with well-directed humor when they deemed it necessary. I could follow Darleen's infectious laugh to where the entertainment was happening. More often than not I was the one getting roasted. I miss them and their humor.

After I arrived, the boss assigned the three newest agents to work with a senior agent. My senior partner was Tom. I was assigned a Chevrolet Silverado truck as my OGV, Official Government Vehicle. The truck worked great for surveillance and undercover assignments.

My undercover driver's license

One day Gary said he was going to the Bureau of Motor Vehicles to get an undercover driver's license and asked if I wanted to go with him. Together we went to a special section of the BMV.

The instructors at the academy suggested we use our real first names when selecting our UC, undercover identities. If we met an acquaintance while undercover and they greeted us using our real first name, our undercover name would match. We should also use a common last name. The woman helping me at the BMV asked what name I would be using. In the moment, all I could think of was J. Howard Johnson. Her expression, as she looked at me over the top of her glasses, was 'Seriously?' My son was Jacob, and we called him Jay. My thought in choosing J. Howard Johnson was that

I could adopt my son's nickname, Jay. However, my senior partner Tom had a different plan, and my work nickname became HOJO.

I added life to my undercover wallet with bogus cards and pictures. I found a glamour photo of an extremely unattractive woman and put her in the front of my wallet. She became my 'wife.' When I opened my wallet, her photo was front and center. Anyone looking at that photo would shudder at the thought of being married to such a homely woman. It was a great distraction. The name worked too. Suspects assumed it was made up and it was!

Tom

My senior partner, Tom, was a Marine Corps Vietnam veteran and former Indianapolis Police Detective Sergeant. His last assignment in the police department was supervising a drug squad. Tom was involved in putting together a complex historical conspiracy case. That type of investigation moves slowly and is mostly a one-man operation. However, he always had other active investigations that I helped him on. Agents typically work several investigations simultaneously, carefully managing and juggling their time.

Working with Tom gave me the opportunity to watch and learn his style. He paid close attention to every detail and had no patience for anyone who cut corners. Undercover operations had to be done strictly by the book. He was especially demanding when it came to handling CIs. He drilled into my head, "Shortcuts lead to mistakes and mistakes lead to problems. I don't want to fix your problems, especially stupid ones. Remember, your work product will establish your reputation with the prosecutors and judges. Don't screw it up."

Tom had a well-established rapport with the United States Attorney's office, in particular the Organized Crime Drug Enforcement Taskforce, OCDETF. The task force specialized in prosecuting drug cases and hosted a complement of talented attorneys led by Jack Thar. Jack earned widespread recognition as one of the best attorneys in Indiana.

We held frequent after-hours strategy meetings in the basement bar at the Knights of Columbus near the federal building. It was there that friendships and trust flourished. Tom brought me into that circle and being a part of those 'meetings' was a privilege. Having unfettered access to our attorneys in an informal setting was priceless. Being able to call them my friends was an honor. It was also a lot of fun.

Tom could be difficult. He didn't like explaining himself, so when he did, I paid attention. He wanted things done his way, which admittedly most often proved to be the right way. One of his former IPD narcotics detectives once told me that Tom was the best investigator he'd ever known, but dealing with him could sometimes be "harder than woodpecker lips."

Once an operation was running smoothly, he was fun to work with, like the time we were in his car waiting for a buy/bust signal. He was telling me about a Vietnam War movie he'd watched called *Apocalypse Now*. He said there was a scene where a squadron of helicopter gunships launched an attack while playing Richard Wagner's *'Ride of the Valkyries.'* It was summer. Tom had the windows down and the sunroof open on his Nissan Maxima. When the arrest signal was given, he punched his CD player and the accelerator, and we raced across the parking lot blasting *'Ride of the Valkyries.'* That song is etched in my brain and linked directly to Tom.

My First Time Undercover

NY Thom, not to be confused with my senior partner Tom, was a GS-12 with three years on the job. Thom started in New York with Indianapolis being his first permanent assignment. He had just begun a new case and offered me the undercover role that I promptly accepted. It's common for new agents to be tested for their willingness to work undercover. The senior agents don't like it when new agents are reluctant to do undercover assignments. It's considered a rite of passage.

As the case agent, it was Thom's responsibility to manage the investigation and the CI. The CI lived in Gnaw Bone, Indiana, about 50 miles south of Indianapolis near the Hoosier National Forest. Thom and I drove to the CI's home to introduce me to him. We took his Chevrolet Impala that he had customized with a CD player and powerful speakers. As we drove down I-65 at slightly less than triple digits, he was blasting Bruce Springsteen's song *Glory Days*. To this day, that song takes me back to that wild ride in Thom's car.

The CI lived in a dilapidated shack somewhere deep in the forest. After he turned off the car's headlights, it was pitch black and dogs were barking around us. The CI came out with a flashlight, telling us to stay in the car as he got in the back seat. The CI said he had recently met a new cocaine source. The source was from Kentucky but came to Nashville, Indiana, frequently to visit a mutual friend. NY Thom told the CI that the objective was to introduce me to his source.

The plan called for the CI to tell his source he had a customer/buyer (me) willing to pay $2,000 for an ounce of cocaine. Thom told the CI to tell his source that the buyer wouldn't front the CI the money. Thom told the CI, "Set up a meeting between the source, you and Howard."

About a week later, NY Thom told me the CI had put the deal together. We planned to meet at a rest area on I-65 south of Columbus, Indiana. Thom assembled a team of agents from our office to provide surveillance for later that evening. I followed Thom in my truck to the CI's residence so we could wire him with a body transmitter.

Leaving from his house, the CI and I drove in my truck to the rest area. He spotted the suspect's vehicle, and we parked next to him. The CI got out and talked with him for a few minutes, then motioned me over. The CI introduced me as a trusted friend and the guy with the money. We talked for a few minutes before the suspect asked me if all this cocaine was for personal use. I told him no, "I'm trying to work my way out of debt, and this is the quickest way I know how to do it." He was satisfied with my answer.

We exchanged phone numbers, and I paid him $2,000. He gave me a small baggie of white powder that later tested positive for cocaine. I told the suspect that, coming from Indianapolis, it was really out of my way to pick up the CI. The suspect agreed to deal directly with me, but I would still have to pay the CI his finder's fee for connecting us. The suspect left the meeting and drove south on I-65. The surveillance team got his license plate. Armed with a plate number and his phone number, Thom began doing his background research. Our second deal went much the same as the first, except the informant wasn't involved. I bought another ounce for $2,000.

Thom was ready to make the arrest. He had me call the suspect and order four ounces. The suspect quoted a price of $6,000. The street term for four ounces is a quarter pound. This time the suspect didn't want to meet at the rest area. I surmised he was nervous because the deal involved $6,000. Smart dealers are always wary of being robbed, a legitimate concern for anyone in this business. Drug traffickers can't report it, and the rest area provided a perfect place for a robbery.

This time he wanted to meet in the truck stop restaurant on I-65 near Taylorsville at 9 PM. On the night of the deal, Indiana was in the midst of a major ice storm with high winds. When I pulled into the truck stop, there were 10 marked police cars in the parking lot.

The suspect's vehicle was there, but he wasn't in it. I went inside and saw a large table in the middle of the restaurant with 10 uniformed officers having dinner. The suspect was sitting in a booth. We made eye contact, and I gave him a 'what the hell' look. He smirked and flipped his head toward the door, signaling me to go outside. As we walked out, he said, "It's freezing out here. Let's get in your truck." Once inside, he told me to drive north on I-65. In less than a mile, he told me to pull into an emergency turn-round and stop. He asked if I had the money. I handed him a brown lunch bag with $6,000 in it. In exchange, he gave me a small block of white powder wrapped in plastic. While his attention was on counting the money, I gave the bust signal, and the team descended.

Both doors were simultaneously ripped open creating a 60-mph wind tunnel through the cab of my truck. When the agents grabbed him, he threw the money in the air which blew out of the open door. That was the last thing I saw before I was dragged out of my truck backwards. The agents quickly gathered the cash before it blew away. They placed the suspect and me over the hood of my truck facing each other and handcuffed us. I still remember the look on his face. It was a mixture of shock, confusion, extreme fear and despair rolled into one expression.

If all drug dealers were like Al Pacino's character Tony Montana in the 1983 movie *Scarface*, arresting them would be rewarding. But there are plenty of dealers who don't fit the *Scarface* profile. This suspect was one of them. He had no arrest record and no history of violence. He was a middle-aged man, married with children, living in a modest home in rural Kentucky. I don't condone drug use or drug trafficking and spent my career fighting it. One simply cannot deny the lure of easy money or the need to feed an addiction can lead otherwise honest people down the wrong road. I've seen it many times.

Thom took custody of the suspect and transported him to our Indianapolis office. The rest of us returned to the office. Thom attempted to get the suspect to cooperate and identify his source(s) and other co-conspirators. The suspect was not cooperating with them telling him, "Putting my friends in hot water so I can get out isn't who I am."

When asked about the other guy in the truck, me, he replied, "That guy had nothing to do with the cocaine. He was loaning me some money. The cocaine in the truck was mine." Thom came out of the interview room and said the suspect was lying about everything. He was even trying to cover for me. Thom told me to go in and tell him who I was and maybe then he would cooperate.

When he saw me, he got a sick look on his face as it sank in that I was an agent. He said, "You know, I thought you were my friend." As he looked down in defeat, he said, "Ah, it's OK. I know you were just doing your job."

As I walked out of the room, I didn't feel triumphant, I felt guilt. I never saw that emotion coming. It blindsided me. He wasn't supposed to be a nice guy. He was a drug dealer. And yet, he was willing to take the blame to protect me, and in return, I had double-crossed him. That paradox messed with my head. As a police officer, I arrested lots of criminals, but this somehow felt different.

As the night came to an end, Thom congratulated me on a 'job well done.' Then ribbing me, he said I reminded him of the character Pinto from the classic cult movie *Animal House.* ChatGPT described Pinto as, "The earnest, but naïve freshman swept up into the wild world of fraternity life in Delta House." Looking back, Thom had me pegged. I was still that small-town police officer not yet fully prepared for the crazy world of the DEA.

This was my first time undercover and it was exhilarating. It was like acting and I was good at it. Everything we did was by the book and in accordance with federal laws. But in the quiet after math, I felt conflicted. Fortunately, not all drug dealers are nice guys. It didn't take long to overcome my misgivings.

My First Time as a Case Agent

My senior partner, Tom, maintained a close relationship with his old IPD, Indianapolis Police Department, now IMPD, drug squad. They visited our office regularly and would often discuss their investigations with Tom, seeking his advice. Occasionally their investigations would reach beyond their jurisdiction or the upper limits of their funding resources. When that happened, we would pool our resources and work on the investigation together.

On one such occasion, the squad arrested a well-known inner city cocaine dealer who had agreed to cooperate. The dealer, turned CI, explained that his supplier would only sell two ounces or more of cocaine at a time. Two ounces of cocaine translated to $4,000, an amount above the IPD's spending limit.

Tom decided we needed to get involved. He told me to, "Open an investigation and run with it." I opened the case and signed the defendant up as a federal informant. The IPD detectives and I soon made a controlled purchase of two ounces of cocaine from the CI's supplier for $4,000.

DEA has strict protocols for purchasing drug evidence, including monitoring and recording all phone calls while setting up the purchase. By properly controlling the phone calls, we successfully recorded incriminating conversations between the CI and his source. When the transaction took place, the source didn't show up and instead sent his adult daughter. We got an arrest warrant for the source and a search warrant for his house. We found over a hundred thousand dollars in cash and a kilogram of cocaine. He surrendered while we searched his home. After arresting him, he agreed to cooperate with us in exchange for not charging his daughter.

During the search of his house, we found among many other things, a radio frequency (RF) detector. After testing it, I determined it was 100% capable of detecting our body wire. This device could silently alert him if anyone wearing a wire entered his house. This device created an extremely dangerous situation for an undercover agent or informant. At the academy, the instructors told us no such device existed and yet, here it was.

After he began cooperating, he showed me another body wire detector the size of a pager which alerted him by vibrating. He purchased it from a 'spy shop' that was advertised in *High Times* magazine. To my amazement, this device was also capable of detecting our body wire. This device could detect a wired undercover agent without the agent knowing he'd been discovered. An RF detector

Radio Frequency (RF) Detector

was like kryptonite to Superman. I think this is what first sparked my interest in technology. Years later, I would dive deep into it in an effort to help improve DEA's technology program.

His cooperation led to the arrest of several interstate drug traffickers resulting in the seizure of 6-8 kilograms of cocaine, guns and several hundred thousand dollars in cash. He was probably the smartest, most sophisticated informant I ever worked with. He spent his entire life learning how to deal drugs and not get caught. He not only knew the drug trade but studied how narcotics investigators operated. He told me he knew his 2-ounce minimum purchase exceeded the cops spending limits. But he never expected to become a target of the DEA.

The first time I used him as an informant to buy cocaine, he vehemently complained that I had given him too many hundred-dollar bills. He only wanted twenties. "I've been dealing drugs all my life and nobody has ever paid me using that many hundreds. That would stand out to me like a zebra in a horse race." I came to understand that street dealers are mostly paid with 10-and 20-dollar bills. They use those same bills to resupply. All those small bills move up the distribution chain. No one exchanges them for hundreds. In an exasperated voice he said, "Look. Unless we agree to do this right, I'm done. You're gonna get me killed, and I'd rather go to prison." I thought to myself, OK, lesson learned.

As the years went by, I was involved in numerous cash seizures, the largest being $900,000 seized from a marijuana dealer. He had stashed the cash in a suitcase hidden in his parents' garage attic. We had a local bank count the money. Three counting machines were used, and it took over two hours to count. Interestingly, the lion's share of the currency was twenty-dollar bills.

Many years later after being transferred to the Science and Technology division ST, I met an agent named Steve. Steve was the case agent who indicted General Manuel Noriega, the de facto leader of Panama. Steve is featured in a book titled 'Shooting the Moon' by David Harris. Arresting Noriega required a U.S. military invasion of Panama dubbed 'Operation Just Cause.' Steve told me that one of his informants in the Noriega case had described flying planeloads of cash from south Florida to Panama to be laundered. The currency was transported in suitcases and consisted mostly of twenty-dollar bills. It's safe to say my informant in Indiana knew what he was talking about with regards to small bills making their way up the distribution chain.

One evening my informant called me with information about a new target. He provided me with the suspect's phone number. This was before cellphones when people only had landline phones in their homes. The telephone company issued phone books. Anyone could have their number unlisted and not published in the phone book. It was called a 'non-pub' or a non-published number. The agents' home phones were non-pub numbers.

The CI's new target had a non-pub number. I told him we'd have to wait until I could get his name and address using a subpoena. He said, "You don't need a subpoena. I can get his name and address right now."

"How are you going to do that?"

"I supply a coke addict who works at the phone company. I can get any number I want."

I told him not to do that. The next day I told my co-workers what the CI had told me. Agents in the office canceled their non pub numbers and got new numbers using bogus names and addresses.

Informants are a necessary tool for agents, but they can be extremely insidious. Within a week of striking an agreement with this CI, he asked me to meet him in a parking lot. When I got there, he handed me an 8 ball of cocaine. Remember, that's 3 ½ grams, roughly the equivalent of three Sweet and Low packets. He said he found it in the console of his car and, wanting to be completely honest, he was turning it in to me. When I got back to the office, I told Tom what happened. He instructed me to process it as a surrendered drug exhibit.

When a defendant becomes an informant, their charges are placed in a pending status in court. When their work as a CI is over and the cases requiring their testimony are adjudicated, they are brought back into court to be sentenced on their original charges. After nearly a year, all the defendants, in this case from Texas, Florida, and Kentucky, were found guilty and sentenced.

Now it was time for our CI to appear in court and be sentenced on his original charges. Through his attorney, the CI requested a review of all the evidence accumulated as a result of his cooperation, an unusual request. I assumed he wanted to flaunt his accomplishments before he was sentenced.

It was a pain in the ass collecting everything. I had the lab send me the drug evidence, six kilograms of cocaine from three separate arrests. I gathered all the non-drug exhibits which included guns, cash and other miscellaneous contraband. Once I had everything, we set up the show and tell and placed all the evidence on a conference table in the U.S. Attorney's office.

The CI and his attorney only looked at the fifteen bags of drug evidence. While we were in court for his sentencing, I asked him what his deal was with viewing the evidence. He admitted he was looking for the 8 ball he had given me in the parking lot the prior year. If the 8 ball hadn't been included as an exhibit, his lawyer planned to file a motion to have the case dismissed, based on missing drug evidence and my misconduct. He was hoping I had 'flushed it down the toilet and forgot about it.' He was also hoping I would deny that he had ever given it to me. "I know it was a long shot but if I could catch you in a lie and destroy your credibility, I might get my case dismissed." Had his plan worked, all the cases he had helped me make could also have been dismissed. I knew then he had probably recorded our meeting in the parking lot when he gave me the 8 ball. He apologized, "Sorry, but I was desperate. I was just trying to save myself." I learned a valuable and sobering lesson that day about just how cunning and calculating a desperate informant can be. His plan didn't work because my senior partner Tom wouldn't tolerate short cuts or sloppy work.

Desperate People Do Desperate Things

It was 2 AM when my bedside phone rang. It was Tom. "We've got a problem. Meet me at the truck stop on I-70 at the Greenfield exit."

When I pulled in, he was already there. I parked my car and got in with him. As we drove southeast, he told me the informant we had recently signed up was at a sheriff's office in a remote part of the state. The informant told the deputies he was a DEA informant and that someone had tried to kill him.

He told the deputies a car chased and then shot at him. He escaped and drove to a sheriff's office, seeking protection. He was a defendant informant, the kind Tom liked to work with, but this sounded like a phony story for several reasons. First, we had kept his arrest secret. Second, he had no reason to be in this rural county 60 miles from Indianapolis. Finally, his criminal associates were from Indianapolis. None of his story made sense.

When we arrived, we saw his BMW in the parking lot. Bullets had shattered the back window and riddled both sides of the car. If he was chased and shot at, it would be logical for the back window to be shot out. Looking closer, the angle of the bullet entry holes in the car's body made no sense. The holes were perfectly round, which meant the bullets entered at a 90-degree angle. Coming from behind, they should have entered at a sharper angle.

The deputies told us they would help in any way they could. They took us to the room where our CI waited. When we entered, he was trembling, shedding a few tears, Porky Pig talking. Tom was furious, telling him his story was bullshit. The guy was pleading with Tom to believe him, but Tom repeatedly told him to shut up. The guy was terrified of Tom. Tom finally said to him, "Have it your way. But when it turns out that you've lied to me, the only thing that's going to beat you to prison will be the headlights of the bus."

With that, Tom walked out, slamming the door behind him. I never said a word until Tom left. After the door closed, I looked at the informant and said, "Wow! I've never seen him that mad before." Which wasn't true. I had seen him that mad at me.

Tom had set the stage for the oldest trick in the book, the Good Cop-Bad Cop routine. I went to work on him. "Look, here's the deal. He knows you're lying. I know you're lying. You know you're lying. If you tell me the truth right now, I'll try to talk to Tom to straighten this mess out." He said, "Yeah, it's all bullshit. I did it myself. I'll show you where I ditched the gun."

"Okay. Let me see what I can do." I left the room less than two minutes after Tom and said, "The guy admitted it's all bullshit and he's going to show us where the gun is." Tom simply said, "Well done." We had not discussed or planned the routine, yet Tom expected me to play off his bad cop act. The CI showed us where he had thrown the gun in a ditch. We picked it up and Tom and I headed back to the city.

I chose this story because it's a good example of how irrational a person can become when they are in a seemingly hopeless situation. Here was an intelligent, successful 35-year-old man who got busted by the DEA for dealing drugs. He was given an opportunity to cooperate, which meant turning against his co-defendants, likely friends or family. When the reality of what he had to do overwhelmed him, he became so irrational that shooting his BMW and concocting a story made sense to him. In his state of mind, he could just as easily convinced himself that shooting Tom might have also made sense. In part, that's what made our work so dangerous. We were in the business of creating desperate people.

There is a footnote to this story. About a year later a nearly identical incident occurred. This time it was real. My informant's son-in-law was driving the informant's truck. Someone began chasing and shooting at the truck, probably thinking it was my informant. A

Bullet hole in CI's car

bullet entered through the back of the cab, hitting the kid in his back. The bullet lodged in his lung and very nearly killed him. The kid survived, but we were never able to identify who did it. There was a long line of people who wanted to kill my informant. I was reminded once again that this 'game' isn't really a game.

The Sniper

Gary was from the Bloomington area and graduated from Indiana University Bloomington. Prior to joining the Indiana State Police, he had been a University Police Officer. He joined DEA three years before me. He was well-connected within the law enforcement community in Indiana and had a steady stream of cases. I liked Gary for the same reason other cops liked him. He was a genuinely nice guy and easy to work with. By the time we finished our first case together, I'd figured out he was also deceptively clever. He was one of those guys who would be two moves ahead of you in a game of chess and you wouldn't know it.

One day Gary asked me if I would be interested in doing some undercover work. He had an informant who knew a methamphetamine dealer in Bedford, Indiana. During this time, meth labs were rampant in southern Indiana. I was all in. We met with the informant and laid out a story-line. I was a bouncer at a strip club in Indianapolis and was supplying the dancers with coke and meth. The dancers in turn sold it to their patrons. We were selling the stuff so fast we couldn't keep up and needed a better supplier.

Gary had the informant set up a one ounce buy, telling the suspect it was just a sample. The informant and I met the suspect in a public park in Bedford and the purchase went without a hitch. The target believed our story line. I told him if his product was good, we could both make a lot of money. We exchanged phone numbers. Mine was an undercover number. The lab results came back indicating the meth was high quality meaning the sample hadn't been diluted. This likely meant the suspect was getting it directly from a meth lab. We talked several times, and he was eager to do more business.

My senior partner Tom suggested we introduce a second undercover for safety reasons and volunteered himself. I told the suspect his stuff was so good that the owner of the club wanted to talk to him. I explained to him that the owner, my boss, owned two clubs and may be interested in having him supply both clubs. I said this was our chance to make some really big money. Greed is a powerful tool in this business.

I ordered a second two-ounce sample and this time Tom came with me. We met in the same park. Tom explained that his dancers could easily sell a couple of pounds a week. Before he agreed to do business, Tom needed to be sure the supply would be steady. Tom said, "I'll be honest with you. We've been getting our supply from bikers and I'm tired of dealing with their biker bullshit. Before I blow them off, I have to know you can handle this."

The suspect guaranteed his people could easily make that much a week. His choice of words clearly implied he was directly connected to a meth lab. We bought the two ounces and Tom told him we needed two pounds by the end of the week. We agreed on a price of $50,000 for two pounds as long as it was the same high-quality stuff. Tom warned him that if he tried to cut the purity, there would be serious problems.

A week later I called the suspect and he had the two pounds. We agreed to meet in the restaurant at the Howard Johnson motel in Bloomington at 5:00 PM. At 10:00 AM a surveillance team had rented two rooms, installed a hidden camera in the undercover room and the surveillance equipment in the adjoining room. The boss called the group together and said this would be an all-agent operation. We had three agents in the monitor room adjoining the undercover room with another five set up on the outer perimeter along with four Indiana State Police units.

I arrived a couple of hours early and hid my gun in the undercover room, stuffing it between bathroom towels. At 5:00 PM, with everything in place, I walked down the hall to the hotel restaurant.

The target was sitting in a booth, and I sat down across from him. I noticed he was jittery, and that's not a good sign for a meth dealer. I broke the ice by saying, "I don't know why, but I'm a little nervous."

"Yeah, me too." There was an odor of alcohol on his breath. There was a tab on the table for his coffee. I told him, "I got this," and left money on the table. As we walked down the hall to the room, I stopped and said, "Look, all we need to do is get this first deal behind us and things will settle down. I don't want anything to break bad or go crazy. I don't have a gun. You can search me."

I turned face-to-face with him and held my arms out. He said, "That won't be necessary." I made the offer and that was good enough for him. When we entered the room, he pulled a gun from his waistband and placed it on the television. He looked at Tom and said, "Because Howard is being honest with me, I'm willing to do this unarmed."

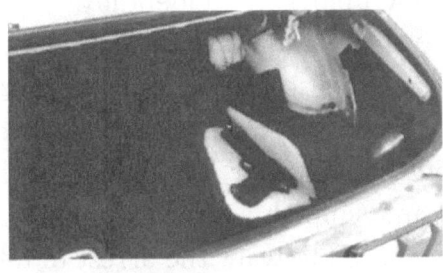

Gun and drugs in the trunk of the car

He asked to see the money. Tom handed him a paper bag full of cash that he quickly thumbed through. His mood changed. He turned intense and serious. "I've got what you ordered. It's a short drive from here. But I'll tell you right now. If you big city guys think you're dealing with a couple of hill jacks, you're making a big mistake."

He then gave Tom a stone-cold death stare and said, "Howard and I are going to take a little ride. I'll show him the stuff and when we get back, we'll finish the deal. This is how it's going down. I have a sharpshooter watching the product. If y'all are thinking about ripping me off, my guy is going to put a bullet right through his head." He turned and looked at me and said, "Are you ready?"

"Hey, I have an idea. How about Tom goes instead of me?" Tom looked at me, and without saying a word, I knew he was thinking 'you smart-ass.' The suspect looked at me and said, "No fucking way! You got me into this. It's you and me, buddy."

It was obvious the suspect was more scared of Tom than he was of me. So, crap. "OK, but I need to pee first." I went into the bathroom and pulled my pistol from the towel rack, putting it in my waistband in the middle of my back. Now I had a gun, and he didn't. The plan was coming together. Well, except for the sniper part.

We got in my truck and were driving east on Highway 45 for about a half mile when he told me to turn right into the IU Bloomington football stadium parking lot. He told me to park next to an old beat-up yellow car. The arrest signal was for me to take off my hat as soon as I saw the drugs. The wind was whipping across the parking lot. Before I got out of my truck, I pulled my hat down as tight as I could, making sure it didn't blow off accidentally.

He opened the trunk of the vehicle and moved a leather coat covering two bags of white powder. He also inadvertently revealed a 45-caliber pistol lying next to the meth. Wow, what a trickster. He left one gun at the hotel but had another one hidden in the trunk. He picked up the pistol and slipped it into his waistband. Even though I had seen the dope, I didn't want the arrest to take place in that moment. The defendant would see the approaching vehicles, which might have resulted in a gunfight. I knew I could take him but there was still a sniper in the mix. I opted to change the plan and didn't give the signal. I told him, "OK, that's good enough for me." I left the drugs in the trunk, and we returned to the hotel.

Unbeknownst to me, after we left the hotel, Tom radioed the perimeter team and alerted them to the sniper. The team spotted an open CJ-7 Jeep in a church parking lot across the road from the stadium. They swooped in and found two suspects and a fully loaded 30-06 caliber rifle with a

Snipers in custody

high-powered scope on the floor between the front seats. From the sniper's vantage point, he had a clear view of me in the parking lot. The shot would have been a relatively easy 400 yards that a skilled deer hunter could have made. The surveillance team took them into custody. When we returned to the hotel room, the suspect was arrested by Tom and the agents from the control room. Nobody roughed me up this time. The suspects didn't cooperate, and the meth lab was never located.

There's an informative book titled Tweeker Parade *by retired DEA agent Philippa LeVine. Philippa spent much of her career working meth lab cases in southern California. Her book is a fun read plus it's informative and humorous.*

This Isn't Even My Pot

I was at my desk catching up on reports when Gary called. He told me he was in Madison, which is a small quiet town on the Ohio River in southern Indiana. He was in the middle of a reverse undercover deal working with the ISP, Indiana State Police. A reverse is when the police pose as sellers instead of buyers. It wasn't used very often. Normally we work our way up the distribution chain not down unless there's special circumstance to justify it.

He told me he needed some help and since it was Gary, I knew it would be an adventure. He said, "I need you to take our undercover Corvette and pick up 300 pounds of marijuana from the State Police Lab. We've called the lab and they're expecting you. Get down here as quick as you can."

When I arrived, a lab tech was waiting with two dollies stacked with bricks of compressed marijuana. We started loading the bricks into the car. I filled the passenger side floorboard up to the seat. Then I had to close the passenger door and finish loading them from the driver's side to stack them against the closed door. The bricks were stacked halfway up the window. I could barely see out and the smell was pungent. I left the lab and headed around I-465 to connect with I-74 toward Cincinnati.

As I came down the ramp onto I-74, Bruce Springsteen's *Glory Days* came on the radio. It made me think of my first undercover deal with NY Thom and the night the money blew out of my truck. It made me smile. I felt great. I opened the throttle and hit triple digits

Me and the Corvette

as I cranked up the volume and passed everything on the highway.

Suddenly I noticed the flashing red lights of an Indiana State Trooper on my bumper. I pulled over and lowered my window as the trooper walked up and looked inside. "What in the hell are you doing?"

"I was probably going a little fast, but I can explain."

Then he saw the marijuana bricks. "Damn! Is that marijuana?"

I laughed a little. "Yeah, 300 pounds and it really stinks. I think it's skunk weed."

"Get out of the car and keep your hands where I can see them."

"Whoa, no wait! I'm a DEA agent and I'm working on a case with your narcotics guys in Madison. Here's my badge and credentials."

"WHAT?"

I could tell he was processing this absurd situation and trying to decide if I was for real. Like a dummy, I thought I could ease the tension by joking with him. "In case you're wondering, this isn't even my pot. Technically speaking it's more yours than it is mine."

"Oh really. Wait here, smart-ass."

"Hey, I wasn't trying to be a smart-ass."

"Well then, I guess you're a natural."

I don't know, maybe he was in a mood. He appeared to be a well-seasoned trooper, no doubt having seen and heard it all before. He got into his car, talked on the radio for a few minutes and walked back. "All I can say is sometimes you DEA guys aren't right in the head. You're free to go."

As I drove away, I realized he had a point. Here I was with my scruffy hair and beard, wearing a leather jacket driving a Corvette loaded with pot, not to mention speeding at nearly 100 mph. Thankfully he hadn't seen the 14 shot 9mm pistol tucked under my thigh. It was at that moment I realized I had evolved from that small-town police officer to an undercover DEA agent.

When I got to Madison, I knew something was happening. A State Police SWAT team was there standing by. Gary told me the informant actually belonged to the State Police, and he hadn't been following their instructions very well. He was too easily swayed during the undercover phone calls

From 1984 to 1987

which resulted in the bad guys calling the shots. The lead investigator and Gary wanted these guys taken down because they were suspects in a decade old homicide of a police officer. They were also old-time career criminals with a history of violence including bank robbery.

Gary said, "The informant told them he had 500 pounds of pot coming in from Texas which he'd sell for $1,000 a pound. The suspects went for it, so now we're trying to put together a plan that's going to be reasonably safe. But this snitch is a pain in the ass. We can't get him to follow our script on the phone. I swear this snitch could give a woodpecker a headache. The plan has changed. We've been able to change the load vehicle from the Corvette to a truck. They won't tell him where the off-load location is. All they've said is that it's a warehouse and they want the truck to pull inside."

I said to Gary, "Oh boy, this sounds bad. There are more red flags here than a Chinese parade."

"I know, but these detectives want this to work. They've been after these guys for years." Gary didn't have to say it. We'd stick with the detectives. I then asked, "What's the plan?"

"They've rented a U-Haul truck and are drilling peepholes for the SWAT team to see out. They're also rigging the overhead door so the team can open it from inside."

Me: "Are they really going to pull inside the warehouse? I smell an ambush."

Gary: "I know. Here's what I'm thinking. You and I drive the truck but instead of pulling inside, we stop in front of the building. Maybe we can draw them out."

"Are the state guys OK with that?"

"Yeah, I've already talked to them."

"OK, let's give it a go."

Now neither the pot nor the undercover Corvette was part of the plan. I transferred custody of the stinky pot to one of the detectives to get it out of the Corvette before the smell got embedded. With the SWAT team set up in the back of the truck, the informant made his call. The suspects gave him directions to an old warehouse on a hill overlooking the Ohio River about 30 minutes away. The warehouse was a perfect location for a robbery or an off-load site. My gut was telling me robbery.

Gary drove. As soon as we pulled in and parked in front of the building, a guy came running out of the door yelling at us to pull the truck around to the side overhead door. I said to Gary, "It's show time!" We needed to get control of the situation quickly I jumped out of the truck and launched into him like a Texas tornado.

"Do you think I'm stupid enough to pull inside a warehouse with a half million dollars of grass? I don't know you from Adam, so that's not happening. And where the hell is your moron partner who set this whole mess up? He's supposed to be here." His 'moron partner' was our informant and we knew he wasn't coming because we planned it that way.

"Calm down, man. He's on his way. He'll be here soon. Come on. Pull the truck inside."

"No way. I want to see the money first. This whole deal stinks. I don't know who you are and we're not doing anything until your idiot shows up. I'll throw the pot in the river before I pull into that warehouse."

By now, Gary was next to me. The guy tried to plead his case to Gary. He didn't want to deal with me anymore. He said to Gary, "Come with me. You can come inside and look at the money."

It was all happening very fast. Gary and the guy started walking and just as they reached the doorway, Gary looked back at me. In a split second, the guy grabbed Gary from behind, pulling him off balance. Now he had Gary in a headlock and was pulling him backward into the doorway. I ran over and punched the guy in the side of his head. He dropped like a sack of potatoes. Gary and I began dragging him back across the parking lot toward the truck just as the SWAT team ran the other way toward the front door.

I looked back and saw them charge into the building. Seconds later, I heard a couple of pops from inside that I could only assume was gunfire. I watched as the SWAT team engaged in a tactical retreat out of the doorway. As they made their exit, a canister of tear gas was tossed into the building. When the gas cleared enough for investigators to go inside, they found, among other things, duct tape and plastic zip ties. No doubt it was going to be a robbery. The suspects had fled out the back of the building.

State Police investigators later identified and arrested the two defendants that had escaped and charged them with attempted robbery. They were the career criminals as the State Police had suspected. The suspect we had in our custody admitted their plan had been to steal the pot. There was never any money.

Eat a Banana

It was late summer, early fall. Farmers would soon be picking corn and soybeans. Their harvest coincided with that of the outdoor marijuana growing season in Indiana and Kentucky.

The topography of southern Indiana is entirely different from the flat farmlands of northern Indiana. Glaciers stopped moving south halfway through the state during the Ice Age, creating a drastic difference in the landscape. The terrain of southern Indiana is very rugged with a mixture of rolling hills, ravines, forest and farmland. There are several rivers and waterways, perfect for growing and concealing marijuana. The point being, there are endless locations where marijuana growers can operate with nearly a 0% chance of being discovered. A small clearing in the middle of the Hoosier National Forest could easily provide enough sunlight to support a dozen or more hybrid marijuana plants. Some can grow as tall as a large Christmas tree and yield several thousand dollars of finished product.

Every year, the Indiana State Police, supported by the Indiana Air National Guard and DEA, conducted outdoor marijuana eradication operations. The operations started before the harvest when the plants were big and lush, making them easier to see by aerial spotters. A typical operation consisted of a helicopter crew and a ground crew armed with machetes to hack down and destroy the plants. One of the biggest challenges was guiding the ground crew to the patch. Sometimes they could get to it with four-wheeler, but more often they had to hike in. On rare occasions, the pilot might find a suitable spot to land and the helicopter crew could cut and load the plants.

I made the mistake one afternoon of not looking terribly busy. The boss strolled through the group room looking for a volunteer, saw me, and asked if I had time to help the eradication team. The boss had a way of phrasing a directive like it was a question. I readily volunteered, and he told me to report to the Indiana Air National Guard Office located off I-74 on the southeast side of Indianapolis at 8:00 AM the next day.

After arriving, I gave my name to the receptionist and she escorted me to a kitchen area where a pilot in his flight suit was drinking coffee. I told him I had always wanted to be a helicopter pilot when I grew up. He laughed and asked if I'd ever flown in one. I told him no. He laughed again and asked if I was prone to motion sickness. I said riding in the backseat of a car made me queasy. Pointing at some bananas he said, "Why don't you eat a couple of bananas and call that breakfast?"

The inference was that the bananas were an antidote to motion sickness. "I didn't know bananas could prevent motion sickness."

He replied, "They can't, but they'll taste the same coming up as they do going down, and that's a bonus."

It wasn't long before the co-pilot and crew chief arrived and he said, "Ready. Let's go."

We walked to a waiting Huey helicopter with the doors re moved. The captain and his co-pilot fired up the aircraft. The crew chief fitted me with a helmet, showed me how to use the intercom headset and locked me in with a safety harness. We lifted off, tilting forward slightly, and began to gain speed and altitude. It was a bumpier ride than I expected. Suddenly, we broke into what is called 'clean air,' a much smoother ride. Sitting in the jump seat next to the open door looking out and down was thrilling.

I heard the captain's voice through my headset telling us we were early. We had time to kill. He asked, "Anyone up for a stroll down memory lane with me?"

The crew chief replied, "Yeah, let's go. Hit it."

I didn't know it, but the captain was a former Vietnam combat helicopter pilot. We dropped into a riverbed flying 30-40 feet above the water, below the treetops, following the river. Suddenly 'Ride of the Valkyries' began playing in my head. With the precision of an Indianapolis 500 race car driver, he followed the river, banking right then left. It was absolutely exhilarating.

We suddenly popped back up into the open sky, headed over to the target area and began working a grid search. I have a slight color deficiency in that I can't distinguish between pastel shades of green. This small, mostly irrelevant issue became a major problem for spotting marijuana plants. The crew found several small patches that day with no help from me. My career as a spotter abruptly ended. I participated in other eradication operations but only as a machete-swinging ground stomper.

Marijuana growers put in a tremendous amount of arduous work all summer cultivating their plants. Some growers had to backpack in water and fertilizer to keep the plants healthy.

Likewise, the eradication crews hiked in and out of the same rugged terrain,

Our house in Indianapolis

making it some of the most physically demanding work in law enforcement. It was not a surprise when occasionally a National Guard helicopter returned with a random bullet hole from an angry pot farmer who had lost a year's worth of work.

On our return flight, I asked the pilot to make a pass over our house so I could get a picture. I had put a pool in the backyard for the kids. Even I could spot that. It was a memorable day.

Indiana State Trooper Terry

I went out with the eradication ground crew a few more times that fall. I met an Indiana State trooper/investigator, Terry. He grew up on a farm and had become especially knowledgeable about growing marijuana. Cultivating and growing marijuana was something I knew little about. Most of the DEA offices had an agent assigned to manage the marijuana eradication program. The requirements to open a marijuana investigation under DEA guidelines required a huge amount of marijuana. Most agents kept busy working on hard drug cases like cocaine and meth.

Terry had a big personality and it was fun working with him. While we were chopping down pot plants, he spotted an area infested with poison ivy. He volunteered to chop that area, protecting the rest of us from exposure. I watched as he cut it down and carried bundles of marijuana out bare-handed. He told us he was immune to it and showed his fearlessness by rubbing it on his arms. Laughing, he pulled up his shirt and rubbed it on his belly. I was sure he would break out in a nasty rash by the end of the day, but he didn't.

Wackin' and stackin'

I had planned to meet him the next day to talk about some indoor marijuana grow operations he was investigating. He was late for our meeting. When he showed up, he told me he had to stop by the pharmacy to get a prescription for poison ivy. I laughed and said, "So, you're not immune after all?"

Terry: "I am, but apparently my wife isn't. She woke up this morning covered with a nasty rash. She's really mad at me. How was I supposed to know it was contagious?"

Me: "It's not contagious, its oil can transfer skin to skin. Let me guess what you two were doing last night."

With his best Bart Simpson imitation, he said, "Yeah, it sucks, man. She's acting like it's all my fault." I laughed and said, "I can't imagine why."

Terry went on to tell me the DEA was missing the boat. "The focus is on outdoor eradication. In my opinion, the more sophisticated indoor cultivators are being overlooked." He said he had been executing, on average, two or three search warrants a month on indoor grow operations. I asked, "That many? How are you finding them?" He said he routinely checked UPS shipping records looking for packages shipped from hydroponic grow shops that advertised in *High Times* magazine. Once he found multiple deliveries or large packages being shipped to an address, he began investigating the recipient. There was a pile of *High Times* magazines stacked in the corner of his office. He picked up a copy and showed me the advertisements for several stores. There were two such stores in Indiana with several more across the country. I was impressed that Terry knew the value of studying his opponent. What better way to get inside their head than to read what they read.

After I retired from DEA, I worked for over 10 years as a contract instructor for the State Department's Anti-Terrorism Assistance program, ATA. During my time as an instructor, I participated in teaching counter terrorism courses in 17 countries worldwide. The single most important message we taught the students was to study and learn the mindset of the terrorists they were pursuing. I often talked about my Indiana State Police detective friend Terry and how he studied the tactics and methods of the marijuana growers he was pursuing. Terry was always looking for vulnerabilities where his suspects had no choice but to expose themselves in order to complete their objectives. This is known as a proactive investigation where studying your opponent is the first step. If there is any hope in preventing a terrorist attack it's going to require a proactive approach.

The next step was to look at the possible grow location. Sometimes he found the windows covered or blacked out. He would subpoena a year's worth of electric bills for the house or building in question. Indoor grow operations consume a large amount of electricity. A sharp increase in electricity usually signaled the start of the operation. Indoor operations use the electricity to power the grow lights and other equipment. He also compared electric bills from equivalent sized houses in the area.

Sometimes he used a specialized camera capable of detecting heat called a FLIR, Forward Looking Infrared. The heat signature of the suspect house often glowed compared to the neighboring houses. He would wrap up his probable cause search warrant by conducting criminal history and background checks on the occupants.

I reviewed several of his completed investigations and was impressed by his success and ingenuity. He explained that many of his defendants were far more sophisticated cultivators than most of the outdoor growers. The indoor guys were not just growing pot. They were using sophisticated plant development techniques like cloning, cross pollination or selective breeding and importing hybrid seeds from all over the world to produce high quality plants.

Indoor cultivators, seeking to optimize their confined areas, have turned to specialized equipment, such as advanced grow lights and high-efficiency fertilizers. Terry said he had also found some cultivators using hydroponic systems, eliminating the need for soil. Terry determined that most of the confiscated equipment and supplies had been purchased and shipped from hydroponic shops that were advertised in *High Times*.

I helped Terry with a couple of his active investigations to learn how he did it. Later, we executed a state search warrant on a suspected grow operation. While the state police were collecting and recording their evidence, and dismantling the set up, I talked with the defendant.

I developed a rapport with him that led to a guided tour of his hydroponic setup. In detail he explained the techniques he used to develop hybrid super plants including things like cloning. His enthusiasm for his work was like that of a proud parent. He was extraordinarily knowledgeable and did an excellent job explaining the operation to me in simple terms. The police videographer, using a shoulder-mounted VHS camera, started recording as the suspect gave me the tour.

I regularly updated the DEA Marijuana Eradication Coordinator on our activities. I also gave him a copy of the video interview, which became known as *The Timmy Tape*. That tape was used several times in police training classes. The Indianapolis Eradication agent, Steve, reported our progress to the Marijuana Desk at DEA Headquarters. Eventually *The Timmy Tape* made its way to headquarters and helped establish the justification for DEA's *Operation*

Green Merchant initiative. Headquarters redoubled their focus on the indoor cultivators and specialty stores.

The Indiana State Police Major Drug Unit and I opened a joint federal investigation into one of the specialty stores in Indiana. The store was a regular advertiser in *High Times*. We needed to determine if the store personnel were promoting and supporting marijuana cultivation. An undercover Indiana State Police detective entered the store several times, seeking advice on technical issues related to the hydroponic cultivation of marijuana. The detective recorded several conversations with store personnel openly providing guidance.

In 1991, DEA launched a nationwide initiative aimed at combating marijuana cultivation, specifically targeting specialty shops collaborating with growers. The initiative was called *Operation Green Merchant* and contributed to the increase of indoor cultivation seizures from less than 1,000 per year in 1985 to 3,849 in 1992.

THC is the active compound in marijuana that produces the high from ingesting it. In the 1960s and 70s THC levels measured between 1%to 4%. These sophisticated cultivators were able to increase the levels to nearly 10% by 2000. With today's marijuana, THC levels often exceed 20% making modern marijuana more potent than ever thanks to American ingenuity.

By far, my most memorable indoor grow operation took place at a pig farm. A financially strapped farmer allowed some aspiring young cultivators to conceal a grow operation in a portion of his hog barn. By the time investigators identified and raided the operation, the young cultivators had produced a crop of high-quality marijuana plants. The problem was they never made a profit and had to refund customers' money.

By co-existing with the hogs inside the barn, the plants absorbed the odor of the pig poop. When customers smoked the pot, it smelled and tasted like pig poop, and they wanted their money refunded. Apparently, the high wasn't worth the gag. You can't make this stuff up.

Crack Arrives in Indianapolis

In 1991, Tom's old IPD narcotics squad executed a search warrant on what is now known as a 'crack house.' Crack was a new phenomenon in Indianapolis. The raid resulted in the arrest of a couple of young men from Los Angeles who had come to Indianapolis on a mission to expand their crack cocaine distribution network. They self-identified as members of a Los Angeles street gang.

How does an LA street gang infiltrate and expand their crack cocaine network into a new city? In this case, one of the young men was visiting his aunt in Indianapolis and introduced his cousin and his cousin's friends to a new form of cocaine called 'crack.'

Crack is a smokeable form of cocaine. Smoking provides a more efficient means for the body to absorb the drug, creating a more intense high. There is a process for converting cocaine HCL to crack and part of their mission was to teach the Indianapolis guys how to convert the drug, package it and sell it.

Once crack was introduced into a neighborhood, it quickly spread throughout the city. During the 1990s, as crack spread across the U.S., it brought with it a staggering increase in violent crime and homicides. Several police departments experienced a sharp increase in homicides following the introduction of crack into their cities. Likewise, Indianapolis experienced a major spike in the early 1990s.

That night was the first time I saw crack cocaine. When we executed the search warrant, a batch of crack was drying in a frying pan and looked like white paint chips. I successfully recruited and interviewed one of the young defendants from that arrest. Unfortunately, he didn't know the name of the cocaine source from Los Angeles but was able to describe him in great detail.

On one of many trips to Los Angeles, I spent several hours looking through dozens of self-adhesive photo albums containing hundreds of pictures of known gang members. The LA street gang unit from the Compton station collected

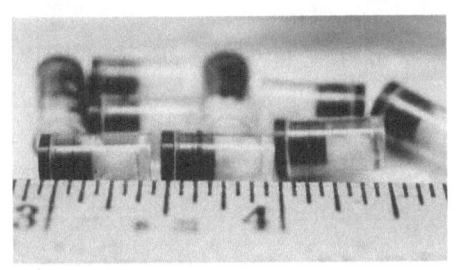

Crack vials

them. I finally identified the source from his picture. Later, armed with a warrant, we found him working in a recording studio in Hollywood, California. We arrested him and brought him to Indianapolis where he was found guilty of conspiracy to distribute cocaine.

Simultaneous to my investigation, ATF Special Agent Pat Donovan was leading a multi-agency task force targeting another LA street gang that was also infiltrating Indianapolis. That gang was using money from crack sales to purchase guns which were shipped to California. I was assigned to work in that task force under Pat's command. We worked on both investigations in tandem.

Pat was known throughout the law enforcement community for his work in solving the Speedway Bomber *crime in the late1970s in Speedway, Indiana. That investigation involved a series of eight random bombings over a seven-day period. His efforts were crucial to unraveling the mystery, leading to the arrest of the bomber. One of my favorite memories of Pat and Emmit, another ATF agent assigned to the task force, took place during one of our California trips. We found ourselves on Topanga Canyon Boulevard, a popular scenic drive. It was a beautiful sunny day when we came across a roadside stand selling strawberries. We stopped and got a quart and stood by the side of the road eating them. At one point I said,*

"You know, if this job was easy, everybody would want to do it." We all laughed, and it became a running joke over the years.

At the conclusion of the investigation, the task force received a certificate of appreciation from the city of Indianapolis. The police chief presented certificates to each of us in the mayor's office. Years later, after Pat and I had both retired, we reunited on the tennis courts. We played together many times at the Indianapolis Racquet Club, IRC. Tragically, he died in a traffic accident. I've lost many friends over the years, but losing Pat was especially difficult. I know it was also tremendously hard Pat's taskforce on his family and everyone who knew him.

The Indianapolis portion of my investigation took place mostly in the east side neighborhoods near where we lived. The case culminated with a dozen or more east-side street gang members being arrested. My last name appeared on legal documents required to be provided to the defendants and their attorneys.

Pat's Task Force members

About a week after the arrests took place, my neighbor, Brad, knocked on my door one Saturday morning. He wanted to show me what he thought was a bullet hole in his front bay window. It was indeed a bullet hole, and the bullet had passed through his living room into the kitchen where it lodged inside a microwave. There was no way of knowing for sure, but it was likely meant to intimidate me. Whoever did it, shot the wrong house. I decided it was time to move out of the city. We had a house built and moved to a neighboring county.

About a year after that, following a long and difficult day that ended about 3:00 AM, I pulled into my driveway only to find my garage door opener didn't work. As I got out of my car, I realized I was in the driveway of my old house. I recount this story to emphasize how exhausted and pre-occupied agents can become.

While working on this investigation I saw a popular new 1991 movie titled *Boyz in the Hood* starring Cuba Gooding Jr. The national news stations reported that several theaters in Los Angeles had erupted in gang violence on opening night of the movie. A psychologist featured on one news station suggested that the movie was triggering violent primal instincts in young men and argued that the movie should be banned.

I was talking with my defendant informant from this case about his gang life in Los Angeles. In a lighthearted moment I asked him, "What's up with you guys shooting each other in theaters?" He told me the movie promoters caused it. I laughed and said that was ridiculous. "You're actually trying to blame the movie executives for a bunch of gang bangers shooting each other?"

He explained that the very purpose of street gangs in Los Angeles was to control and run their neighborhoods. Most neighborhoods had a movie theater. "When the movie came out, we all wanted to see it. The movie execs released the movie in select theaters only. Due to limited locations of selected theaters, some gangs had to enter rival territories to watch the movie. What do you think is going happen if rival gangs are in the same theater at the same time?"

While I find it hard to believe the select theater release was done for that purpose, it can't be denied that his explanation was far more logical than the expert psychologist had explained on the news.

Tigger

The boss walked into the group area one morning and said he needed four senior agents to conduct an applicant interview at 1:30 PM. Tom said, "That sounds like a job for the least senior, senior agents." The boss readily agreed. "I need Howard, Noel, Paul and Gary in my office at one."

In his office, he handed each of us a copy of the applicant's SF-171 background application. I was reminded of my interview in Chicago seven years earlier. Everything I was told and warned about had been spot on. I now understood what was meant when I was told it's not a job, not even a career. It is a lifestyle.

The boss explained the interview process was a pass or fail and the decision had to be unanimous. I asked if there was a list of questions. He told us, "No. You're experienced agents. Ask him whatever you want. If you think he'll make a good agent, pass him. If not, fail him." He added, "There will be no split decisions. If one of you chooses to fail him, he's done. Non-supervisory senior street agents must make the decision."

The applicant was waiting in our interview room dressed in a crisp black suit, looking intimidated. I remembered that feeling. We walked in wearing blue jeans and polo shirts with no actual plan. I saw a little of myself in him and knew what he was going through. The first thing that struck me was his youth. He was 26. I was 10 years older.

Noel began by asking him to tell us about himself. While he lacked law enforcement or military experience, he had a master's degree with a high GPA. The fact he was not married was a plus for dealing with long hours and travel. He was a devoted runner and fitness guy. That would help him get through the academy. He spoke well. I could see his confidence grow as he got more comfortable with us. He had a leadership quality in his demeanor that would serve him well working with other agencies and informants. Noel asked him if he had applied to other departments or agencies. He had but said that was his backup plan in case the DEA did not select him. He was candid and honest.

Gary asked him if he understood what the job involved, referencing the long hours, nights, working in questionable places, going up against dangerous people. He said that he had looked hard at DEA and knew this was what he wanted to do.

After about an hour, we told him we would step out for a bit and make our decision. It only took a minute for us to agree to pass him. I told the guys I had one more question, but it wouldn't affect our decision. When we walked back in, I wanted to ask him if he could drive drunk, but that line was old. I told him that I had one thing to clear up regarding his prior employment.

Looking at his SF-171, "On the application, you stated you were employed at Disney World as a character actor. What character were you?" He looked at me, puzzled, like what's that got to do with anything. Stopping in mid-sentence, he realized I was messing with him saying, "I can't say because Disney has a non-disclosure..." He said, "Fine. I was Tigger. Are you happy?" As we all broke out laughing, I announced, "I like this guy. He's going to make a great agent."

Years later, while I was a GS-13 instructor, I ran into Tigger at the DEA Academy in Quantico, Virginia. We were both glad to see each other, shaking hands. Tigger was now a GS-14 Group Supervisor. I couldn't help but feel a sense of pride that I had played a part in selecting him. He laughed when he told me it took five years and two transfers to shake that damn nickname. He then added, "Let's keep that between us." I laughed and said, "Your secret is safe with me." He shook his head, rolled his eyes and smiled.

The Ghost Train of Mechanicsburg

Bill McCallister, an Indiana State Trooper Detective Sergeant, would call me a few times a month, usually whenever he and his guys were getting ready to serve a warrant or as he would say, "kick a door." I was happy to join him. It was reminiscent of my childhood when I would sneak out to play with my friends. Bill and his team were talented investigators, and occasionally, I made a federal case out of their work.

The infamous
Ghost Train

It's a well-known fact that law enforcement is full of pranksters and I love cop humor. It's embedded in my DNA. My dad and grandfather were both former officers and loved pranks. I've played many pranks in my day and have been the victim of even more.

In the 1970s, cassette tape recorders were high-tech for cops. My department had one we used to record witness statements and confessions. A guy in our department found that by playing a recording using fast forward, the voice sounded like they had inhaled helium. Adding an inappropriate comment played in fast forward cracked us up. Cops tended to discover this kind of stuff when they were bored.

Meanwhile in Indiana, a young state trooper named Bill McCallister had recently bought his own tape recorder. One night while on patrol, he got stuck waiting for a passing train. As the train went by, the engineer, seeing a police car, blasted his horn. That gave young Bill an idea. He raced ahead to meet the train at the next intersection and waited. As the train approached, it blasted its horn again. This time Bill was ready. He held his recorder out the window.

He now knew his mission. There was a small town in his assigned area that was 10 miles from the nearest railroad tracks. At about 2 AM, he raced down Main Street, playing the recording over his patrol car's loudspeaker.

The next morning, he sauntered into the local coffee shop on Main Street. He listened to the buzz from the locals talking about the train they heard the previous night. One person who had slept through it assured everyone that it was just their imagination. Another guy, angry because he wasn't being believed, decided to up the ante. "I not only heard it, I saw it." One of Bill's friends, the late Judge Greg Caldwell from Noblesville, Indiana, wrote a poem about it.

Mechanicsburg had no tracks
No place for a train to go
A fact which brought Bill
Entirely too much woe...
Late one night he used his recorder
To capture a great sound
For to share it with the people
Of that small trackless town,
When he arrived at the edge of town
His PA system on
He fired up his tape recorder
And down the street he was bound
At 50 mph with his PA on full blast
He made everyone in town think
A train was coming fast

at 2 a.m. the lights came on
All over this small town
as Bill and his home-made sound
Came quickly bearing down...
for days to come in Mechanicsburg
There was not a single face
That did not claim they heard or saw
the train come through their place...
for sure they heard the whistle
but no answer was ever found
from where that train came
or where it was bound

Greg Caldwell, Municipal Judge
Noblesville, Indiana

Judge Caldwell's poem

Cops weren't the only ones playing with cassette recorders. As the story goes, in 1973 astronaut Owen Garriott recorded his wife's voice and this conversation took place between Skylab and Mission Control.

Houston:"Skylab, this is Houston, Do you read?"

A woman's voice responded from Skylab:"Hello Houston. This is Skylab."

A short silence. Houston: "Who is this?

Skylab: "Oh, Hi Robert. It's Helen, Owen's wife."

Houston: "What? How? What? Helen? What are you doing up there?"

One of the greatest pranks in astronaut history.

Then there was Lenny. Lenny was a retired Navy underwater demolitions specialist who served as the bomb expert for our ATA training classes. Lenny didn't need a tape recorder. He was a ventriloquist of sorts in that he could imitate the sound of a metal detector wand. I learned of his skill in the Ninoy Aquino International airport in Manila, as I was being scanned by a Philippine Immigration agent. Every time the wand was passed over my butt, it squealed indicating the presence of metal. Coincidentally Lenny was right behind me in line. Fortunately he revealed his talent to the inspector before they got too invasive with their inspection.

Top Gun the Movie

Once again, Gary looked across the group room and motioned me to his desk. "I got a new informant. He's in with a group that's dealing Ecstasy." Ecstasy is methylenedioxy-methamphetamine, MDMA, sometimes called molly. It comes in both tablet form and blotter paper, both providing a powerful stimulant with psychedelic effects. It was popular at rave parties. People ingested blotter paper by dissolving it on their tongue. The paper often had cartoon characters imprinted on it.

The informant was a defendant in an Indiana State Police arrest. They didn't want to use him, so they gave him to Gary. The informant was in his early 20s, short, maybe 5'2", a bodybuilder and gym rat. He looked like a high school wrestler.

The investigation ended up having two parts. First, the CI was supplying a couple of young girls with Ecstasy. The girls were also buying, selling and using cocaine. Because the CI was now under our control, he could no longer provide them with drugs. DEA strictly prohibits their informants from breaking any laws, leaving it up to the agents to figure a way around it.

The informant's source for Ecstasy was a guy in his 40s who was also a bodybuilder. They belonged to the same gym. The target was well-built, heavily tattooed and was using copious amounts of steroids to build muscle. Excessive use of anabolic steroids can lead to a condition known as 'roid rage' defined as 'sudden mood changes, irrational behavior coupled with outbursts of anger, aggression and violence.' After seeing this guy for the first time, he could have been a poster child for an anti-steroid campaign.

Gary instructed the CI to arrange for Gary and me to meet the cocaine dealing girls. The meeting took place in their apartment on the west side of Indianapolis. They were in their early twenties, bubbly and excited to see the CI. When he told them he didn't have any Ecstasy for them, they weren't so bubbly.

When we arrived, they were about to leave but stayed for a bit. They appeared to be stoned and were snorting lines of coke off a coffee table. One girl was breastfeeding her baby before going out for the evening. There was also a third young teenage girl who was the babysitter. The girl with the baby offered to share a line of coke with me. "Want some?"

"That's tempting, but I'm on probation and have a piss test tomorrow, but I'll take some for later."

"Sure. How much do you want?"

"I've got $500. How much will that get me?"

"I'll give you a ¼ ounce for $500. It's fantastic too."

"OK, we got a deal. Let me get your number so we can hook up again."

The strategy for making small purchases is to establish a criminal charge that can be leveraged to recruit new informants. Most will agree to cooperate and make controlled purchases from their suppliers. In principle, it's a simple game.

I knew Gary wouldn't want to use her as a CI because she was young, naïve and too unpredictable. The only reason I bought the evidence was to give Child Protective Services an opportunity to intervene on behalf of her baby. She would soon hear from us again and it would be one of the worst nights of her life.

I was out of town when Gary made the first buy with the suspect from the gym. When I returned, he told me he had bought a couple hundred hits of Ecstasy. The deal went smoothly, and he could cut the CI out of the picture. CIs are essential in introducing undercover agents, but the best strategy is to eliminate their involvement as soon as possible. This makes the case less complicated.

The month of May and the Indianapolis 500 race were approaching. People called the infield of the 500 track the Snake Pit because it was like the Wild West. Drugs were everywhere and people acted wild and crazy all night long.

The story line Gary laid out to the suspect was he had people distributing large quantities of drugs and Ecstasy in and around the 500 racetrack. Gary told him he needed five thousand hits as soon as possible. Within a few days the suspect contacted Gary and told him he had the 5,000 hits. Gary agreed to meet him the following night in the junkyard where he worked. The junkyard was kind of cool. There was a giant machine that crushed cars into blocks of scrap metal.

We surveyed the location and found it was isolated and not open to the public. It had only one way in and out, making it a perfect location for a robbery. The situation forced us into a corner. We couldn't change the meeting location without alarming the suspect.

The suspect told Gary he'd come alone and expected Gary to do the same. After we reviewed the location, I said, "It's your call, but I'd feel better if we did this one together." Gary agreed. "He won't like it, but he'll have to get over it."

We spent the next day preparing for the buy/bust. At 7:30 PM, Gary and I left the office in his undercover vehicle followed by six surveillance units. Since the location was so isolated, the surveillance team wouldn't be very helpful if the deal turned into a robbery. As the saying goes, "It doesn't matter if help is a minute away when all you have are seconds."

As Gary and I drove into the parking lot, there was a vehicle in a back corner that flashed its parking lights. We pulled up, driver door to driver door. The suspect looked inside and saw me in the car and said to Gary, "I thought I told you to come alone."

I leaned forward and saw there was someone in his passenger seat. Gary responded with, "And I thought you said you'd be coming alone." I'm not a psychologist, but I could tell this wasn't starting out well. His passenger got out of the vehicle, walked around, and stood between the cars. He wasn't particularly aggressive, but his demeanor clearly aimed to establish control. I had no choice but to do the same thing, ending up face-to-face with him standing between the cars. It was then I realized this guy stood about 6'6," a good eight inches taller than me and weighed in at 300+ pounds. As intimidating as that was, what really scared me were his unnaturally huge biceps. His biceps had to be from serious steroid abuse, which meant he was a prime candidate for 'roid rage' if things didn't go well.

At first, nobody said anything. It was intense. I saw my opportunity to break the ice, like Hector did with me at the academy when we first met. Hector saw my Milwaukee Brewers hat and told me how much he loved the Brewers, creating a connection. I even ended up giving him my hat.

There I stood face-to-face with Mr. Biceps, who was wearing a cool Tom Cruise *Top Gun* movie hat. I looked him dead in the eyes and said, "I got one question for you." I was trying to sound like a tough guy.

"What?" said with an inflection that let me know how insignificant he thought I was.

"Where did you get that hat? That's a cool hat. And that movie was the best."

"You like this hat, huh? Here, it's yours." He took it off and handed it to me. I put it on. Surprisingly, it was a perfect fit, which made me wonder if my head was too big for my body or if his head was too small for his. I suppressed the big head-little head thoughts and said, "And Meg Ryan was so hot."

"Yeah, but Kelly McGillis is more my type."

I noticed the suspect in the car was looking a bit annoyed, mixed with some bewilderment at the surreal moment we were having in the middle of this drug deal. "Enough. Let's get this done."

We both returned to our respective cars after being properly scolded. Gary and the suspect exchanged packages. While Gary checked the drugs, the suspect thumbed through the money.

While we were driving out of the parking lot, we passed the cavalry coming in, two marked police cars with red lights flashing and four of our surveillance team following behind. As we drove away, I had a feeling there was about to be a 'roid rage' episode waiting for them, one I was glad not to be part of.

We had a warrant for our young nursing mother. I had her number and called to ask what she was doing. She told me they were on their way to Union Station. Union Station was an old train depot that had been revitalized with new décor, restaurants, bars, and shops. It was a hot spot in Indianapolis. I told her Gary and

I would meet them there. They were more interested in scoring drugs than they were in us.

When Gary and I arrived at the club, they saw us and came over. I told them the place was too loud and asked if we could go somewhere more private. They probably thought we had drugs. When we got to the parking lot, I identified myself and told her she was under arrest for dealing cocaine. She freaked out and didn't believe me until I handcuffed her. "You're not being very nice right now. Am I going to jail?"

"Yes."

"Are they going to take my purse away?"

"Yes, but you'll get it back."

"Can I at least keep my lip gloss?"

"I don't know about that. You can ask when you get there."

Gary and I transported her to the Marion County Jail. The jail was best described as a modern-day dungeon. The receiving area was underground and doubled as a loading dock. When we entered the jail, we passed through a steel exterior door into an isolation chamber. Once inside, the interior door opened after the outside door closed. From inside the chamber, the jail control center was visible through a glass window. The interior door opened into a large booking area across from the suicide watch cells.

During the booking process, the incoming prisoners were in full view of all the 'crazies' in the watch cells. When we walked in, the crazies began yelling obscenities at her. It was like a scene from the TV show *Scared Straight*. Her knees buckled and she started crying. I discreetly held her up, and in a quiet voice, told her to ignore the crazies. "They can't hurt you. Look straight ahead and keep walking."

It was a hard lesson for a young and naive girl. However horrible it was, I hoped that it might result in turning her life around. I don't know whatever became of her. Unlike the movies, agents don't have time to keep track of their defendants or informants after a case is concluded. There are always more investigations waiting.

My Glock

The Glock is an Austrian manufactured semi-automatic pistol with a synthetic polymer-frame making it ultra-lightweight. The pistol came in multiple models and calibers. The most well-known was the Model 17. Glock also produced a slightly smaller version the model 19. By the mid-1980s DEA approved the Glock pistols for agents. However, DEA's officially issued weapon was the Sig Sauer P220 9mm semi-automatic pistol known for its accuracy, reliability and safety. I liked my Sig Sauer, but it was not as comfortable to carry as the Glock.

In about 1988, Gary, our designated firearms officer, purchased a Glock17. The company was offering law enforcement a steep discount. I liked Gary's gun but decided to buy the smaller more concealable model 19 and ordered one. To qualify for the discount, the gun had to be shipped directly to the agency's address. I was like a little kid waiting for my gun to arrive, checking the mail every day. I was at my desk when Gary entered the group room and announced my gun had arrived and handed me the box. I tore open the box like it was Christmas only to find a chrome-plated 32 caliber piece of shit Saturday night special covered with packing peanuts.

I went from confused to disappointment followed by anger. I'd been ripped off. The guys in the office were looking at the box, checking for a tracking number, offering condolences. I should have known. They were way too involved and compassionate. I found the telephone number for the company and started to dial, Gary said, "Hold on, we're just messing with you. Here's your gun." They got me good! Karma was paying me back for every prank I'd ever played.

I usually carried my gun tucked in the back right-side of my waistband. The Glock was smooth and flat making it easy to conceal and carry. It didn't shoot as well as the Sig Sauer, but it was good enough. What I didn't like about it was the lack of a safety switch. Somehow the safety was supposed to be part of the trigger, which I never understood because pulling the trigger fired the gun. This lack of a traditional safety switch nearly ended in a disaster for me.

One night about 3 AM while checking into a hotel in Evansville, IN, two plainclothes off-duty police officers working security noticed my gun and jumped me from behind to take it, which they did quite effectively. They didn't know who I was and remember, I didn't look like a choirboy either. Fortunately, when they ripped the gun from my waistband, they didn't accidentally pull the trigger. But from that day on, I never carried the gun with a chambered round. I would rack the slide and chamber a round just before I needed it.

The second problem I had with the gun occurred at the start of a quarterly qualification. When the whistle blew to draw and fire, I pulled the trigger and all I got was a click, a misfire. I cleared the round and tried again, yet another misfire. I pulled the magazine, cleared the round and caught it in the air. The primer hadn't been dented. I picked up the first round and it's primer hadn't been struck either. With a clear and safe weapon, I exited the firing line and disassembled the gun only to discover a broken firing pin. It must have broken when I fired the very last round during our previous qualification three months earlier. Even though the odds were astronomical, there was no other explanation. Since owning the gun, I'd fired well over 10,000 rounds through it flawlessly. I thought about all the doors kicked and the people we'd arrested over the last three months, done with a broken gun. I sent the gun to Quantico where the armorers fixed it, but I never carried it again. Gary gave me my Sig Sauer back.

Bucky Comes to Town

After six years in Indianapolis, Bucky called and said he was flying a mission and would be staying overnight in Indianapolis. "I'll call you when I set down and you can pick me up at the airport."

I picked him up about 7:00 PM. He, of course, wanted seafood. We ended up at *Joe's Crab Shack*. In typical Bucky fashion, he ordered beer and raw oysters on the half shell with extra red sauce. I was happy to see him and ordered the same. We laughed hard that night, reminiscing about Glynco and catching up on old classmates. Bucky told me about one guy in our class who accidentally shot a hole in the floorboard of his supervisor's car in Miami.

He also heard that Brian, our class cadence caller, had gotten into a gunfight in Detroit and somehow had shot out his windshield during the fight. One of the other guys in our class joined *Operation Snowcap* and got some kind of waterborne jungle amoeba or worm in his brain. Bucky said the guy was in terrible shape but had survived. We both knew about William getting shot and killed in Texas.

Bucky Beavers with his pet monkey on his shoulder

After dropping Bucky off, I got home about 3 AM. I went straight to bed, but apparently not before throwing up. Four hours later, I woke to someone shaking me. Completely disoriented, I panicked. Oh crap, I'm late for gym class. I then recognized my wife's voice, "Howard, come on. Wake up. There's blood all over the kid's bathroom. Are you hurt?" After a few blinks, my brain slowly kicked in and things started to make sense. I must have used the kids' bathroom when I puked those slimy oysters. I mumbled, "It's not blood. It's just cocktail sauce." All I heard was, "My god, are you ever gonna grow up?" I closed my eyes and let my head sink back into the pillow.

The Grab and Go

Mike, fresh out of the academy, was our replacement for NY Thom. Mike didn't have prior law enforcement or military experience, but he was smart and had a lot of enthusiasm. He reminded me a little of Bruce Willis as the wisecracking cop in *Die Hard* who always had a smart-ass comeback. I liked that about him. He could also be mischievous.

On one occasion, I returned early from lunch to find him forwarding all of the office phones to Tom's desk. Mike was getting even with Tom for something. When the staff returned from lunch, all the incoming calls were redirected to Tom's desk. For 30 minutes, Tom was answering non-stop incoming calls and had to transfer them back to the desk where they were supposed to go in the first place. It was very entertaining since I knew what had happened.

Mike learned a hard lesson that messing with the IPD narcotics guys would result in retaliation. One night he left the office to find his car filled with Styrofoam packing peanuts. Although I never heard what he did, I'm sure he provoked it.

Gary told me he had a new case in Bloomington and needed an undercover agent. I hated to pass, but suggested Mike get his feet wet. When Gary and Mike left for Bloomington, I felt like the kid who was going to miss the circus.

After a week, Gary called to say he needed some help. Their investigation had led them to a cocaine source that was temporarily living at the Holiday Inn in Bloomington. Gary's CI couldn't buy directly from the guy at the hotel, but the CI could buy from one of his customers. Gary's plan was to buy/bust the middleman and use him as a CI to buy/bust the guy at the Holiday Inn.

Gary and Mike had set the first buy/bust to take place in a parking lot near the hotel so the arrest had to be done quickly and quietly. He didn't want to use uniformed police. Gary asked me to bring the undercover surveillance van along with agent Noel and meet him in Bloomington. The plan was to park the van next to the suspect's vehicle. After the buy was completed, we would grab the suspect and load him in the van. A 'DEA grab and go.'

The first buy went as planned. As the middleman was walking to his car, we jumped out, overpowered him, and stuffed him into the van. It went perfectly or so we thought. As we were making the getaway with our prisoner, Gary got a page to call a friend at the State Police. The detective asked if we were in the area and had just kidnapped someone. Gary told him we had just arrested someone, but that it may have actually 'looked like a kidnapping.'

The detective heard an All-Points Bulletin, APB, broadcast over the radio reporting an apparent abduction. Someone driving by saw the incident, called 911. Now every cop in southern Indiana knew about the 'kidnapping' and was looking for our silver van. Fortunately, they didn't know it was us. The detective, after having worked with us many times, had a hunch it might have been us. The detective told Gary he'd get the APB canceled.

After I 'had the talk' with the new defendant, he agreed to cooperate. When I briefed Gary, he asked, "Did you flip him?" I said, "Like a pancake. It's show time." The new CI told me he would cooperate and make a controlled purchase but warned me the guy was high on crack and dangerously crazy.

I offered to do the rest of the undercover, but Mike wanted to finish the job. Gary had the new informant call the hotel room and set up a buy for one ounce of coke, $2,000 worth. Gary instructed the CI to tell the source his buyer wouldn't front the money, so he would have to bring him along.

It was supposed to be a simple buy/bust inside the hotel room. I put a body transmitter on the new CI. Gary got a key from the front desk clerk. After Mike and the CI entered the room, Gary, Noel and I took a 'snake' position in the hallway outside the room.

I was monitoring the conversation happening in the room over a headset. I could hear Mike counting out the money, signaling the deal was done. I then heard Mike make a comment about 'the gun on the bed.' Mike was using the body wire to tell us there was a gun in play and its location. I whispered to Gary and Noel there was a gun on the bed. Gary quietly unlocked the door, and we charged into the room. The suspect lunged for the shotgun lying on the bed.

As I cleared the doorway, I jumped on top of the suspect. We were both grappling for control of the gun. I was holding it down as he was trying to raise it up. The gun pointed toward the wall of the adjoining room. I knew if it discharged, it could penetrate the wall and injure or kill anyone on

The bed where we 'struggled'

the other side. I was doing everything I could to hold the gun down and keep his fingers off the trigger. It was the struggle of a lifetime. There is no participation trophy in this league, you either win or lose. That said, a little help from your trusted partners can sway the results. This time it was Gary who punched the suspect in the head, ending the struggle.

After the suspect was in custody, Gary examined the gun and found it was a fully loaded 12-gauge pump shotgun with a round in the chamber and the safety switch was off. We were only a trigger pull from disaster. We later learned the gun had been stolen from a police cruiser in Florida.

It may surprise you to know DEA agents encounter confrontations like this on a regular basis. Most of the time they survive because of our training and experience. But not always. DEA has had 57 agents killed in the line of duty since the agency was created in 1973. That's not counting the number of state and local officers killed doing the same kind of work. And, I have no idea how many have been seriously injured.

The Airport

Every year, the boss assigned an agent to work full-time with the Indianapolis Airport Interdiction group. The unit consisted of officers from the Indiana State Police and the Indianapolis Police Department. The mission of the group was to interdict airport drug smuggling. Most major airports in the country had an interdiction unit. These units often coordinated with each other.

My time at the airport was in the late 1980s, long before the 9/11 attacks changed protocols. Things were quite different then. People could smoke on airplanes. There were no metal detectors and the TSA didn't exist. I had a defendant who, as a joke, purchased his plane tickets using the name Ronald Reagan, never having to show any identification. He showed me his stack of ticket stubs.

You may wonder how we could pick out a smuggler from the other people in a crowded airport. It can't be done just by observation. Over time an experienced investigator could spot suspicious behaviors that justified closer examination. As an example, an individual making a last-minute cash purchase for a one-way flight to Miami may draw an investigator's attention, especially if they only have a carry-on bag. An individual purchasing a ticket late at night with a return flight the next morning may draw attention.

Investigators look for things that don't fit normal human behavior.

Normal behavior for a drug trafficker would be to get there, take care of business, and return quickly. They don't want to linger around Miami with thousands of dollars in cash or bricks of cocaine in their possession. The longer their stay, the greater the risk of robbery or discovery and arrest.

It's no secret that drug dealers make a lot of money. They often showed off their high roller lifestyle, especially to attractive female ticket agents. We recruited some ticket agents to spot drug smugglers for us, and they were masterful at it. They knew by flirting with the suspects, they couldn't help but brag, practically telling the ticket agents what they were doing. Their tips were invaluable. Sometimes we would pay them cash rewards for their assistance. But most of the ticket agents considered it a game and it was a fun way to break the monotony of the job. All the women who helped us were good people who chose to do something to curb drugs.

But it still comes down to the investigator's interviewing skills and understanding of human behaviors. The most successful drug traffickers are not stupid people and have tactics and techniques to protect themselves. One common tactic is to use an accomplice as a 'mule' to carry the drugs or money while they watch them from a distance.

My most memorable airport case wasn't an impressive seizure or a major trafficker. Rather, it was how it happened. It began with a phone call from the Houston Interdiction unit informing us a suspect would be arriving on a particular flight. They described him and told us he had two checked bags with 50 pounds of marijuana in each one. They chose to let him board his flight without approaching him, giving us the opportunity to expand the investigation. We spotted him as he deplaned and followed him to the luggage carousel.

I had a small rolling bag to look like a fellow traveler. I positioned myself next to him at the carousel. Our team members took up positions around us. He was like General Custer at Little Big Horn, surrounded but didn't know it yet.

When his first bag came around, he pulled it off the carousel and placed it at his feet. I knelt down, pretending to play with the zipper on my bag. With a perplexed look on my face, I stood up. In an inappropriately loud voice, I announced to the surrounding people that I thought I could smell marijuana. I asked people near me if they could smell pot.

I asked the suspect if he could smell it. Actually, I was testing him to see if he would show any sign of guilt when I claimed to smell the marijuana. He said nothing, but he looked like he wanted to tell me to shut the hell up. He picked up his bag and walked to the other side of the carousel to wait for his second bag. When it came around, he grabbed it and hurried for the exit only to be intercepted by the team as he tried to get in a taxi. I can only imagine what that must have felt like. His expression was total despair, knowing that he had almost made it.

The scene reminded me of my favorite childhood war movie, the 1963 World War II POW film *The Great Escape* starring Steve McQueen. In my favorite scene, McQueen attempted to jump a motorcycle over the last remaining fence to freedom. The jump failed and left McQueen tangled in a barbed wire fence as German soldiers captured him.

The team took the suspect to our office and found 100 pounds of high-grade marijuana in his bags. When I walked in, he looked at me and blurted, "THAT WAS YOU." I laughed and said, "Come on, you've got to admit that was kind of funny."

"No, it wasn't!"

"OK, maybe not to you, but it was to me."

After we discussed options and consequences, he decided it would be best to cooperate and work with us. We had him meet with his associate and complete the delivery which led to his arrest and the seizure of over $100,000 in cash. In the 90s, a pound of marijuana in Texas sold for about $700. That same pound in Indiana would be worth about $1,200. His hundred pounds would have made him a $50,000 profit. Not bad for a few days' work.

The Old Man and the Kid

While working at the airport, I got a call from a detective in the Indianapolis Metro unit. He asked if I would go with them on a search warrant. They wanted me to do a federal forfeiture action on some cash they were expecting to find. I made a point to help whenever I was asked. I learned a long time ago what goes around comes around.

They had arrested a small-time pot dealer in his early 20s who rolled over on his source. The kid told the detectives an interesting story about his source which turned out to be his stepfather I'll call the 'old man.' The old man was a 50 something, divorced truck driver living alone in a trailer court on the east side of Indianapolis. He was living a quiet life and had no criminal history. He was a lifelong truck driver who drove a round-trip route from Indianapolis to McAllen, Texas hauling fresh produce. The wholesale produce company paid him about $50,000 per year.

After one of his trips, the trucker told his family about some guy who had tried to sell him five pounds of pot at a truck stop near the Mexican border. He said he just laughed when the guy guaranteed the best price in Texas at $600 a pound. Sometime later the kid proposed to the old man, "You buy it, I'll sell it, and we'll double our money." The two of them pondered the idea, did some math calculations, and decided to go for it.

Soon he was bringing five pounds of pot back every week from Texas in his lunch bucket. He gave it to the kid who sold it by the ounce. This was a small operation that DEA would rate a notch below jaywalking. But the story had an interesting twist. For nearly six years the old man had stashed most of his profits.

Let's do the math. The purchase price was $600 per pound and sold for $1,200 per pound. That's $600 profit per pound, times five pounds equals $3,000 a week, or $156,000 a year. Multiplying by six years equals $936,000 with no expenses or overhead. A 50/50 split meant they each made about $468,000. The kid, living life large, spent his share. Here's where it got interesting. The kid told the detectives the old man was paranoid. All he ever bought was a big screen plasma TV and a Nintendo. The rest of it he stuffed weekly into a safe under his trailer where it stayed until we confiscated it.

As the detectives were counting the money on the kitchen table, the old man said, "I knew this day would come. I'm glad it's finally over." I'm convinced he meant every word. He told me he worried day and night about getting caught. "My trailer was ransacked twice. I suspected it was either my kid or one of his friends looking for my share of the money."

It was actually sad that he had put himself through a living nightmare all for a TV and a Nintendo. I did a federal forfeiture action against the money. He lost it all. The detectives took the TV but left him the Nintendo. He had no criminal history and the amount of marijuana in the case was

Just another cash seizure

insufficient to qualify for a federal charges. The metro investigators brought state charges against him.

I smile when I show my non-agent friends the money photo. I know they are doing exactly what Milwaukee John taught me never to do, fantasize. The drug business is a game best left to the people who have no conscience. I know a truck driver who would agree with me.

The Saltwater Cowboys

Tim McBride graduated from Delavan-Darien High School in Wisconsin in1976. Two years later he moved from his parent's home on Delavan Lake to start a new life in south Florida with his friend. When Timothy arrived in Florida, he began working on a crab boat but soon became involved in smuggling marijuana.

Tim tells his amazing story as a marijuana smuggler in his book titled *Saltwater Cowboy,* co-authored by Ralph Berrier, Jr. Tim writes that on the first night of smuggling, he and his associates offloaded several tons of marijuana from a Columbian cargo ship onto their crab boat. They transported the marijuana to Chokoloskee Island where it was transferred to vehicles that carried it to Miami for nationwide distribution.

In that same year I was a 24-year-old police officer on the Delavan Lake Police Department, married, and my salary was $8,000 per year. Per his own words, Tim's rookie salary was $5,000 per night. After completing two nights, his pay jumped to between $25,000 and $50,000 per night. Tim provides a good accounting of how their marijuana smuggling operation functioned in south Florida. He also does an excellent job of explaining the profit margins and the business side of the house.

According to Tim, from 1979 to 1988 he and his crew handled 90% of the Colombian marijuana coming into the United States. He earned and spent millions of dollars during his run. It came to an end when he was arrested by the DEA in 1988 along with over a hundred of his associates during *Operations Peacemaker* and *Black Rock.* For his part he drew a 10-year prison sentence of which he served eight years.

I began my career with DEA in 1985. I never knew Tim. but I was good friends with his older brother Mike. We played on two championship football teams and graduated from Big Foot High School in 1972. It was on that gridiron where I learned one of the secrets to success in life. Surround yourself with talented people whom you can trust. DEA provided me with an abundant supply of talented associates.

Mike was a good man. He worked hard, was married and had a family.

Mike, Thom, me, and John

He said, "I knew you were a DEA agent, and I knew what my brother was doing. I'm sorry I never told you, but he was my brother." Mike died in 2022. At least he had a chance to clear his conscience with me, and I was able to tell him that, "I understood." I read Tim's book and watched a U-Tube video interview of him and was taken by how much his mannerisms and even his voice reminded me of his brother.

The' Just Click It' Ticket

Indiana is known as the Crossroads of America in part because I-65 crosses I-70 in the center of Indiana. I-70 provides a direct route from California to New York and I-65 starts in Chicago and ends in Florida. Both highways are major commercial transportation routes and serve the same purpose for smugglers. In an effort to reduce drunk driving, police have deployed DUI, Driving Under the Influence, check points at random locations. In the late 1980s an Indiana state trooper took this concept a step further. He made a sign announcing a 'Drug Check Point Ahead.' He placed his sign along I-70, positioning it just before an emergency turn around. The turnaround provided drivers with a guilty conscience a convenient opportunity to avoid the non-existent 'inspection.'

After setting up his sign, he simply waited in the dark on the opposite side of the highway for the guilty parties to reveal themselves by making an illegal U-turn. While issuing the driver a traffic citation, he probed the reason for their evasive maneuver. In most instances, someone in the car was in possession of an illegal substance, usually marijuana or cocaine. Quantities ranged from personal use to trunk loads. These operations netted several drug shipments coming from the southern borders. It was a simple yet successful tactic.

Yes, I have revealed a little secret but rest assured it won't help you. I participated in a few of these investigations, so I knew the game well. Fast forward the time machine to 2003. I was living and working in northern Virginia. My wife and I had returned to Indianapolis for our daughter's wedding. As we were getting into the car the day before the wedding, I was on my phone dealing with some DEA issues in Washington. Involved in my conversation, I neglected to put my seat belt on. With my wife driving, we left our hotel, traveling eastbound on 96th Street near I-69. That section of 96th street was a busy 4-lane road surrounded by strip malls.

My wife saw a seat belt check point ahead. She broke into my phone conversation to say I needed to put my seatbelt on. Juggling my phone, I reached back and quickly snapped it on. As we entered the check point, a Fishers police officer motioned her to pull over. A young Fishers officer came to my window and asked, "Did we forget our seat belt this morning?" With a touch of smugness, I showed him my seat belt was fastened. He said, "Well, it is now, but it wasn't back there when my spotter saw you put it on."

I could hardly keep from laughing. They got the old fox. I never told him who I was because they got me fair and square. Besides, I was so impressed with how these young officers had resurrected that old trick, with a new spin. So, he got his ticket and I got a kick out of it.

Fast forward the time machine again 22 years to 2025. My wife is working hard editing my book. When she got to this story she said, "I don't remember this. Do you have a copy of the ticket?" "I don't think so. I haven't seen it in any of my papers. I might have even mailed it back with the payment. I don't know."

While she was editing at the kitchen table, I was completing an HOA application to install a gazebo. I needed a copy of the house plot plan for the house we had built in 2019. I was going through the real estate closing documents. In the

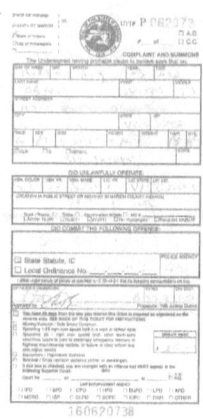

My ticket

back of that 2019 real estate folder was the original passenger seat belt violation from 2003 with a fine of $25. It was issued to me two days before my daughter's wedding in 2003 listing my address as Woodbridge, Virginia. The circumstances and timing of its appearance was to say the least uncanny. I can't explain it. Unless maybe my guardian angel enjoyed an occasional playful prank.

Back to the Academy

Most field agents have little interest in disrupting their lives to do a three-month Temporary Duty assignment, TDY, as a Basic Agent Counselor. In March 1992, our office received a Teletype from Chicago Division Headquarters instructing us to provide the Quantico Training Division with a senior agent for a counselor assignment. I ended up with the assignment which meant living three months at the FBI Academy in Quantico, Virginia.

The DEA moved its academy to Quantico in 1986, the year after I graduated. For 11 years the FBI shared its resources and facilities with the DEA. In 1997 the DEA built their own academy on the grounds of Quantico within walking distance of the FBI's facilities.

I was one of four counselors to mentor the new agents through their training process. We arrived a week before the recruits for orientation and to meet with the Class Coordinator and staff. The coordinator is a permanent staff member assigned to the academy. Their role is like that of a ringmaster in a circus. The training was divided into sections: Academics, Practical Exercises, Firearms, and Physical Training. A grade 14 Unit Chief supervised each section.

The coordinator briefed us on the rules and requirements. Most of it was common sense. I remember him telling us, "Things have changed. This isn't Glynco. You're not here to wash out recruits. You are here to mentor them through the academy." He explained that we could have a trainee dismissed for cause by using the Basic Agent Review Board known as a BARB. He cautioned us that the BARB process was like a nuclear option, as it was irreversible once it started. "DEA has invested a lot of money in these trainees, and you better have a good reason to wash one out. These trainees are going to become agents and one day you may need their help."

Since counselors have significant control and influence over recruits, the coordinator warned us the academy prohibited hazing, harassment, or bullying. During prep week, we underwent a psychological screening to ensure we were mostly normal. To my amazement, I passed. Before the students arrived, we had a round table review of all the trainees' personnel folders, page by page. Their backgrounds were impressive. One counselor said he was glad he didn't have to compete against this batch of trainees. I was thinking the same thing.

DEA's move from Glynco to the FBI's Quantico campus and co-housing the two agencies clearly influenced DEA's training philosophies. It had been seven years since I was a trainee, and I remembered it like it was yesterday. I was looking forward to experiencing the academy from the inside, a chance to see behind the curtain in the Land of Oz.

The academy housing consisted of high-rise dormitories. Our class was assigned to the sixth floor of one of the buildings. Each bedroom accommodated two trainees with a set of twin beds. Two rooms shared a Jack and Jill bathroom. Counselors had private rooms but shared a bathroom with another counselor.

DEA classroom on day one

One interesting aspect of the training was the weekly student review. When I attended Glynco, rumors circulated among the trainees that the staff held reviews of the students with their pictures on a large screen. I can confirm it is true. I participated in those reviews. In the first few weeks, the staff and instructors may not have matched names to faces, so the photographs were essential to the review process.

Following the example from Glynco, the class was divided into four teams: Red, Blue, Green, and Gold. I was assigned the Red team. I had two students that stood out. One was a former Navy SEAL. He would prove to be polished and yet humble. He was one of the most physically fit individuals I had ever known.

The trainers administered a baseline physical fitness test the first week. Pull-ups, push-ups, sit-ups, bench press, and a mile and a half run were part of the testing. The SEAL came within seconds of breaking the fastest time ever recorded for DEA in the mile and a half run. At the finish line, a PT instructor was calling out the times. I was standing next to him. Several other PT instructors from both DEA and the FBI gathered near the finish line to witness his feat.

We all assumed he was going to set the record, but in the last lap, he appeared to run out of gas. I asked him why he had slowed down. He told me, "Sometimes breaking records puts a target on your back, and I don't want to start out on the wrong foot." He added, "But if you want me to, I'll break the record the next time." That never happened. About four weeks into the program, he resigned. Since he was on my team, I oversaw his departure. I remembered back in Georgia when the staff abandoned Bob at the front gate. Times had changed. I was instructed to drive him to the airport.

My fondest memory of him took place one evening while I was waiting for the elevator. According to academy policy, trainees were not allowed to ride the elevators. Our rooms were on the sixth floor. As I was getting on the elevator, the SEAL was walking by. I held the door and invited him to ride with me. He reminded me that students were not allowed. The door closed and moments later, as it opened on the 6th floor, he casually walked by. My head jerked back as I thought, how did he do that? He must have flown up the stairs. Not saying a word, he nodded and walked on, not the least bit winded.

I talked with him while he packed. He told me he had been a Technical Advisor for the 1990 action movie *Navy Seals*. They hired him to teach Charlie Sheen how to act like a SEAL. He said the director gave him a small speaking part. I watched the movie and, sure enough, he was in it.

I tried to talk him into changing his mind and finishing the academy, but his mind was made up. I drove him to Dulles airport where he flew back to California. He said the academy, the staff, and the training were very professional. He never told me why he dropped out. I heard later he accepted a position with the CIA.

My other trainee that stood out was a graduate of Harvard Law School. He was young, 23 years old. His academic grades were nearly perfect. He was quick to learn, a sponge for knowledge.

Becoming a DEA agent is often a second career. Many new agents come from the military, law enforcement, paramedic or some other stress-filled career where they've learned to control their emotions. The age range for most Basic Agent Trainees is 28-32. Through no fault of his, Young Harvard simply lacked experience. He wasn't immature. It was more a matter of youthful exuberance.

I observed him during the practical exercises involving mock arrests and raids. I could tell his heart was racing long before the action started. This was a potential problem that needed correction. I talked to him about turning down his intensity and stress level. He was respectful and receptive to my constructive criticism, but I didn't think he could see that trait in himself.

Counselors have a lot of influence if they choose to use it. I requested to play the role of a bad guy in an exercise that I knew was going to end with Young Harvard arresting me. In this scenario, he wouldn't know whether I had a gun or not. I did not. He ordered me at gunpoint to raise my hands slowly. As expected, he was full of adrenaline. I gave him a deadly stare, and we locked eyes. This was his first crucial mistake. He was using his peripheral vision to watch my hands. Tactically, this is flawed. Watching the hands always come first. I raised my hands slowly but then jerked them up. He did exactly what I expected. He shot me. According to the script, this drill was not supposed to result in deadly force. The staff instructors immediately entered the scene. "Who in the hell fired?" Young Harvard readily admitted, "It was me. I did it."

Practical exercises simu-
late real-world scenarios
and are in tense. He shot an
unarmed suspect. This was
about to turn into a problem for him. I asked to speak
privately with the training
supervisor. I told him it was
my fault, that I had baited
him into shooting me. I

Bedroom at Quantico

didn't tell him why I did it. He was not happy with me. He told me,
"From now on, stick to the script, no improvising allowed." My
'confession' put the matter to rest with no further actions against
Young Harvard.

Later that night, I sat with him and said, "Now you understand
what I'm talking about. You're going to make a good agent, but you
must learn to control your adrenaline." I explained that most of
his classmates were older, and many had stress filled jobs where
they learned to maintain their composure under stress. "Remember, calmness is as contagious as panic." This time I was sure he got
the message. As the training progressed, I could see him mature.

The FBI's famous Hogan's Alley facilities replaced the tract
houses we used for raid training at Glynco. Hogan's Alley is a
mock-up of a town with full-size houses, stores and buildings used
for practical exercises. I discovered it was fun playing the bad guy
in the tactical exercises with the class. I volunteered to play a bad
guy in a scenario calling for us to take a trainee hostage during an
undercover deal. The script called for the trainees to make a dar-
ing rescue by assaulting our building. For this exercise, paintball
guns replaced the blank guns. We had a helmet and eye goggles
but only lightweight body protection to absorb some of the bullet's impact. We also had paint guns and were free to shoot back

during their assault. In the beginning, we did OK. We could take out one or two of the BATS before they gunned us down.

The instructors ran the scenario over and over, each time correcting their mistakes and adjusting their tactics until they could overwhelm us without casualties.

I had always known DEA trained us well. But, facing off against my fellow agents caused me to appreciate just how well we were trained. I'm not suggesting we're in the same category as the FBI's Hostage Rescue Team, HRT. But for working street agents, we were exceptionally good.

When I got back to my room, overheated and sweaty, I took a shower. That's when I found the paintball hits had left me covered in red welts, a sign of how good the BATS had become.

The high-speed driving class had become much more sane and safer. The cars were equipped with an anti-roll feature comprised of what looked like training wheels extending from under the vehicle. The students enjoyed the extreme driving despite the training wheels.

Overall, I enjoyed my time as a counselor. The staff and I spent much of our spare time playing ping pong or basketball. One of the PT instructors gave me hours of boxing lessons. I completed the famous FBI Yellow Brick Road obstacle course with my class. The course is a 6.1mile cross-country trail with a dozen or more challenging obstacles.

It was over as quickly as it started, and I soon was back in Indianapolis with my investigations waiting for me.

~ 6 ~

A BRIDGE TOO FAR

Good guys aren't all good. Bad guys aren't all bad and agents must learn to navigate in that fog.

Today a Google search of Vladimiro Montesinos yields volumes of information about this ruthless, corrupt official. He held positions at the highest levels of the Peruvian government in the 1980s and 1990s. His criminal activities included bribery, arms trafficking, drug trafficking, and assassinations.

He was the trusted confidant to the Peruvian President Alberto Fujimori, in office from 1990 to 2000. Montesinos' official title was Director of the Peruvian National Intelligence Service, Peru's version of the CIA. He was the most powerful man in Peru and was a mixed bag of good and evil. U.S. government officials considered him pro-American. While cooperating with the U.S., he was secretly extorting Peruvian politicians, taking bribes from drug cartels and facilitating weapons sales to terrorist organizations.

Fujimori also entrusted Montesinos with tremendous power and influence over the military. Montesinos used that power to promote his corrupt associates into military command positions. From those key positions, his associates did his bidding with drug traffickers, smugglers and other criminal enterprises.

Why would the U.S. government collaborate with such a criminal? That's a complex question that doesn't lend itself to a simple answer. First, he officially represented the Peruvian government.

More importantly, he was a smart man and concealed his criminal activities well. As an example of his prowess, he used his powerful position to support DEA's hugely successful *Operation Snowcap*. It was Montesinos who authorized the Peruvian Air Force to shoot down smugglers' aircraft if they refused to surrender, solidifying him a kick ass supporter of DEA.

However, according to our informants, he was collecting pay-offs from drug traffickers that may have included Pablo Escobar's organization. Those payments were to ensure safe passage for select aircraft departing Peru loaded with coca base. Base is the raw material used to produce crystal cocaine HCL. The fee he charged for this arrangement yielded him hundreds of thousands of dollars.

Snowcap was a DEA joint operation that ran from 1987 to 1994. DEA agents along with U.S. Special Forces and Peruvian military and police worked together to disrupt drug operations. These DEA para-military operations took place predominantly in Bolivia, Peru and Colombia. The goals were to destroy coca fields, production labs and disrupt cartel smuggling operations. They used explosives to blow craters in hidden jungle landing strips and hunted down clandestine labs to destroy them. These efforts proved enormously effective to the point of creating a cocaine supply shortage in the U.S., at least for a brief time.

If what our informants told us about him was true, he was a classic example of what DEA considered a profiteer. Remember, a profiteer professes their motive for cooperation as financial gain. In this case, Montesinos offered his anti-drug support to America to gain trust and favor.

Complicating matters, terrorism was rampant in Central and South America during this same period. Several countries were struggling to contain a dozen or more viable terrorist organizations bent on overthrowing their governments. The Peruvian government was facing the real possibility of falling into the hands of Chinese Communists under the leadership of Abimael Guzman and his Sendero Luminoso organization, also known as the Shining Path. The Shining Path, Sendero, was a ruthless and extremely violent group responsible for thousands of deaths in Peru. In part, they relied on the illegal drug trade to fund their revolutionary activities.

The Sendero wasn't the only revolutionary group in Peru. Tupac Amaru movement, MRTA, was also conducting their own terrorist activities inside Peru. It was the MRTA that seized the Japanese Embassy in Lima on December 17, 1996. Initially they held a couple hundred hostages but released many of them in the days following the takeover. A commando style raid by the Peruvian Armed Forces ended the crisis 126 days later. During the raid, two commandos were killed along with one hostage and all 14 militants.

It's widely accepted that Montesinos played a key role in the September 1992 capture of Abimael Guzman, leader of the Shining Path. Years later human rights organizations would condemn Montesinos for the tactics he used. There are three civilian massacres attributed to Montesinos' and his death squads which took place in La Cantuta, Barrios Alto and Santa. His ruthlessness landed him several nicknames including El Diablo, 'The Devil.'

Even after Guzman's arrest, the city of Lima remained a hotbed of terrorist activities, including bombings, kidnappings, and street violence. Terrorists attacked the U.S. Embassy twice, first with a car bomb and again with a rocket-propelled grenade, RPG. Why did the U.S. government tolerate Montesinos? In order to protect U.S. interests, there was no other option.

If the Peruvian government fell to the communists, a destabilization of the region would likely have occurred. The U.S. could not let that happen. To prevent that, the CIA needed Montesinos to stay in power. Very few people, including me, understood how critical the situation was, and those who did kept it quiet. The U.S.

government's foreign policies can be complicated causing agencies within the government to have conflicting objectives. In this instance, the CIA's objective was to stabilize the country, while DEA's mission was to hunt down drug traffickers.

Operation Pig Ear

In 1992, Bill, a U.S. Customs agent assigned to the Indianapolis DEA task force, asked if I'd be interested in working on a Customs led joint investigation. He told me the investigation had been initiated by a Dan, a Customs agent. Bill thought I'd be a valuable addition to their investigation, and that I would work well with Dan. Dan started his career as an Indiana State Trooper, joined DEA as an agent and later transferred to U.S. Customs. He was a talented investigator. To this day, both Dan and Bill are two of my most trusted friends.

Bill and I met Dan at the Customs office. Dan and I hit it off immediately. We talked about his informant, Tito, not his real name, and the potential for the case. At one point, I asked Dan if he was married. He took out his wallet and showed me a picture of his attractive wife and two children. I told him I was married and also had two children. I had my real wallet in my right rear pocket and my undercover wallet in the left one. I couldn't help myself. I took out my undercover wallet and proudly showed him the picture of my pretend wife, Coyote Ugly. There was a pause, the kind that happens when one is momentarily speechless. He struggled but finally said, "Wow, yeah, now there's a keeper." I smiled proudly and said, "Yeah, I'm lucky. She could have had any guy she wanted, and she chose me." Dan, gaining his equilibrium, said, "Well then, I think she's a keeper."

Bill was in his office when that conversation occurred. He later told me that after I left, Dan came into his office and asked him if he'd met my wife. Bill said he hadn't. Dan told him that from the picture he saw, my wife had to be one of the ugliest women he'd ever seen. He said, "I feel bad saying this. When he showed me her picture, I almost laughed. It was awkward. I honestly didn't know what to say." I later learned Dan was the king of pranks in his office. My prank delighted the office when they heard about it. Dan liked it so much he talked me into giving him the picture so he could use it.

Dan's CI, Tito, was a naturalized U.S. citizen from Peru. He told us he knew a drug smuggler from Peru whose organization was sending hundreds of pounds of cocaine into Houston, Texas hidden on ocean freighters. His acquaintance also knew of a corrupt Peruvian government official, later identified as Montesinos, who was involved in criminal activity including drug trafficking. This was our starting point for this investigation in 1992.

Tito said the smuggler, later identified as Juan, not his real name, was coming to the U.S. for a family vacation. Juan wanted to sell Tito a couple of kilos of cocaine so that he could have spending money while in the U.S. It's not unusual for traffickers to do separate 'side deals,' a kind of an 'off the books' arrangement. We recorded a series of phone calls between Tito and Juan that resulted in Juan delivering two kilos of cocaine to Tito. Juan was arrested and agreed to cooperate.

Juan was a Peruvian citizen and now an undocumented incarcerated criminal. U.S. Immigration did not grant permission for his release to work as an informant. His wife and two children remained in Indianapolis living as undocumented immigrants. On her own, his wife rented an apartment, got a job, and enrolled her kids in school. She accomplished that without help from us. We simply ignored her illegal status.

Dan and I spent months debriefing Juan. His information led to what would eventually become a Targeted Kingpin Organization, TKO, investigation, a designation reserved for DEA's highest priority investigations.

Once a federal investigation reaches a certain level, it's given an operational name. This case was named 'Pig Ears' after a misunderstanding. The sketch artist thought the CI said, 'pig ears' when he was trying to say, 'big ears.'

Inside a small office in the Federal Court House in Indianapolis, Dan and I began interviewing Juan. Multiple interviews resulted in volumes of intelligence reports and were the impetus for the U.S. Attorney's office to initiate a Federal Grand Jury. Prosecutors would eventually charge all the defendants with conspiracy to import cocaine into the United States. Federal conspiracy laws are a powerful tool used by prosecutors in complex criminal investigations. The law states that anyone who commits an overt act toward the commission of a crime is guilty of conspiring to commit the actual crime. The law provides a means to charge criminals who might otherwise escape prosecution.

During the interview Juan told us about a smuggling operation involving crew members on an ocean freighter and provided the name of the ship. He said these men typically brought in several hundred pounds of cocaine per trip.

As the interviews continued, Juan told us about a high-ranking Peruvian government official named Vladimiro Montesinos, who used his political influence over the military to promote his puppets into military command positions. One key position was in the Huallaga Valley region. This region was well-known for growing and processing coca plants into base material. It was also the area where planes from Columbia landed, using primitive jungle landing strips to pick up the coca base. Juan explained Montesinos was an attorney and former military officer. While Montesinos was in the army, he had a designated driver, named Antonio, not his real name, who was his trusted confidant. He was using Antonio to collect and transport bribe money from the jungle to Lima. Juan claimed to have direct knowledge about these smuggling operations from conversations he had with Antonio, the courier. Juan told us Antonio had bragged about dealing with Pablo Escobar's people. With the information supplied by Juan, DEA Agent Mike from the Lima country office was able to identify the courier.

In July 1992, at the same time our investigation was progressing, Pablo Escobar escaped from a Colombian prison. This led to the largest manhunt in Colombian history lasting 17 months. It ended on December 2, 1993, when Colombian National Police killed Escobar. While on the lam, Escobar, already a designated Kingpin, was declared the most wanted drug trafficker in the world.

The U.S. government offered a $2 million reward for information leading to his capture. Our U.S. military added resources to the hunt including a highly sophisticated airborne cellphone interception team known as Centra Spike. At the same time, the CIA was using their cellphone tracking equipment code-named Majestic Eagle to do the same. A Delta Force team was dispatched to Medellín to support Columbia's Special Forces in the hunt. DEA wanted to block any possible escape route or potential safe haven and Montesinos was in a position to provide that. As a street agent in Indianapolis, none of these classified operations in Medellín, Columbia were known to me at the time. It would be years before the full story of the hunt for Escobar became known.

Given that my intelligence reports indicated a possible link between Escobar and Montesinos, DEA headquarters wanted this potential connection either confirmed or refuted. Consequently, our investigation was elevated to a TKO, Targeted Kingpin Organization, status. The pressure was on. Investigating Montesinos on his home court would be risky, but agents don't quit because the odds are stacked against them.

First we needed to authenticate Juan's reliability. To this end, we instructed him to find out when the next cocaine shipment would arrive in Houston. He was jailed in Indianapolis which made his assignment even more difficult. But it was up to him to prove his credibility. We surmised he was using his wife as an intermediary between him and his criminal associates. A few weeks later he told us the name of the ship and the exact date it was due to arrive in Houston. Dan did a customs search, and everything matched.

Houston, Texas

Dan, Bill and I traveled to Houston. Dan coordinated the operation between the Houston Customs agents, the Port Authority Police and us. Initially there was a small turf struggle, and we had to agree to take a supporting role and a secondary surveillance position. The local Customs agents wanted the front row seat.

About 4:00 AM on the 2nd night of 24-hour surveillance, we heard frantic voices over the portable radio. Assuming the cocaine would come off the gangway, the Customs agents hadn't adequately covered the stern of the ship. The smugglers had set a zip line from the ship's stern to the dock and were sending sea bags of cocaine down the rope.

The ground crew was throwing them into the back of a pickup truck when they were spotted by Port Authority Police. The suspects took off in their truck leading a procession of police vehicles through the shipyard. To our dismay, the suspects escaped, but fortunately four sea bags containing about two hundred pounds of cocaine were left behind.

The Houston Customs office seized the ship and initiated a civil forfeiture. The U.S. government resolved the forfeiture by selling the ship back to its owners for two million dollars. This was a customary practice

Bags containing 200+ pounds of cocaine

since it would cost the government more than that to store it in dry-dock.

Despite no arrests, we established Juan was being truthful. Our lead prosecutor John was impressed with the informant but not so much with us since we failed to make arrests. We were gaining confidence in Juan's credibility. This investigation was leading toward serious allegations against a high-ranking Peruvian official. We all agreed Juan needed to prove himself once more. Dan and I told him Houston was good, but not good enough. We needed him to set up another deal. He explained that the people he dealt with knew each other and were probably suspicious about the close call in Houston. He would need to be sure they weren't suspicious of him, and he needed time to figure out how to pull off another deal.

Soon he told us about another man named Carlos, not his real name. Carlos had recently fled Peru and was living somewhere in Florida. Juan told us he had contacted Carlos, and Carlos agreed to sell Tito two kilos. He said Carlos would contact Tito to finalize the details.

Within a week Tito received a call from the new suspect, Carlos. They negotiated a price of $50,000 for two kilograms of cocaine to be delivered to Indianapolis. None of the participating agencies had $50,000 to spend on cocaine. Customs approved a $50,000 flash roll which meant we could only show it. This was getting complicated. Our objective was to identify Carlos and find the source of the cocaine. A buy/bust would expose both informants, Tito and Juan, and end the investigation.

The Customs Resident Agent in Charge, Mike, endowed with a serious set of balls, decided to let the flash roll 'walk.' That meant giving the money to the suspect and letting him drive away with it, a very risky call. The objective was to let the suspect get far enough away from Indianapolis so he wouldn't suspect our informant had double-crossed him. A surveillance team was assembled using ten cars from four agencies and a helicopter equipped with night vision. Losing the flash money was not an option. The deal went as planned in a hotel room on the west side of Indianapolis. When Carlos left, our surveillance team was on him like white on rice.

When Carlos reached Lexington, KY, we had arranged for a Kentucky State Trooper to stop him for 'speeding.' The trooper needed the stop to appear as a routine traffic stop and then 'discover' the suspicious cash. Most importantly, the trooper must identify Carlos. We weren't ready to arrest him because we didn't want to risk exposing Tito and Juan. The trooper informed Carlos that he would confiscate the cash because he suspected it could be linked to drug activity. He explained how to appeal the seizure in court, which he never did. These kinds of interdiction stops and seizures were well known to traffickers who often accepted them as the cost of doing business.

Our Peruvian defendant CI Juan was now batting two for two, officially making him a credible and reliable witness. Our prosecutor John took the investigation to a grand jury, obtaining indictments against Juan, Carlos, and Montesinos' courier Antonio. All we had to do was find Antonio in Peru, arrest him and bring him back to the United States. He was the final link in the bridge we needed to cross.

Federal Prison Camp, Pensacola, Florida

It wasn't long before Miami agents located and arrested Carlos. I flew to Miami on a Monday morning for the removal hearing. When I got back on Friday, my wife told me my 10-year-old son hadn't even noticed I was gone.

Carlos, being an undocumented immigrant, was transferred to the Federal Prison in Pensacola, Florida. Once imprisoned, he agreed to talk to us. Dan and I flew there to interview him. He told us he fled Peru because he had gotten into serious trouble with Montesinos. He feared Montesinos was going to have him killed.

Dan: "How do you know Montesinos?"

With the help of a translator: "My friends and I worked for him. We eliminated the people he declared to be enemies of Peru. When he wanted somebody killed, we did it quickly. He called me Meteor."

Dan: "Montesinos directed you to kill people?"

Carlos: "Yes, many times."

Me: "How did you get in trouble with him?"

Carlos: "The last time I made a mistake and killed the wrong people. He is furious with me."

Dan: "How did you get from Peru to the United States?"

Carlos: "My brother is a pipefitter in the port of Callao. He was working on a Russian freighter when he found out the ship was bound for Houston. He snuck me onboard. I hid under a drain grate in the engine room. When the ship came into port, I ran up to the open deck and jumped. Eventually I made my way to Miami.

After Dan and I returned to Indianapolis, it was time to go after Antonio, the courier. He was the only person who could confirm or dispel the connection between Escobar and Montesinos. DEA headquarters upgraded our investigation into TKO status providing us with the support necessary to find and arrest him. A TKO designation brought with it direct oversight by a headquarters supervisor. I called the TKO supervisor and told him we had the courier identified, including a photograph and a warrant for his arrest. "This is the guy who can connect the dots between Montesinos and Escobar."

HQ: "What do you want to do?"

Me: "I need to go to Lima with my co-case agent and find him."

HQ: "I have no problem with you going, but we're not giving country clearance to a Customs agent."

Me: "Why not?"

HQ: "Because it's a DEA investigation."

Me: "Hold on. That's not true. This is a taskforce investigation. In fact, it's a Customs led taskforce.

HQ: "Not anymore. It's been re-classified."

This put me in a trick bag with Dan. I had to tell him DEA head-quarters wouldn't approve his travel to Peru. This had been an ex-tremely challenging investigation from the beginning. Whenever things got complicated, Dan and I relied on each other to find a so-lution. At the most critical point, I had to go it alone. When I told him he simply said, "Don't worry about it. We're all one team. Go get him."

Lima, Peru

It was April 1993 when I flew from Indianapolis through Miami to Jorge Chavez International Airport in Lima, Peru. Special Agent Mike picked me up at the airport and told me he had changed my hotel reservations. The Lima police bomb squad found and dis-armed a bomb near my hotel.

Mike: "I don't think it had anything to do with you, but I moved you anyway. Besides, the Las Americas hotel is much nicer."

I asked Mike if he had any leads on my fugitive. "My best cops are working on it. If he's here, they'll find him. For now, get checked into the hotel but do not leave the hotel. The threat level here is off the charts, especially at night." Just as we've seen here in the U.S during periods of civil unrest, nighttime is when the greatest amount of violence takes place.

Mike: "You have a security briefing scheduled for 9:00 AM. After that, the Spooks wanted to talk to us before we do anything."

"The Spooks, you mean CIA?"

"Yeah."

"What does the CIA want with me?"

"I don't know. We'll find out tomorrow. We're meeting them at a cafe in the Miraflores neighborhood of Lima."

"You're sure you don't know what they want?"

"No. Don't worry about it. It'll be fine. Remember, don't go any-where tonight. I'll pick you up at 8:30 AM."

The next morning Mike picked me up and as we were driving, he pointed to a building located a short distance from my hotel. It had plywood covering the damage caused by a car bomb.

We went to the Embassy Security Office to meet with the RSO. The Regional Security Officer is like the Police Chief for the Embassy. He's responsible for the safety and security of all embassy and visiting personnel. All official visitors entering any country on official business must attend a security

Plywood covering the blown-out
windows

briefing on the current conditions. It was a Monday morning and there were four or five people in the room with me. I didn't know who they were or what their business was.

The RSO described Lima as the most dangerous city in the world. He told us to stay off the streets at night, not to drink the tap water and to call in an emergency. "Questions?" With no ques-tions, we got up to leave. As I started toward the door, he subtly pointed at me, gave me the stop-sign hand, and said, "Not you."

After the room cleared, he reminded me that I didn't have diplomatic immunity. He was concerned that I may be targeted for abduction by criminals posing as police. He told me not to al-low myself to be 'arrested' by anyone, under any circumstances. He said, "If you allow that to happen, there will be little chance of us ever finding you or your body. Do whatever is necessary to es-cape." He handed me a piece of paper with a number, "If you get in a jam, call this number. Our team will find you. Stay close to Mike. He knows his way around."

When I got back to the DEA office within the building, Mike asked, "Did it go OK?"

"Yeah, he told me not to get kidnapped." Mike responded, "He's not exaggerating. People disappear all the time. These Sendero characters are crazy dangerous. A few days ago, they gunned down one of our task force cops at a bus stop and then blew his body up with a stick of dynamite. Stone cold, ruthless and they definitely don't like us."

Mike and I went to the cafe to meet with the CIA. It was a sidewalk café across the street from a community park. The CIA officers, a man and a woman, were pleasant. They asked what I thought Montesinos was up to. I told them, "My information is he is taking bribes from drug traffickers to allow safe passage for their aircraft."

CIA: "How do you know that?"

Me: "The cash arrives on the same plane that transports the coca paste out of the jungle. Our informant says the courier carries the cash from the jungle to Lima. He claims that Escobar and his people are affiliated with Montesinos'."

CIA: "What is your plan?"

Me: "Once we get the courier arrested and to the states, hopefully he'll cooperate. We need to determine if there is a direct connection between Escobar and Montesinos. If there is, we want to make sure Montesinos doesn't help Escobar escape. I think Montesinos is as big of a crook as Escobar and the courier can confirm that. Plus, he could provide valuable information on active smuggling operations."

CIA: "Is this a grand jury investigation?"

Me: "Yes, the Southern District of Indiana."

CIA: "That's a federal grand jury?"

Me: "Yes."

CIA: "Do you know where the courier is now?"

Me: "No, that's why I'm here."

CIA: "Montesinos is an important asset to the United States. He is also a supporter of DEA's *Snowcap* program."

Me: "I understand, but he is also a double-dealing criminal."

CIA "Is there anything else you can tell us?"

Me: "We've also interviewed another informant who claims he's killed people at the direction of Montesinos."

CIA: "What's his name?"

Me: "Are you going to share any of your information?"

CIA: "We knew nothing about these accusations until we read your intelligence reports. So, like you, we're trying to determine if any of it could be true."

After we left, I said to Mike, "That felt more like an interrogation than a meeting." "Don't worry about it. Let's go for a ride."

Once we left the city, the houses led to shacks and the roads turned to dirt. As we drove Mike said, "We're entering Sendero country. The Sendero controls most of the rural areas. The cities remain under government control." What struck me were all the communist Chinese flags openly displayed, like campaign posters.

I asked him what we were doing out there. He said, "I wanted you to see how fractured this country is and how it could fall to the communists."

Looking back, I understand Mike was trying to show me how unstable the country was. But it didn't register. I had tunnel vision. Like a typical DEA agent, I was only focused on my target. I asked him, "When are we going to look for my fugitive?"

Mike: "My cops tracked him down, but he's fled the country. But that's OK, because if your information is good, Montesinos would never let us extradite him. My instincts tell me he'll show up in Bolivia, and we'll have a better chance of getting him there."

Later that night, Mike dropped me off at my hotel, again reminding me not to wander around outside. My room was on the seventh floor. When I got to the room, I turned on the TV and tried to find an English-speaking channel to no avail. The scenes on the local news station said it all. I didn't need to understand the words. I pulled the drapes open. I could see a column of thick black smoke billowing up from where insurgents were burning tires in the street. There were police and military vehicles racing in every direction. When I opened the window to let in some air, I could hear periodic bursts of automatic gunfire in the distance. I thought, how did a small-town cop end up with a front row seat to a would-be communist revolution in South America? It was eerie how the insurgents and the violence faded away in the light of day.

A few days later, I was in the DEA's communications center when I heard a familiar voice over the radio. I asked if that was Bob Hartman talking. Bob was the agent I worked with in Milwaukee who advised me not to draw attention to myself at the academy.

Radio operator: "Yeah, he's the team leader for the group down range."

Me: "Where exactly is down range?"

Radio operator: "The base camp, Santa Lucia, on the other side of the mountains inland toward the Amazon."

Me: "I need to go out there and talk to him."

Mike: "There's a resupply flight on Thursday. I can get you a seat. Just to give you a heads up, the peaks of the Andes Mountain range exceed the plane's maximum altitude capabilities. Two auxiliary jet boosters were installed to provide the aircraft with the additional lift needed to clear the mountain peaks. You sure you still want to go?" I wasn't sure if he was serious or tweaking me. I responded, "Yeah, I'd like to talk to him."

Flying in this region was inherently dangerous. A year after my mission in Peru, a DEA aircraft crashed near Santa Lucia, killing all five agents on board.

On Thursday morning, I boarded the supply plane. The plane had two turbo-prop engines, and its nickname was *The Burro*. There were two rows of jump seats that ran the length of the fuselage along the walls. Already onboard were a dozen Peruvian passengers who looked like camp workers.

The Burro

After landing, I exited through the back door and was smacked in the face by the hot, humid jungle air. It was like the rush of hot air when opening an oven door to see if the cookies were done. The pilot never turned off the engines. The plane was on the ground for a few minutes before returning to Lima. The Sendero wanted to destroy that plane, so it didn't linger. Bob greeted me on the tarmac, "Howard, what in the world are you doing here?"

Me: "I was in the neighborhood and thought I'd stop by to say hi. Actually, I need to talk to you."

Bob: "Great! I'm in the middle of something right now. I'll get with you when I'm done. In the meantime, make yourself at home. There's bread and peanut butter in the kitchen if you're hungry."

While we were conversing, a pair of old Vietnam era Huey helicopters landed. I commented about how old they were. He laughed and said, "Those are our only source of transportation out here. If we try to use the roads, sooner or later the Sendero will ambush us."

As I was wandering around the camp, I found a coca plant processing lab. Bob later told me it was an actual captured lab, brought back to camp, and set up for display. DEA's *Snowcap* operation was drawing a lot of attention. He used the lab as a prop for visiting VIPs which included some Congressional delegates and news reporters, the likes of Peter Jennings. The lab served as a backdrop for a few major news stories.

Snowcap was one of DEA's most successful cocaine suppression programs. It disrupted the flow of cocaine into the U.S. to such a degree that, for a brief time in the early 1990s, the street price of cocaine rose, a sure sign of a supply shortage. Bob authored an informative book about his experiences as a *Snowcap* operator titled *Inside DEA* by Special Agent Bob Hartman.

Entrance to Base Camp Santa Lucia

The coca plant has been growing in this region for thousands of years. It's embedded in the culture of the Indigenous population like corn in the United States. It's a temperamental plant that will only grow in certain locations. For centuries, the natives have been chewing the leaves, providing them with a mild stimulant. They also believe the plant has healing properties. The coca leaves are used to make tea which helps stave off altitude sickness.

The leaves also provide the raw ingredient for cocaine. The process starts by stomping the leaves with bare feet in a large vat filled with a mixture of water and nitric acid. Next the liquid is poured into barrels, adding lime and gasoline to produce a syrup. The syrup is then poured onto a drying table where it eventually becomes a paste that is 30 to 90 percent pure cocaine.

The remaining liquid is often dumped in a river contaminating it for miles. That paste, called base, is the material smugglers take back to Colombia. Refineries in Colombia convert the base into cocaine HCL, known as street cocaine.

In Peru, some natives smoke the dried coca base which is a horribly contaminated crack in a practice referred to as 'basuco.' Once the cocaine is processed into HCL, it becomes water soluble and is no longer smokable. In HCL form, it's dissolvable and must be absorbed through the mucous membranes of the nose or injected with a syringe.

The process of making crack cocaine turns the water-soluble HCL back into base, making it smokable. Crack gained popularity in the early 1990s because smoking provided a more efficient means for the body to absorb it, resulting in a more intense high.

The camp looked like a Vietnam era fire base. I climbed one of the observation towers. When I got to the top deck, I found a Special Forces soldier sitting on the floor, leaning back against the wall, knees up. He had an M-16 rifle propped upright, squeezed between his knees. When I saw him I said, "Hey, how are you?"

SF: "Fine, who are you?"

Me: "DEA waiting to meet with Bob."

SF: "What are you doing up here?

Me: "Nothing, killing time."

He kept watch on the perimeter. Suddenly, he spun around, took a kneeling position, and fired his M-16. I ducked down behind some sandbags. When I peeked at him, he was settling back into his relaxed position. I asked, "What the hell was that?"

Guard tower in the background

SF: "Dog. We don't let dogs in the camp. Rabies. You ever see a man die from rabies? I have. It isn't pretty."

He was talking with a terse, tight-lipped delivery reminiscent of Clint Eastwood's character, Harry Callahan in the 1971 movie *Dirty Harry*. I couldn't tell what was up with this guy, but I wasn't sticking around to find out. I walked back to the team house where I met Bob. He was finished dealing with his problem and was available to talk. I briefed him on Montesinos. He listened intently and then in a defensive tone said, "These PNP (Peruvian National Police) guys put their lives on the line out here. Hell, I trust them with my life every day."

I told him this wasn't about foot soldiers. This was corruption at the highest levels. Bob said, "You know it's Montesinos allowing this mission. He might even be the only guy who can keep this country from falling into communist hands."

Me: "That may be, but just so you know, he's pulling the same crap Noriega did in Panama. What I'm telling you is, I think he's playing everyone."

Bob then told me what he had been dealing with involved a Peruvian Air Force pilot who had refused an order to shoot down a smuggler's plane. The smuggler had refused to turn back and surrender. The Peruvian pilot claimed his guns had jammed. "I test-fired them myself and they worked fine. Then he changed his story and said it was his conscience that wouldn't allow him to do it." Bob said he was going to discharge him from the mission and send him home. I suggested re-interviewing him because he may have been pressured to let that plane go.

We went back to the group room where I saw the Special Forces guy from the tower. He called over to me, "Hey Howard, did you notice how much weight Bob's lost?" "Yeah. Bob, you look like a high school basketball player."

This prompted Bob to step over to a scale, the kind that had weights that slide back and forth. As he stepped on the scale and started moving the weights, the SF guy stood behind him and secretly put his foot on the scale. Bob got his reading and in total exasperation, rhetorically asked, "How the hell can I gain eight pounds in a day?" The SF guy looked at me with a sly smile and said, "Come on, Bob, you sound like a girl crying about how fat you are." I got it now. He's a prankster. Was there a rabid dog? I don't think so. It was one of those Green Beret pranks. Dan would have enjoyed that. With nothing more to do in Santa Lucia, I caught the next supply plane back to Lima.

I talked with Mike and there was nothing more we could do in Lima. I scheduled my return flight to Indianapolis. With one night left in Lima, I went back to the cafe where we had met with the CIA. There were three little kids trying to sell carved stone animal figures to the patrons. The servers kept chasing them away. They

Animal figures

were dirty, dressed in little more than rags and barefoot. Two were older, about seven or eight , and a little guy around five. I winked at the little guy. He knew he had a potential sale. I watched as they huddled up and formed a plan. The two older ones distracted the servers while the little guy snuck over to me. He had a shoe box with a half dozen animal figures mostly chipped and broken. I bought them all for more than he was asking.

When I got back to Indiana, we held a team briefing. I related what happened in Peru. Now it was a waiting game. Mike predicted our guy would surface in Venezuela or Bolivia.

La Paz, Bolivia, Two Months Later
I got a call from the country attaché in La Paz, Bolivia. "I think we found your fugitive. I'm sending you a picture to verify." It was him. He told me they've had him under surveillance for the last few days. The attaché told me there was a provision in the Bolivian law that permitted the expulsion of non-Bolivian criminals

by the most expeditious means possible. If we provided the means to remove him, we could have him. This was a legal alternative to a formal extradition hearing. I called my TKO coordinator in DC and told him what our plan was. He said, "Got it. Tell them there's a plane on its way now."

I called the DEA attaché in Bolivia to tell him a plane was on its way. He said they were going to snatch him the next morning after he dropped his kid off at school. It was happening so fast that I didn't have time to get there. He assured me my presence wasn't necessary. The next morning, I got the call. "We got him."

Several years later, while assigned to ST in Lorton, Virginia, I worked with Frank, a fellow agent. Frank was a pilot who had transferred into ST from the air wing. Frank and I were talking, and this case came up. He said, "Hey, wait a minute, I remember that case. I was the pilot that flew there to pick him up in La Paz. I was flying over Texas in the DEA Lear jet when I got an urgent message to fly directly to La Paz for a prisoner pick up. After landing in La Paz, headquarters instructed me to stand by. No one ever showed up." After several hours, he received clearance to return to the U.S. never knowing what had happened until I told him.

I was at my desk in Indianapolis when the country attaché called to tell me they had hit a snag. The Bolivian police officer running the operation received a call from his commander ordering him to bring the fugitive to court. His commander told him if he put the fugitive on our DEA plane, his career was over, and he would go to prison.

The attaché said he couldn't jeopardize the officer. They took the fugitive to court. Inside the courtroom were several people he didn't recognize. He said what happened next was something he'd never heard of. As soon as court began, the judge ordered all the Americans removed. The Bolivian fiscal (prosecutor) assigned to their office was allowed to remain in the courtroom. The fiscal later provided the attaché a written account of the events that took place.

Without hearing any testimony, the judge criticized the American 'imperialists' for arresting a poor Peruvian citizen who had done nothing wrong. The judge ordered that he be immediately returned to his native country of Peru. This took place while the agents were waiting in the hall. The attaché told me he couldn't believe it. He could only surmise that Montesinos must have found out about the arrest and made a phone call to some influential person inside the Bolivian government.

Years earlier Montesinos, also an attorney, had represented some of the largest drug traffickers in Bolivia. There was no doubt he had connections in Bolivia. His influence there would become indisputable once the infamous 1999 *Arms-for-Cocaine* scandal was brought to light. Montesinos had used the Peruvian military to conceal the distribution of 10,000 AK-47 rifles in exchange for cocaine. Rifles ended up in the hands of Colombian terrorists. In that case, it's believed that the Russian manufactured rifles were allowed to pass through Bolivia en route to Columbia with the help of corrupt elements of the local military and/or Customs officials.

This courtroom disaster foreshadowed what was in store for DEA in Bolivia. In 2008, Evo Morales, the former head of the coca grower's union and well-known proponent of legalized coca cultivation, was elected president. Morales ordered the DEA to shut down all their offices and leave the country. The exit from Bolivia constituted the largest evacuation of DEA personnel in the history of the agency. In just 77 days the DEA closed all their offices and relocated 109 agents and their families, as reported in the DEA's 50th Anniversary publication.

In a last-ditch effort, I called Mike to tell him what happened in Bolivia. He already knew about it. I asked him if I could come down to interview the courier now that he was back in custody in Peru.

Mike said, "Sorry, brother. It's over. That was our only chance, and we lost him. We'll never see him again and it's probably not safe for you to come back here either."

By the end of the year, Escobar was located in Colombia and killed while attempting to escape arrest. The only chance we had to keep our investigation alive ended with the loss of Antonio the courier. The same was true for any shot we might have had at exposing Montesinos. I overestimated DEA's reach and influence on foreign soil. This time I was the one who brought checkers to a chess game and got out played. In the real world you're judged by results not effort.

What matters most is how the story ends. In 2000, President Fujimori's administration began unraveling amid allegations of corruption, leading the president to flee the country. A court eventually convicted him of several crimes, including bribery, embezzlement and human rights violations that included torture and murder. At the center of it all was the head of his secret police, Vladimiro Montesinos.

Peruvian prosecutors filed over 60 criminal charges against Montesinos, causing him to flee the country. In June 2001, Montesinos was located and arrested by FBI agents in Caracas, Venezuela and returned to Peru to stand trial. His first conviction was for Abuse of Power. The judge sentenced him to nine years and four months and fined him $2.8 million. The sentence was far more severe than the prosecutor had asked for. He served his time in a maximum-security prison in the city of Callao, Peru. In an ironic twist, Montesinos was in the same cell block as Abimael Guzman, the former communist leader of the Sendero.

Around 2000, after I was transferred to ST, I received a phone call from an INS, Immigration and Naturalization, agent. He was investigating a Peruvian military pilot seeking political asylum. The pilot had fled Peru in a military aircraft and landed at the

Homestead Air Reserve Base, ARB, in Florida. According to the agent, the pilot claimed to have previously smuggled cocaine into the U.S. onboard military aircraft at the direction of his commanding officers. Now those same commanders were threatening his life. The agent said a 1992 intelligence report I'd written seemed to independently corroborate his claim. He asked me if I had any additional information not included in the report. I didn't. I never heard if the pilot was granted asylum, but it just irritated an old wound for me.

Remember Steve, the agent from the General Noriega case? He and I talked about past cases when we worked together at ST. Often our conversations centered around his Noriega case and my Montesinos case. He told me I was lucky that our investigation short-circuited when it did. He said, "You cannot imagine how the Noriega case took over my life. I fell prey like so many agents, and let the job consume me, a mistake that cost me my marriage."

He gave me a copy of the book *Shooting the Moon* by David Harris. Steve told me the title came from a comment he had made during an interview with the author. The author asked Steve, "Where did you want the case to go?" Steve responded, "I'm gonna shoot the moon with it." After I finished that book, I understood what he had gone through. Looking back, maybe I was lucky I never got to dance with the Peruvian Devil. Every agent in DEA knows the adage: *Big cases - Big problems, Little cases - Little problems, No cases - No problems."*

~ 7 ~

WIRES AND PLIERS

The Telephone Box

In the mid 90s, Tom was promoted to a GS-14, Group Supervisor. He assigned me to take over his Tech responsibilities as a collateral duty. A collateral assignment is in addition to regular duties. Tom had attended DEA's Advanced Tech Agent School in Lorton, Virginia. Tech was a specialized school and was offered only once or twice a year with a long wait list. I was selected to attend four years later.

Tom had been coaching me on how to set up and use various pieces of covert equipment. He taught me how to install a pen register on landline phones. A pen register is a device that intercepts the phone numbers of all incoming and outgoing calls on a targeted line. Agents analyze those numbers to help identify the target's associates.

The case agent managed the investigation and obtained court orders authorizing telephone intercepts. It was the tech agent that worked the wires and pliers to make the magic happen. During my time as the tech agent, I installed several pen registers along with a few Title III voice intercepts. A Title III intercept is the legal term for a 'wiretap.'

Before cellphones took over the world, most households had a landline home phone. There used to be big green metal telephone junction boxes on most streets. Inside those boxes were the interlacing wires that made the telephone system work. A special tool was needed to open the box. Tech agents had that tool plus the same tools as telephone technicians.

One day Noel told me he had a court order for a pen register on an auto repair shop that was a 'front' for a drug trafficking operation. After completing the prep work, I headed out to install the device inside the junction box. The box I needed to access was located across the street from the target's auto shop.

Typical junction box

The door to the box was on the side facing away from the shop. I thought I would go unnoticed working inside the box. I parked my truck, walked over and opened the box. It was a big box with hundreds of wires going in every direction. I was completely focused on finding the correct wires. Out of nowhere a big booming voice behind me barked, "Who the hell are you and what are you doing?" When I turned around, standing behind me was the target and two of his buddies. Fortunately, my gun and badge were in the bottom of my tool bag, out of sight. I said, "I'm a sub-contractor for the phone company. I'm doing an emergency repair for a doctor's office."

Surprisingly, that satisfied him. If he had pursued it or tried to look in my tool bag, it would have been game on for all of us. He nodded and walked away. I called out to him as he was crossing the street, "Hey, how much would it cost to replace the exhaust on my truck?"

Without looking back, he said, "We don't do exhaust pipes. Take it to a muffler shop."

I finished installing the device and left. By the end of the day, his incoming and outgoing calls were being monitored. Within a week Noel had upgraded the pen register order to a Title III wiretap. That order allowed us to listen to and record his phone conversations.

By the mid-90s, cellphones were a mainstay with drug dealers. Despite being quite expensive, they fit with a dealer's business and lifestyle. Money was never an issue for drug dealers. Soon every dealer had one and DEA didn't have the technological ability to intercept them. It wasn't just DEA. Nearly every agency fell behind in cellphone intercept technology. This also marked the beginning of cellphone encryption and privacy issues. Law enforcement was unprepared for this new digital revolution. Gathering telephone communication data had been essential to investigating conspiracy cases.

In1995, our Indianapolis office moved to a different floor in the federal building and our floor space doubled. GS Tom designated three rooms exclusively for technical operations. He knew that technology and the computer age was just beginning, and we needed to catch up. As insightful as GS Tom was, he paled in comparison to my dad.

When I was seven years old in 1961, my dad and I were watching a Dick Tracy TV cartoon. Detective Tracy had a wristwatch phone. My dad told me that someday those wristwatch phones would be real. With the infinite wisdom of a 7-year-old, I told him, "No way. It's just a cartoon." Then 56 years later in 2017, Apple introduced their cellular internet wristwatch.

Terry the Computer Wizard

After we moved into our new space, the Indiana National Guard assigned two full-time guardsmen to our DEA task force. One of the young guardsmen, Terry Ordille, was a computer wizard.

Within a few short years Terry would be hired by DEA as a telecommunications specialist. Like most agents in the office, I knew nothing about computers. I was quick to recognize his valuable talent and asked GS Tom to assign him to me. This was about the time Microsoft released their first user friendly *Windows 95*. The computer age had arrived. Most of my generation were woefully unprepared.

When I first met Terry, I told him his job was to teach me everything he knew about computers. Considering what little knowledge I brought to the table, his work was cut out for him. In our workshop, he taught me about hardware, operating systems, software programs, and networking. I remember the first time I took the cover off a computer. I thought springs would fly out. I was like a gorilla trying to figure out a color TV.

Terry and I built a couple of computers from scratch for people in the office. Around 1996, my daughter told me her high school, Hamilton Southeastern, was selling old classroom computers. I went there on a Saturday and bought five computers for $10.00 each. Back in our workshop, we cannibalized three of them and used their parts to make the remaining two computers work faster.

There were other task-force guys, like Ron from IMPD, who were interested in computers. We shared our collective knowledge to help prepare our office and ourselves for the impending computer evolution.

During that era much of society was unprepared. I recall a night in 1995 when Bill Gates, the founder of Microsoft, appeared on the David Letterman show. Gates was attempting to explain the internet to Letterman claiming it to be 'the next big thing.' Gates told Letterman that soon the internet and computers would allow people to listen to baseball games. Letterman responded, "Ever heard of a radio?" which generated laughter from the audience. Gates then said, "You'll be able to read about all the things you're interested in." Letterman responded, "I already do that with magazines and newspapers," reflecting the public's view of the internet and computers at the time.

Leading up to that era was the 1977 movie Smokey and the Bandit *starring Bert Reynolds and Sally Field that popularized CB radios. Except for truck drivers, the fad lasted only a few years before the majority of the motoring public tired of it. Many people who had seen CB radios come and go equated the internet and computers with the same skepticism.*

In the mid-1990s DEA launched its own internal computer network system called *Firebird*. All DEA employees were required to attend a *Firebird* operators' training class. We were all beginners. The training was basic, including how to double-click a mouse. This wasn't remedial training. This was my generation being reluctantly thrown into the digital age.

We had an older agent who hated his new desk computer and refused to use it. I was the first one to learn about this cool feature called a screensaver. As a joke, I set his screensaver to activate every two hours with a scrolling marquee message, "Fatal Error! Caused by Operator Incompetence." Throughout the day he would yell and curse at it. I'd go over and 'fix' it for him. He told me repeatedly and emphatically, "It's not me. I haven't even touched the damn thing."

Eventually he got so mad he threatened to throw it out the window. Fearing he might actually do it, I returned it to the default setting. Fortunately, he never figured out it was me or he might have thrown me out the window.

The National Intelligence Academy

GS Tom wanted me to figure out how to tap cellphones ASAP. I was learning computers as fast as I could but using them and the internet to intercept cellphones was over my head. I learned about a Cellular Telephone Technology Class taught by the National Intelligence Academy in Deerfield Beach, Florida. GS Tom authorized me to attend the class. The instructors explained how the cellular network functioned. It gave me some ideas on how to bridge analog technologies with digital technologies.

After returning from Florida, GS Tom called me into his office and told me an agent needed a pen register on a cell phone. I was still trying to figure that out. He told me to get some help from our Division Technical Group in Chicago. The Chicago Group Supervisor told me it wasn't possible. DEA didn't have the technical ability to do it.

When I told GS Tom, he wasn't happy. He told me I was supposed to be figuring out how to tap cell phones. Little did we know it would be another few years before DEA headquarters' Science and Technology Section, ST, would solve the issue on a national scale.

Despite the technical issues, GS Tom told agent Noel to move ahead and get a federal Title III court order. He intended to use the power of the court to force the Chicago Tech group and me to make it happen. He knew how to get things done one way or another.

One thing I learned from the NIA class was that cell companies have switch engineers who operate the cellular switch. The switch is the computer-driven control center for the entire network that sorts and connects cellphone calls. It's the digital version of the old green telephone box.

I located the switch engineer for the cell company and introduced myself. I explained we had a federal court order to wiretap a cellphone, and I needed his help. He was very cooperative and told me what equipment was needed. To start with, I needed a computer with a dial-up modem. The $10.00 high school computer we rebuilt had a modem. I got the other device we needed from Chicago and he and I installed it inside the switch. With some program modifications, the switch engineer had the target's incoming and outgoing numbers forwarded to our computer over a regular phone line. We next integrated an audio stream into our recording equipment. It was a cobbled together mess, but it worked. That's the DEA way. It doesn't have to be pretty as long as it works.

Our office was the first in the DEA Chicago division to do a Title III intercept on a cellphone. Amazingly we did it with a $10.00 surplus school computer. The Chicago Technical group sent representatives to see how we accomplished it.

The hero of this story was the switch engineer who was instrumental in figuring out how to make the pieces fit together. He told me he had lost a family member to a drug overdose and was happy to help.

Although we made it work, it wasn't a large-scale solution. The set-up was cumbersome and labor intensive. DEA would eventually develop a sophisticated workable solution on a nationwide scale.

In addition to setting up the wire tap, we concealed a hidden camera across the

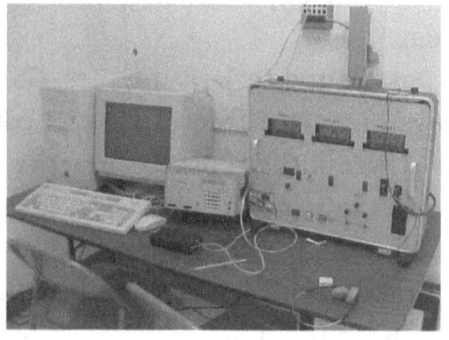

Our cobbled together wiretap

street from the target's residence. We transmitted a live video feed to a monitor in the wire room. The image wasn't great because unlike today the refresh rate was very slow causing the video to be choppy. But it allowed the monitors to watch the house while listening to the suspect's telephone conversations. One day Diane, an IMPD officer assigned to our task force, called me into the wire room to show me what looked like an injured dog lying in the road in front of the target's house. It didn't appear to be moving except for lifting its head up periodically. Diane, an avid animal lover, was distraught that someone had just heartlessly ran over it and another car did the same. She insisted we go out there right away and help it. I have a soft heart for animals too, so recruiting me for the task wasn't difficult. Diane and I drove to the rescue only to find a crushed brown cardboard box lying in the road. The wind was causing one of the flaps to lift up and down. Remember I said the picture wasn't great. Relieved there was no injured dog, Diane and I went out for coffee. Just another day in the wire room.

Tech Agent School

In 1998, I was selected to attend Tech Agent Training in Lorton, Virginia. This was an extensive five-week school. I flew into Reagan National airport and caught a taxi to a hotel in Springfield, Virginia. As I checked in, I saw several of my classmates talking in the lobby. I was happy to see my old friend Mike from Peru was in the class. On our first weekend, Mike and I went to what he described as the 'best Peruvian restaurant in northern Virginia.' I had Peruvian chicken, yucca and plantain for the first time. A couple of years later, after transferring to Virginia, it was one of our favorite restaurants.

Mike told me about the plane crash in Santa Lucia that occurred about a year after my Peru trip. He was on the first helicopter to arrive at the crash site. The jungle was so thick he and a couple other guys had to rappel out of the helicopter with chainsaws to clear an opening for choppers to land. He said the entire recovery process was terribly sad. Although I didn't know any of the casualties personally, I still felt the loss.

The next morning, we boarded a small bus that took us to the Office of Science & Technology, ST. The building was a warehouse in an industrial park with no identifying signage. The roof had several antennas in various shapes and sizes. An instructor from the training unit greeted us and took us to the classroom.

During the five-week school, each of the technologies, Radio, Audio/Video, Telephones, Tracking/Sensors and Computer Forensics supplied instructors who taught their respective courses. Classes began with an overview of DEA's current capabilities followed by plans for future advancements. We received information about the different devices and equipment in each section, along with detailed instructions on their usage. Some devices were simple to operate, while others were more complex. Most classes concluded with a series of practical exercises designed to verify our understanding and ability to use the equipment.

We received a detailed briefing from the radio unit regarding the pending upgrade to DEA's radio network. DEA's radios were old and obsolete, something DEA agents already knew. The upgrade would be a multi-million dollar project spread out over several years.

The Audio/Video section introduced us to the newest covert devices in DEA's inventory. We were shown the disguised transmitters and how to use them. We reviewed the newest miniature cameras and recorders. They introduced us to a new technology called 'Bluetooth' which was slated to revolutionize our short-range covert audio body wires.

There was a full-sized replica motel room built inside the warehouse. We did several practical exercises setting up and installing the covert equipment necessary to run a simulated clandestine surveillance operation. The video and audio signals had to be transmitted to a monitoring station in a nearby control room.

The Computer Forensics instructors taught us how to properly seize a computer while protecting the data. They showed us methods and resources used to bypass or override password-protected computers.

Telephone Unit

The telephone class started with a history lesson on the evolution of the telephone system in the U.S. and how it worked. The telephone unit had a self-contained working telephone network inside the building complete with telephone poles in the back parking lot. We had several wiretap exercises to complete including climbing the poles to splice wires. I already knew how to do most of it, but they were fun to do. We knew that landlines were fast becoming obsolete.

In the cellphone portion of the class, the instructor told us ST was developing a nationwide uniform solution for wiretaps. The solution was a multi-million dollar project and was a few years away from completion. The world of telecommunications was exploding, and we were playing catch up.

In addition to finding a solution for intercepting cellphones, we needed to do the same for Voice over the Internet Protocol, VOIP. VOIP technology allowed users to talk through the internet creating a new set of problems for intercepting. A prime example was the PlayStation2 video game console. This 'toy' gave users the ability to talk to each other using a simple headset and microphone. In a 1999 DEA investigation, drug traffickers were identified using VOIP through the PlayStation gaming machines for secure communications.

At one point, the instructor noticed the name card on my desk. He gave me a puzzled look and said, "Are you the guy from Indiana who did a cellphone wiretap using a surplus school computer?" I smiled and said, "Yeah." He quickly added, "You earned a bit of notoriety with that stunt." That happened three years prior. I didn't think it was that big a deal. Evidently, it was.

FBI Lock and Alarm

We spent a day with the FBI's Lock and Alarm entry team. These agents were highly specialized and exceptionally talented.

They were the guys that carried out court-authorized surreptitious entries, also known as legal burglaries. Their specialty was installing listening devices in difficult locations. We had a lot of fun with them, and they had great stories. They gave us a set of lock picking tools, and we spent the afternoon opening an assortment of locks. They closed the class with a briefing on their capabilities and how to contact them.

Years after retiring from DEA, I was in Kuala Lumpur, Malaysia preparing to teach an international terrorism course for the state department's Anti Terrorism Assistance program. There always seemed to be some kind of hiccup. This time our supplies were locked in a storage cabinet for which we had no key. Fortunately I had my lock picks and within a few minutes the lock gave up its secrets and popped open.

Which brings me to my next story. In the same pocket with my lock picks I always kept a small handheld GPS device which I'd purchased at Walmart. I carried the device in case I ever got separated from my teammates, I'd be able to use the device to find my way back to the hotel or training camp. We had just arrived in Amman, Jordan when I got diverted into a different immigration line. As the agent was going through my backpack, he found the device, held it up and called for assistance. I didn't understand what he was saying but I suspected a problem when they whisked me into a room with no windows. Well, apparently bringing military equipment into Jordan is a felony. Since my Walmart device had a faux camouflage finish, it looked military. Had it been any other color they wouldn't have pay any attention to it. When I didn't make it to the parking lot where the rest of team was assembling, they sent our Jordanian liaison officer to find me. He rescued me just in time to stop them from strip searching me.

Even though I sure it must have been a misunderstanding, my mind wondered back to a movie from 1978 called Midnight Express *where an American tourist got put into a Jordanian prison and became a sex toy for a brutal prison guard. Claud, my teammate, later told me the movie took place in Turkey not Jordan, like that made a difference.*

Pager Intercept

In the 80s and 90s, before cellphones, pagers were the primary means to send instant messages. I carried a pager for years. Most messages were brief, such as 'call Tom' or 'call the office,' which meant find a pay phone and make the call. At that time pagers were state-of-the-art.

The paging system worked differently than the current cellphone system. Cellphones continually register with the closest cell tower. This is how the cell company knows where to send incoming phone calls. Unlike cellphones, pagers only received messages, they didn't transmit. This meant they couldn't register with any towers.

To make the paging system work, the companies built a network of transmission towers across the country. To insure a message reached its intended pager, every tower simultaneously broadcast the message coast to coast. Radio broadcast messages filled the sky. A pin code attached to the radio broadcast insured that only the matching pager would receive the message.

DEA had receivers capable of monitoring the radio frequencies used by the paging companies. The receivers intercepted all the broadcast messages sent to the target's pin code. When I returned to Indianapolis and told the agents about this 'new' capability, it didn't take long before agents began using it. Today, pagers are mostly obsolete.

Tracking and Sensors Unit

My favorite class was Tracking taught by the Unit Chief, Jon. He explained the difference between communication satellites and overhead spy satellites and how they functioned. He explained the history of GPS, Global Positioning System, and how it worked.

Next he introduced data loggers which are devices that self-record their position at preset time intervals. Once activated and attached to a vehicle, the logger recorded its GPS location every 10 seconds while the vehicle was in motion. After retrieving the logger from the vehicle, its' data was downloaded to a computer where mapping software created a breadcrumb trail of the vehicle's travel history. The agent could then study the suspect's historical movements. As a street agent, I immediately recognized its value. This device could do the work of ten surveillance agents. He also showed us a device that could track in real-time. These devices revolutionized surveillance.

He showed us an electronic transmitter nicknamed the 'kill switch,' a device that could shut off a car's engine from about one hundred yards away. I was introduced to a new world of technology that I didn't know existed. This was 1998.

Jon a former army combat engineer and Vietnam veteran rarely talked about any of his many accomplishments. Jon preferred to work behind the scenes. He did tell me once, "There's no limit to what you can accomplish, so long as you don't care who takes the credit." I heard about this accomplishment from a mutual friend.

Tranquilandia

In 1984 a Chicago DEA undercover chemical storefront operation led to the discovery of the largest cocaine processing lab in the agency's history. The investigation began when some Colombians negotiated with undercover agents for the purchase of one thousand 55-gallon drums of ether. Ether is an essential component for processing cocaine. The suspects wanted the ether-filled barrels shipped to Columbia. The agents knew that ether was used to process cocaine. This massive amount of ether could lead them to a bonanza if the barrels could be tracked.

Knowing the Colombians were not stupid and wouldn't fall prey to conventional surveillance, there had to be another way. Jon from ST came up with one of the most ingenious ideas. President Reagan had recently released the GPS satellite network to the public for commercial use. Prior to that it was only used by our military. One needs to understand GPS satellites are nothing more than orbiting transmission beacons in space. It takes a decoder device like a Garmin to receive GPS signals and use them to calculate a location on the earth's surface.

Jon knew that by hiding a GPS receiver in some of the barrels, it could track itself. A GPS Garmin only receives signals, it cannot transmit. For transmitting Jon would need another device that could transmit the GPS coordinates to a communication satellite. His solution was to configure a transmission beacon to work with a GPS device.

Next Jon needed access to a communication satellite. In 1984 there were only 374 satellites in orbit, today there are over 10,000. Since none belonged to DEA, Jon sought help from NOAA, the National Oceanic and Atmospheric Administration. In 1984, NOAA had satellites orbiting earth collecting data from weather sensors in Antarctica. The data collected by the orbiting satellite was downloaded back to earth when the satellite passed over a receiving station. Jon collaborated with the NOAA engineers to modify his GPS device, making it compatible with their satellites. Finally, Jon figured out how to conceal the modified transponders inside two of the first 75 barrels shipped to Columbia.

The final destination was an extremely remote area in the Colombian jungle. Traffickers called it Tranquilandia or 'land of tranquility.' Once the lab was found, agents along with Colombian police staged a raid that yielded nearly 15 tons of cocaine and a wealth of intelligence including ledgers and names. The Colombian police burned everything to the ground. The raid infuriated Pablo Escobar, leader of the Medellín cartel. In retaliation, Escobar ordered the assassination of the head of the Colombian drug police and a participating minister of justice. Both were quickly murdered. To put this in perspective, it's estimated that during his lifetime, Pablo Escobar was responsible for ordering the deaths of as many as 1,000 police officers and political opponents in the Colombian government.

Some of the documents seized during the raid provided crucial evidence in the indictment of General Manuel Noriega years later.

When the school ended we were issued a brown bag full tools and gadgets. The truth is 'black bag operations' are really done with brown bags. Two years later, I would return to ST as an instructor.

~ 8 ~

ST INSTRUCTOR

Lorton, Virginia

In July 2000, I was transferred to the Office of Investigative Technology, ST, in Lorton, Virginia as an instructor. The day I reported, Lou, my supervisor, greeted me at the front door. He was personable and enthusiastic about his job. He told me he was determined to maintain the excellent reputation of the training unit. He introduced me to Gary, the other instructor. Gary and I were the only Senior Grade 13 agents in the building. All the other agents were GS-14s or above.

Lou explained the responsibilities of each section including buying and distributing millions of dollars of equipment to the field offices. DEA uses a centralized acquisition concept to maintain uniformity in equipment. Each of the technology sections was responsible for researching and testing new equipment before purchasing. Last, each section provided field support to both foreign and domestic offices.

Our training unit coordinated the five-week Tech Agent course. In addition, we taught basic agent classes at the DEA Academy at Quantico. Those classes included photography and an introduction to DEA's technical capabilities. We provided support for the Basic Agent's Capstone practical exercise, a mock Title-3 wiretap.

Lou issued me my first DEA cellphone. He said ST was in the process of moving to a new building. The three of us then went to see the new building. It was impressive. There was a security fence with an electronic gate, several cameras surrounding the compound and 24-hour security guards.

Investigative Technology, ST Building

Our classroom had new tables and chairs, and state-of-the-art Audio/Video projection equipment. All the offices and workstations had new furnishings, including ergonomic chairs and computers. The mock motel room was included in the building's construction and was already furnished. It was obvious DEA management was serious about bringing our technological capabilities into the 21st century. Important things were about to happen, and I was in the right place at the right time.

I spent the first month in the old building taking apart the mock motel room and disposing of it. I salvaged equipment that could be used in the new building. The mock telephone system had to be dismantled and discarded. Our goal was to restore the building to its original condition leaving no trace of what it had been used for.

The WITS Symposium

In October 2000, shortly after moving into our new building, Lou told Gary and me DEA would be hosting the WITS symposium in Washington, D.C. WITS was a worldwide technology organization comprised of 15 NATO nations. Representatives from member countries gathered annually to share ideas and new technological advances. It was like a real James Bond "Q" convention.

The training unit would organize the event. We had to find a location to hold the event, a hotel to house the representatives and arrange their transportation needs. By tradition, the host country was expected to provide a cultural experience for the participants. Gary, a colonel in the Air Force reserves, arranged for a private VIP tour of the Pentagon. We organized a group dinner at the JW Marriott restaurant that had a panoramic view overlooking Washington, D.C. We also reserved the Marriott conference room for the symposium and arranged a catered lunch every day. We managed everything, including registration, setting up the Audio/Video equipment and even arranging tables and chairs.

We maintained a 24-hour hospitality room with refreshments throughout the event. I hardly went home for three days. All the participants were experienced law enforcement professionals. Despite the long hours, I thoroughly enjoyed the assignment, especially meeting and talking with the participants. One evening I joined a small group of guys who were drinking, snacking, and telling stories in the hospitality room.

One guy shared an amazing story about an attempted kidnapping that turned into a barricaded hostage situation. The hostages were a prominent family from their country. Police responded, cordoned off the building, shut down the cell towers, cut off electricity and water, following standard procedures. The SWAT team surrounded the building with spotters and sharp shooters. Police gave the suspect a phone that only allowed him to talk to negotiators.

As time wore on, the suspect demanded to speak to the news media and wanted a working cellphone. The negotiators refused. At that point, the suspect became enraged and threatened to kill the hostages. The situation was rapidly deteriorating and the odds of rescuing the hostages unharmed with a SWAT assault were not good.

That was when this tech guy suggested they give the suspect a cellphone, but not just any cellphone. He had modified one just for this kind of situation. It had a tiny piece of plastic explosive hidden inside it. When the suspect dialed the local news station and put the phone to his ear, the guy detonated the phone with a remote switch. The hostages were rescued unharmed. I can't reveal where or when this happened. There are some countries that play by different rules when it comes to terrorists and kidnappers.

9/17/2024 *I watched as CNN reported that exploding pagers killed 32 Hezbollah operatives in Lebanon. As news reporters were speculating about what had caused the explosions, I knew what happened. It sounded remarkably similar to my old friend who used plastic explosives hidden in a cellphone to end the hostage situation years earlier. A second round of exploding walkie-talkies killed another twenty Hezbollah operatives, confirming my suspicions.*

Brussels, Belgium

The next WITS symposium was scheduled to take place in Brussels, Belgium. In preparation for the upcoming symposium, ST was asked to send a representative to confer with the host country organizers. I was selected and traveled to Belgium to share my experiences. The trip was considered a diplomatic mission, and I was permitted to bring my wife. I was responsible for any additional expenses. We were housed in a command staff apartment in the Belgium police headquarters complex in Brussels.

On the first day we watched the Queen's Cavalry perform their drills. Over several days, two Belgium police officers gave us a tour of their country including the North Sea, several castles, ancient churches and the room in Ghent where the treaty of

Queen's Cavalry

Ghent was signed. The treaty was between the United States and Great Britain to end the War of 1812. I met with the coordinators, reviewed their plans, and offered minor suggestions. It was primarily a goodwill mission.

Paris, France

The following year, the symposium was held in Versailles, France. I attended as a speaker on behalf of the DEA. My topic covered our newest mobile covert surveillance vans and their capabilities. Again, this was a diplomatic mission, and my wife was permitted to accompany me. After we landed at the Charles de Gaulle airport, there was a lengthy line of people waiting to go through immigration. I saw a Paris police officer walking down the line carrying a sign with my name on it. I held up my hand and he motioned for us to come with him. He led us to a waiting pair of Paris police cars that drove us across town with lights and sirens singing wee-woo, wee-woo. I was self-conscious about the attention, but my wife loved it.

The cultural experience was a private night tour and catered dinner at the Roland-Garros Tennis complex. We also saw a demonstration by the French Gendarmerie's GIGN commandos, considered to be one of the world's best SWAT teams. They gained that reputation in 1994 after rescuing the passengers of the hijacked Air France Flight 8969 in Marseille airport. By executing a lightning assault, they killed all four terrorists without injury to the passengers, a stunning accomplishment.

There was a demonstration of a mock lightning assault, beginning with a fast rappel (face first) from a pair of helicopters followed by clearing a barricaded hostage situation. The show was impressive with lots of flash bangs and simulated gun fire. Following the demonstration, the commandos held a Q&A session and gave us an opportunity to test fire their weapons.

My wife and I stayed a couple of extra days after the conference. We successfully navigated the French underground train system to visit the Louvre Museum, the Eiffel Tower and the Notre Dame Cathedral.

ST Instructor

My job as an instructor included organizing classes and scheduling instructors and speakers. I became a building-wide ambassador to all sections. I relied heavily on my field experience to ensure the course material was useful to the field agents. I also spent a lot of time developing my own course curriculum.

I was lucky to be working with some of the most knowledgeable and talented people in DEA. I was in the perfect position to get personalized tutoring from an array of technological wizards. I was especially good at spotting things I knew would be useful to field agents. It was an exciting time to be part of the technological revolution that was taking place.

Dale, the head of ST was a resourceful guy. He had a knack for finding much-needed funding for projects ST had in development. He was also aggressively recruiting and drafting the most qualified technical people he could find hidden in the field divisions. He knew, by pulling them into ST, they could work collectively to advance DEA into the 21st century.

The Miami division had the most advanced cellular technology capabilities of any DEA division. Dale drafted the Miami Group Supervisor to head the Telephone Section. Once inside ST, his knowledge benefited all divisions.

ST had many extraordinary people in the building. One Telecommunication Specialist assigned to the Radio section was a former Air Force officer that had worked for the White House communications team. He kept the President of the United States in communications at all times. We had another agent who was a former Signals Intelligence, SIGINT, Specialist at the National Security Agency, NSA. Claud, one of my close friends in the building and one of the smartest agents I knew, also transferred in from Miami. Prior to Miami, he'd spent 10 years in Bangkok, Thailand and had experience dealing with foreign operations. He was a self-taught computer software wizard. I would never discourage anyone from going to college but never underestimate someone self-taught. Some of the world's most ingenious and destructive computer hackers are self-taught or tutored by more experienced hackers.

DEA is managed and led by agents. The only non-agent supervisor in the building was Jon, an engineer and head of the Tracking unit. Jon was DEA's only resident expert on satellites and sensors, making him all but irreplaceable. Remember, it was Jon's unprecedented and ingenious use of satellite technology that located the cocaine processing lab in the *Tranquilandia* investigation.

The Day the World Changed

Tuesday, September 11, 2001, at 8:46 AM the first of four hijacked airplanes crashed into the North Tower of the World Trade Center complex in New York City. I was at my desk when my daughter Sarah called to tell me a plane had crashed into the World Trade Center. While still talking to her she told me a 2nd plane just hit the South Tower. It was9:03AM. I knew then this was no accident. I told her I'd call back once I heard what was going on.

I went to the classroom where we had access to cable television and a live news feed. Several people had gathered to watch as the events unfolded. By 9:37 AM, reports were coming in that another plane had crashed into the Pentagon. At 10:03 AM another report emerged that a fourth plane crashed into a field in Pennsylvania. I went back to my desk on the east side of the building. I happened to look out the window and saw a pair of fighter jets flying low and fast in a northerly direction toward Washington DC. In the end 2,977 people lost their lives with thousands more injured in the most horrific act of terrorism in the history of our nation.

I knew my adult son Jacob was working somewhere in downtown DC. Thankfully he was able to contact me to say he was OK but traffic on I-95 was at a standstill. By 9:45 AM President Bush ordered all airplanes grounded. I got home to our townhouse in Woodbridge shortly after 7:00 PM. My wife and I along with several neighbors were in the parking lot talking and listening to a lone aircraft high in the sky. It was undoubtedly a military AWACS surveillance plane. At about that time, the President's helicopter Marine One flew over us heading north toward Washington. It was escorted by a pair of Blackhawk helicopters. Of course, there was no way of knowing if the President was onboard or not.

The following weekend my wife and I visited Arlington Cemetery where we had a clear view of the Pentagon. We could still smell the smoke from the fire. Within a month, my teaching partner Gary, a Major in the Air Force reserves, was activated and deployed in support of *Operation Enduring Freedom*.

Yet Another DC Surprise

Beginning in October 2002, the greater DC area including northern Virginia and Maryland came under attack by what became known as the *Beltway Sniper*. Over a three-week period, John

Muhammad and Lee Boyd Malvo killed 10 people and injured three in a series of seven separate sniper attacks. Initially, law enforcement thought the sniper attacks were coming from a white box truck and reported as such by the news media. Any white box truck within a 100 miles stood out like a clown at a funeral and the region was saturated with law enforcement. Coincidentally our son Jacob was working for an outdoor event company and was stopped in a search of the company's white box truck. I don't think anybody figured it out until the suspects were caught by a fluke. I didn't believe the white truck theory, but, like everyone else, a mobile sniper's nest in the trunk of a car never occurred to me.

The attacks were deadly and random. The entire region was terrified, bringing DC tourism to a halt. Two of the seven shootings took place less than 30 minutes from our home in Woodbridge, VA. One of the shootings occurred at a gas station where my wife and I had purchased gas. Following that shooting, several gas stations hung canvas drapes from the awnings over the gas pumps shielding customers from view.

The Kill Switch

During my two years as an instructor, I participated in teaching and facilitating several advanced technical classes. As an instructor, I promoted certain devices and put forward novel ideas.

One such item was the kill switch, a device that, when installed on a vehicle's engine, could instantly shut the engine off. A transmitter from a distant location would activate the kill switch. The kill switch added a measure of safety during controlled contraband deliveries. Following the arrest of a smuggler, agents often used a kill switch to carry out a controlled delivery to identify and arrest their associates.

Sometimes while carrying out a controlled delivery, the smuggler may have a change of heart and try to escape. This happened one night while I was a street agent in Indianapolis. Our 'cooperating' suspect changed his mind and attempted to escape, leading to a high-speed chase.

Fortunately, we had a helicopter equipped with a thermal night vision camera supporting the operation. After crashing his car, the smuggler fled on foot into a wooded area. The pilot, using night vision, could see the ghostly white image of the smuggler's body heat. The pilot also saw us chasing him on foot. He directed us to where the suspect hid in the underbrush. As we closed in, he took off running but we were able to catch him. The camera also recorded the 'wrestling match' as he was taken into custody.

The following day we reviewed the camera footage of the car chase and caught the moment the 'cooperator' threw a gun out of his window. The gun was hidden in his vehicle, and we missed it during our search. Once he was allowed back in his vehicle, he retrieved the hidden gun and made the decision to throw it out rather than use it. He must have held it close to his body because it was warm enough for the camera to see it stand out against the cool night air when he threw it out the window. We were able to pinpoint the exact location and found the gun. It was embarrassing that we missed it in the first place.

Installing a kill switch required a fair amount of automotive mechanical skills. I recruited a certified auto-mechanic from a local technical college to teach an installation class. The mechanic had never seen such a device but quickly understood the concept and figured out how to install it. I allotted him an entire day to teach the class. The agents loved the class, and he was a popular instructor. He enjoyed the class as much as the students did.

This is why I told the pursuit story from Indianapolis. I introduced his class by showing the video taken from the helicopter. I told the class that we didn't know the kill switch device existed then. "Had we used it in that case, we could have stopped the co-operator and prevented the chase." I added, "Today our guest instructor will teach you how to install a kill switch."

DEA Academy Instructor

In addition to my duties at ST, I taught several classes at the DEA Academy, and it was important to me that the students remembered my courses as useful. My first opportunity was with the Basic Photography class. I inherited the existing curriculum from a previous instructor. The course was good, and the basics were covered. At the conclusion of the classroom lecture, the students were issued Nikon N-70 cameras and two rolls of practice film. Yes, film. If you were born after 1999, you may not have heard of film in the digital age.

The only thing I disliked about the course was the practice assignment. Students were required to take specific photographs. The list contained dozens of useless pictures, such as a gun on a floorboard of a car or a gun lying on the ground. The purpose of the assignment was to verify the students understanding of the principles of photography and produce usable photographs. I thought there was a more productive way to achieve the same outcome.

When I handed out the cameras, I told the class they could toss the required assignment. They were free to photograph whatever they wanted. My only stipulation was they couldn't take any pictures that would embarrass their grandmother. I suggested they use the cameras to document their daily life at the academy. I told them, "The photos will be yours to take with you when you leave. Believe me, one day those pictures will be priceless." I had so few pictures from my time at the academy. I knew they would appreciate them someday. I was always impressed with their pictures. There were usually a few students in each class whose pictures didn't turn out. I'd schedule extra time to help them one-on-one.

A typical class was comprised of 45 to 50 students. Each one received two rolls of film with thirty-six exposures. This meant I reviewed over 3,000 pictures per class. I selected three hundred of the best photos, scanned them into a digital format, and created a slideshow with embedded music. I played the slideshow during a follow-up class. It was always popular.

The show highlighted the best, funniest, and most awe-inspiring photographs. Several classes played the show for their families at their graduation parties. Students often told me that the photography class and show were a highlight for them. I gained a great deal of satisfaction knowing that my students left the academy with pictures documenting a unique and once-in-a-lifetime experience. The instructor that followed me transitioned the class to Nikon D1 digital cameras. I don't know if they continued to give the students free rein or not. I hope they did.

Sensitive Investigation Units

Some DEA foreign offices have special units including host country personnel. It is the foreign version of a domestic task force. We call them Sensitive Investigative Units, SIUs. DEA provided training classes at the academy for SIU units from all over the world. The academy's SIU program administrators met with representatives from ST. Students from previous classes were asking for more technical training. ST agreed to develop a one-week curriculum suitable for the SIU classes. The academy would shorten their curriculum by a week and replace it with a week of technical training in our building. The academy would provide transportation. They anticipated six classes per year.

The curriculum we developed included basic photography, cell phone technologies, and tracking techniques. We also included a practical exercise on configuring a break wire alert. A break wire is a transmitter with a fine filament wire hidden inside a box or envelope in a way to break when the package is opened. The transmitter then sends a signal to a receiver. The military uses similar devices but for different purposes which they refer to as tripwires.

Students consistently rated our training as one of their favorite parts of the whole program.

I had some memorable classes, one of which was from Pakistan. I started Day One with my photography class. The classroom lecture filled the morning, followed by a lunch break. The afternoon was dedicated to practice, giving the students the opportunity to roam around outside taking photographs. There was a wooded area and a short walk to the river's edge providing opportunities to snap interesting pictures.

At the end of the afternoon when the class reassembled, I was short a student. His camera was on his desk, but he was missing. Finally, one of his friends admitted to me he had gone AWOL. I called the Program Manager to tell him what had happened. He said he'd deal with it.

The next day I arrived at 7:00 AM to teach an early class at Quantico where the SIU students were housed. It was January and it was cold. As I pulled in, I saw my Pakistani class in the parking lot doing jumping jacks. They were dressed in gym shorts and bare-chested, a steam cloud was rolling off their collective bodies.

When I entered the building, I looked at the security guard who shook his head and told me, "They've been out there since 3 AM." Their commanding officer was angry and embarrassed about the AWOL student and punished the entire class. I don't know what became of the wayward student.

Security desk inside the academy

We had several classes from Mexico. I learned that one of our Mexico SIU classes had ten of their members ambushed and murdered by a drug cartel. Special Agent David Gaddis, now retired, recounts the story in his book titled *The Noble Experiment*.

~ 9 ~

ST UNIT CHIEF

A **Promotion**

After spending a little over two years as an instructor, Jon informed me he had been promoted to a grade 15 Section Chief. His grade 14 Unit Chief spot was vacant. He encouraged me to apply for the position. I liked my job as an instructor, but after thinking it over, I submitted my application.

On November 2, 2002, I was promoted to a GS-14 and assigned to Jon's former position as the Tracking Unit Chief. At the time, I didn't know it was Jon's recommendation that secured my position. It was a small unit consisting of two engineers and one telecommunications specialist.

Before joining DEA, one of my engineers, Dan, worked as a defense contractor for several years. He was part of a team of engineers attempting to develop the technology to hijack control of Russian nuclear missiles after their launch and send them back to Russia. He never told me if they were successful. While telling me about it, he remembered how the SR-71 Blackbird spy plane leaked oil on him while he was mounting devices underneath it. That surprised me and I asked, "The most advanced spy plane in the world leaked oil?" He laughed and replied, "Only on the ground. At altitude, the change in air pressure caused the rings to expand and seal the leaks."

Troy, my telecommunications specialist, was a former US Coast Guard Electronics Counter Warfare Specialist. The knowledge he had regarding satellite technologies, computers and networking was extensive. It was his gift for innovation that eventually paved the way for a fresh approach to DEA's Satellite Tracking program.

I asked Jon about the weird phone on his desk, now mine. He said it was a secure telephone known as STU-III. The National Security Agency, NSA, developed it to encrypt phone conversations over standard public telephone lines. It worked like a Virtual Private Network, VPN, in computer communications. Most intelligence agencies communicated using the STU phone.

Within weeks of starting my new position, Jon told me I'd need to get my Top-Secret clearance upgraded to an SCI, Sensitive Compartment Information status. It was needed to attend various meetings and briefings with other intelligence agencies. After completing the paperwork, I attended the 'Read In' process necessary for the upgrade at a Sensitive Compartment Information Facility, SCIF, located in downtown Washington, DC.

One place I visited frequently was the NRO, National Reconnaissance Office, in Chantilly, Virginia. The NRO manages our US space-based surveillance and reconnaissance satellites. From those meetings, I learned about many of our government's assets and capabilities. I was looking for 'things' that could be useful to DEA.

Jon turned over his ongoing projects to me. One of them involved upgrading the radio frequency short range tracking system. The system was used for both tracking and as the receiver for the break wire kit. Agents often used the kit for controlled deliveries to alert them when a box or package was opened. The upgrade contract belonged to a Canadian company in Halifax, Nova Scotia. In December 2003, while on a trip to Halifax, I peppered Jon with numerous technical questions. He was an encyclopedia of knowledge.

Night Vision Goggles

In January 2003, a few months after starting in my tech position, I received a call from an agent working in the Bogotá, Colombia office. He needed to locate a remote mountain stash house used to store cocaine and cash by a drug cartel. Due to the remote location and challenging terrain, conventional surveillance methods were impractical. Even aerial surveillance would have been easily detectable.

The agent told me his informant was friends with a security guard at the stash house. The guard told the informant it was so dark at night they couldn't see anything. The guard, knowing the informant worked at a US military base, asked if he could 'get' some night vision goggles. The agent's question was, "Would it be possible to hide a tracking device inside a set of night vision goggles?"

One of my engineers said it would take a couple of days, but he could do it. The NOAA satellites that captured the GPS transmissions in Jon's Tranqilandia case were still available. I got a set of goggles from the Audio/Video unit, and we successfully installed a beacon inside the protective case.

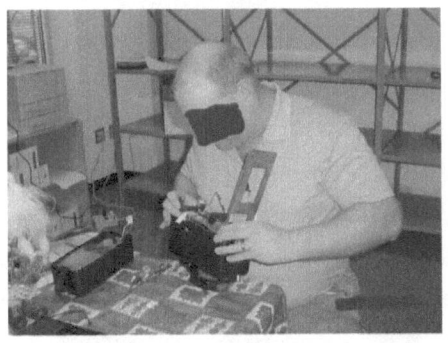

Technician concealing a beacon

The stash's mountaintop location improved the beacon's chance of connecting to the NOAA satellite.

I sent the goggles to the agent. Within a couple of weeks, we were receiving the latitude and longitude coordinates from NOAA. The location was narrowed down to within a 50-foot radius of the hideout. I sent the GPS coordinates to the case agent. The rest was up to him.

Over the next few years, we did several more satellite beacon concealments, including a set of ship-to-shore radios and a money counting machine.

Istanbul, Turkey

In April 2003, Mike, the prankster agent from Indianapolis, now stationed in Istanbul, Turkey, called me. He was working a heroin investigation with the Turkish National Police. He explained that a group of Turkish Nationals were smuggling massive quantities of opium base from Afghanistan into Turkey. The opium and a processing lab were hidden somewhere in the desert. The lab converted the opium into heroin hydrochloride, street heroin. The finished product was being smuggled into Europe for distribution.

The chemical process for converting opium base to heroin requires the use of acetone/ethyl ether and hydrochloric acid. Converting such massive quantities would require hundreds of gallons of chemicals. The Turkish investigators were watching for large purchases of these chemicals, intending to track the shipment. Investigators identified several purchases but could only follow the purchasers to the edge of the city. After that, the terrain turned into an open desert where it was impossible to continue surveillance. Arresting the drivers at the edge of the desert and flipping them was not an option either. The traffickers switched out the drivers repeatedly, preventing the drivers from knowing the final destination.

Mike was hoping we could somehow track the chemical containers. I told him I would get the devices gathered and bring them to him. I got a satellite beacon along with the pieces and parts needed to conceal it inside one of the chemical barrels. As a backup, I brought a short-range radio tracking kit and flew to Istanbul.

This was my first visit to a Muslim country. I spent the first few days adjusting to the time change and the culture shock. I had never heard the Islamic call to prayer broadcast over citywide loudspeakers. It was eerie at first. Once I became accustomed to it, it was equivalent to church bells.

On the second day, Mike picked me up at the hotel and we met with Turkish investigators at their headquarters. I brought the beacon and placed it near a window so it could connect with the GPS satellites. After that, it would need to transmit those coordinates to the orbiting NOAA satellite.

The investigators brought in a couple of empty chemical barrels, and we installed the beacon. Several days later we hadn't received any data from NOAA. The beacon was a failure in Turkey. I later learned the orbit of the NOAA satellite didn't synchronize well in Istanbul. When the satellite passed over Istanbul, it was too low on the horizon for the beacon to reach it.

I had the radio frequency tracking kit, and I showed them how to use it. I gave the transmitter beacon to two Turkish police officers and told them to hide somewhere in the city. With the receiver in Mike's car, we took the Turkish lead investigator on a city-wide grid search. Within an hour, we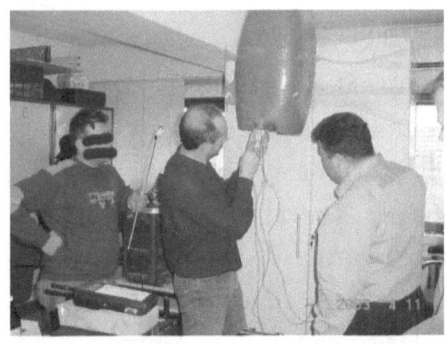

Concealing a beacon in Istanbul

found the officers in an alley behind an automotive repair shop drinking tea with friends.

The investigators were pleased with how well the kit worked. I suggested we put the radio frequency beacon in one of the barrels and take the receiver up in an airplane. We decided that plan wouldn't work. The battery life of the transmitter was too short.

In the end, I was unable to help them. Both Mike and the Turkish police recognized how useful the radio tracking kit would be for other purposes and wanted to keep it. I transferred the kit to the Istanbul office inventory and, within a few days, headed home.

Before I left, Mike showed me highlights of Istanbul, including the underground chambers of the Basilica Cistern, the Dolmabahce Palace and the Grand Bazaar. As a special treat, he introduced me to his future wife.

The Centralized Tracking System - CTS

When I returned from Istanbul, I had a conversation with my Telecom Specialist, Troy. He explained the NOAA satellites could only do so much. The reason why the NOAA satellites worked on the night vision goggles was because the target location lined up perfectly with NOAA's orbit. Plus, that operation was not time sensitive, so the beacon and satellites had time to find each other. What we needed was a new network designed for real-time satellite tracking.

For real-time tracking, we needed to use stationary commercial communication satellites. To clarify, stationary satellites aren't truly stationary. Their orbits are calculated to keep in sync with the earth's rotation. They remain stationary above a specific location and are a fixed antenna in the sky.

There are several privately owned satellite service providers similar to cellphone companies. Each provider offers coverage for different regions of the planet. A satellite tracking device operates like a cellphone except it connects to satellites instead of cell towers. Troy explained we would need to contract services from these companies and connect our satellite tracking beacons through their networks.

We already had vehicle tracking capabilities inside the continental US using cellphone service. These cellular kits could only track one target at a time and could be viewed on a single corresponding laptop. But they worked great and the agents that knew about them used them frequently.

We did have the ability to do some satellite tracking with the help of other agencies like Customs and the Joint Interagency Task Force South, JIATF. More about them later.

What we envisioned was a system that could centralize all our tracking beacons and display them on a single map. We called it CTS for Centralized Tracking System, and the name stuck. To begin, we needed a powerful computer network server capable of receiving the incoming tracking data. The server needed to process the data, turning it into moving icons on a map in real time.

Next, the server had to distribute the live tracking data to the people who needed to see it. Those interested people could be located anywhere in the world and could view the tracking live. I soon realized this was going to be a massive and costly project. When I proposed it to Jon, he understood the concept and liked it. He predicted the cost could reach a million dollars, but it would be well worth the investment.

About this time, US Customs moved their technology center into a new building next to ours. I briefed them on our project, and they wanted to take part. Sharing costs, we worked together. We purchased our own independent servers but together we contracted a software company to write the programming. We signed service contracts with the satellite communication companies. We contracted for the design and development of the next generation of covert tracking beacons. It took us a year to get everything in place. Once we had it working, we emptied a storage room and set up an operations center with two big screen monitors, a control panel and seating for viewing and demonstrations.

I was questioned a few times as to why we didn't use secure government satellites instead of commercial ones. I discussed using secure satellites with the controllers from the National Reconnaissance Office, NRO, but DEA didn't rank high enough on the priority scale for access to those resources. The system we built was secured by a VPN network. For our purposes we didn't need a Top-Secret rating. We built it using the resources we had access to and made it work.

By March 2004, I had become the spokesperson for promoting the CTS program. We needed to recruit DEA's EPIC, El Paso Intelligence Center, in Texas. EPIC is a 24-hour operation center that provides Federal Law Enforcement agencies with a vast array of record searches. We needed EPIC for their ability to provide 24-hour monitoring of the targets.

Troy and I flew to EPIC where I gave a Power Point presentation explaining how the CTS program was designed to work. We also demonstrated an active tracking beacon. My objective was to convince them to support the program. They were the only ones who could offer 24-hour centralized monitoring.

Immediately they recognized the potential of the CTS program and agreed to take it on. They even funded the purchase of a large screen monitor and computer. We returned a few weeks later to set it up in their control room. Field agents quickly learned about this new capability and requests for tracking targets began coming in from agents in Central and South America. Within a year, EPIC was monitoring a dozen targets, mostly boats and airplanes in the Caribbean.

In April 2004, I got a call from an Assistant Special Agent in Charge at DEA's Air wing in Texas. DEA had about 125 different aircraft. The ASAC had seen the CTS system in operation at EPIC. He was interested in using the system to keep track of our aircraft. To differentiate aircraft, suspect aircraft became red airplane icons and DEA aircraft were blue icons. The same color combinations were used for boats.

DEA Headquarters Crisis Center

By October 2004, the program was getting much attention. We regularly gave demonstrations to other law enforcement agencies. There was interest from elements of the military, including the Defense Intelligence Agency, DIA. The DEA Deputy Administrator was given a demonstration during one of his visits to our building. He must have been impressed because, within a week we were told to install a monitoring system inside the Crisis Center at DEA headquarters.

On May 1, 2011, long after my retirement, I watched news reports of the Osama bin Laden raid in Pakistan by our Navy SEALs. What caught my attention was the President and his cabinet members were watching a live video feed in the White House Situation Room coming from drones flying over bin Laden's compound. Simultaneously, CIA director Leon Panetta and his people watched from the 7th floor conference room at CIA headquarters in Langley, Virginia while the Joint Special Operations Command, JSOC, at Fort Bragg, North Carolina were also watching. This provides a dramatic example of what our CTS platform was designed to do for DEA's live satellite tracking program.

Operations Bahamas - OPBAT

During the 1980s and 90s, smugglers routinely transported cocaine from Colombia into the US by way of the Caribbean. This route covered 100,000 square miles of ocean, half the size of the United States. The Caribbean is home to 700+ islands, many of which are uninhabited. Smugglers used some of those islands as way points to rendezvous aircraft and boats.

OPBAT was a task force comprised of DEA, the Coast Guard, US Customs, the State Department, the US Army along with the Royal Bahamas, Turks and Caicos police and others. It was a combined effort to intercept and arrest smugglers. While there were several successful interceptions, the mission was extraordinarily difficult because of the vastness of the ocean.

Around June 2003, Jon called me and said we needed to attend a meeting in Dahlgren, Virginia. The next day we drove to the Naval Surface Warfare Center, where he introduced me to the Special Operations Technical group. These were some of the most talented people in the world in clandestine nautical knowledge.

The meeting was to update the group on our joint projects. This was when I first learned that the Dahlgren guys and Jon had been developing a remote acoustic detection system for the OP-BAT operators. The operators figured out smugglers often used primitive landing strips on several islands. The islands were transfer points where loads would be taken from planes and loaded on boats. Smugglers knew if they took their airplanes too far north, US radar would detect them.

Being less detectable, the boats could finish transporting the loads through the Caribbean and into south Florida. It was common for unaffiliated groups to use the same islands. It was often weeks or months between any activity, making human surveillance impractical.

Jon and the Dahlgren group came up with the idea to conceal satellite-based acoustic sensors on the islands. Once the sensors detected a landing plane, an alert message was sent via satellite to the Joint Interagency Task Force South, JIATFS, Command Center in Key West, Florida. JIATFS would then dispatch the closest Coast Guard cutter or plane to intercept the smugglers.

This team's ingenuity and imagination was astonishing. They were working on a solution for detecting smuggler boats as they made their way north through the Caribbean. The purpose of our meeting that day was to discuss those ideas and concepts.

Trouble in Paradise

By January 2004, the CTS project was successful and growing, but we had a bit of a hiccup with the Joint Interagency Task Force South, JIATF South. Unbeknownst to me, JIATF had been installing tracking devices and monitoring aircraft for some of our agents in South and Central America.

JIATF was using their tracking devices and black bag installers. Their beacons could only be monitored by their Command Center in Key West. We at ST were not in the loop and had no knowledge of their activities. They worked directly with our field agents, which wasn't necessarily wrong, but it created a potential problem for Jon and me. A few years earlier, a small plane crashed in the Caribbean and a rumor emerged that DEA had a tracking device hidden on the plane. I wasn't familiar with the incident and had no way of knowing if it was true. That was the problem. It was my responsibility to know what was being tracked by all DEA agents.

Jon, Troy and I flew to Key West to meet with JIATF and explain our new CTS platform. The meeting turned into a power play. The JIATF representatives didn't see the need to make any changes. Their attitude was 'we were Washington bureaucrats interfering in their business.' One of them made it clear that I was not in his chain of command and had no authority within their 'area of responsibility.'

I made it clear to him that any tracking installation requests coming from DEA agents fell into my 'area of responsibility' where I did have authority. Going forward any DEA agent requesting their services without my authorization would face consequences, adding that changes needed to be made.

I thanked them for all their help and reassured them we had no intention of excluding them. Going forward, all DEA satellite tracking will be done on our CTS network. If they wanted to continue working with us, and I knew they did, our system would be linked to theirs for a seamless transition. In the end, the only thing they were actually concerned about was being included in the black bag operations. Once I explained we weren't trying to cut them out, they accepted the change.

On the flight home Jon said, "By the way, boys, you know we don't have any FAA certified aircraft tracking installers." Troy and I had been so focused on creating the CTS platform that we had overlooked the obvious.

In the past, there were a few cases where DEA used covert aircraft tracking, and it was Customs or JIATF who did the installs for us. Had Jon told us this on the way down, I don't think I would have been quite so brazen in the meeting.

Flying home after my last meeting with JIATF, I looked out the plane window and saw a tropical storm approaching Key West. That storm would become hurricane Katrina and hit New Orleans with devastating force.

Creating the CAT Team

Jon told us the Tracking Unit previously had two agents who were FAA certified installers, but both had retired. DEA had the required FAA licenses needed to install clandestine tracking devices. But after those agents were gone, the DEA license expired. I met with a representative from the FAA and got our license reinstated. In addition, the FAA required a 40-hour training course to certify each individual installer.

Customs had an approved FAA school and agreed to train five of our agents in their next class. I didn't have any trouble finding five highly qualified volunteers to attend the class. I required them to have a current passport and be willing to travel overseas on short notice. Once certified, they would be part of a quick response team we dubbed the 'CATS,' Clandestine Aircraft installation Technician Specialists. They would return to their respective offices with the understanding they could be called on short notice for installation requests.

Jon also told me that years ago, the DEA had an undercover aircraft repair company. I searched old files and discovered the expired Certificate of Incorporation and had it reinstated. I designed undercover documentation, including company letterhead, work orders, billing receipts, laminated company name tags and business cards. I also had the company logo embroidered on polo shirts and we issued the shirts at graduation to the newly certified CATS team members.

One of the first to volunteer was Bryon, a Telecommunications Specialist assigned to a South American office. I had met him when he attended the Technical Agent class the previous year. I knew he was a helicopter pilot, a certified FAA aircraft mechanic, and spoke fluent Spanish. He joined DEA after retiring from the Army. Being too old to meet the maximum age limit to become an agent, he opted for a position as a telecommunications specialist.

I knew his military record was extraordinary. He was an Airborne/Ranger in the 101st Airborne and became a Special Forces Green Beret. The Army later selected him for its elite Delta Force. He shared some of his background with me, including his time as an advisor in Afghanistan in the 1980s. He had a slight limp from having been shot in the leg by a Russian Special Forces soldier.

He had also worked in South America as a special operator under the direction of CIA Director William Casey, but he couldn't tell me about that. Jokingly, I asked if he knew Ollie North. Without hesitation, he said, "I didn't know him, but I saw him a few times at Langley." CIA Headquarters is sometimes referred to as Langley because it's located in the unincorporated community of Langley. Langley is actually part of McLean, Virginia.

Bogotá Colombia

By the end of August 2004, our first Aircraft Installers class was completed. Within a month, I got a call from Bryon. "I just heard about the showdown you had with the JIATF boys."

"Yeah, it wasn't pretty, but we're all good now."

"They'll get over it. They're just not used to somebody ballsy enough to push back. Hey, I need you to activate your STU phone so we can encrypt our conversation."

"It's on. I turned the key."

"I have an aircraft installation request from the Bogotá Office. I'm going there today to set it up. It's a unilateral request so no Colombians will be involved. Can you meet me there tomorrow?"

"Yes. What about security? Do we need some agents?"

"No, the fewer people, the better. You and me, we're in and out."

"OK. I'll see you there."

I gathered the parts needed and booked my flight. I contacted the case agent and told him to send the monitoring request to EPIC.

When I arrived, Bryon and I did a reconnaissance assessment at the airport. He told me the plane belonged to a well-known drug cartel who were using it to transport cash. The installation needed to be done that night because the plane was leaving in the morning. This would be our only opportunity.

He told me, "I've already paid the guard not to 'see us.' He's also going to leave the hangar's side door unlocked. If we get there and the door is locked, something has gone wrong, and we'll abort."

We got back to our hotel about 8 PM. I was exhausted and jet lagged. I told Bryon I was going to sleep for a few hours. At 2 AM I woke up to him pounding on my door yelling, "Come on. Let's go." I yelled back through the door, "OK, I'm putting on my pants."

When I met him at the door I said, "I thought we were going at 2:30?" He said with a laugh, "That means 2:00 Delta time. Do you have your gun?"

Me: "Do I need it?"

Bryon: "Probably not but bring it anyway."

Me laughing: "Yeah, I've got it. Do you think I'd go anywhere with you without a gun?"

We drove to the airport, parked a short distance away, grabbed our tool bags and made our way to the hangar. Since Bryon was familiar with the area, I followed his lead. We found the side door unlocked. As he opened it, he said, "It's a go."

The hanger was dark, but we both had flashlight headgear. Once we found the plane, I took several digital pictures of the surrounding area to be sure we put everything back exactly the way we found it. A digital camera back then used a 3 ½ inch floppy disk and could store about ten pictures. It had a small viewing screen.

Bryon made quick work of opening the airplane panel and concealing the beacon. The beacon was powered by batteries eliminating the need to cut into the aircraft's power supply. The installation was quick because Bryon had practiced on a similar plane ahead of time.

Concealing a beacon in Bogotá

Bryon finished by putting the screws back into the panel. He commented as he was doing it that FAA regulations required the screws to go back in the exact holes they came out of. We tested the beacon to be sure it was working. We then collected our tools and compared the area to the pictures I had taken. We walked out locking the door behind us and slipped away into the darkness. The moment was poetic because the slogan the class had adopted for the CATS team was 'The night belongs to the CATS.' I have to admit that little adventure gave me an overdue dose of adrenaline.

We had breakfast and then met the case agent at the DEA office. We set up a CTS laptop on his desk, opened the program and saw a small red airplane icon on the screen. Within an hour, we watched as the plane taxied to the runway and took off. A small group of agents had gathered around his desk to watch. Within minutes, EPIC was on the phone notifying the case agent that his target had gone airborne.

The CTS program revolutionized DEA's tracking capabilities and would soon be recognized as the industry standard for federal law enforcement.

Months later Bryon called to tell me he was going to be 'off the reservation' for a few days. He needed to assist some of his former associates with a covert operation. He wasn't asking permission. He just needed me to know what he was doing in case something went terribly wrong. He explained Al Qaeda had a commercial ship used to move weapons, people and supplies around the world. The ship had been located in a South American port and he and his former associates were going to conceal a tracking beacon on the ship. I offer this tidbit of information only to re-emphasize the extraordinary people DEA had.

Special Operations Command - SOCOM

Jon called me to his office one morning and asked if I was up for a road trip. "Sure. Where are we going?" "Tampa," he replied. "I've got a friend there who asked if we could come and meet with him." Our destination was SOCOM, the United States Special Operations Command located at MacDill Air Force Base in Tampa, Florida. SO-COM commands all the elite military units specializing in high-risk missions like counter-terrorism and unconventional warfare.

By now I was sure everyone involved in satellite tracking either knew or had heard of Jon.

Within a few days, we flew to Tampa, rented a car, and drove to MacDill. Once inside, Jon's friend, an Air Force NCO in charge of the Technical Operations Support Section, greeted us. Jon introduced me as we walked to the workshop. He showed us his supply room full of Pelican protective cases containing all types of technical equipment.

He showed us various satellite beacons and sensors and asked Jon numerous technical questions. He said much of this equipment had never been used. Our meeting took place two years after September 11, 2001 terrorist attack against the United States. He was seeking insight and advice from multiple sources on the latest and best tracking devices available. He knew DEA was at the forefront and wanted our input on what he should be purchasing. "With this new war on terrorism, I've got a lot of money coming in and I want to be sure it's spent wisely."

This didn't surprise me because I had been dealing with the Defense Intelligence Agency, DIA. They were asking the same questions. In fact, DIA was already buying equipment and gadgets from our suppliers by piggybacking off our existing contracts.

Jon and I spent the rest of the day sharing and comparing information. Jon's friend was particularly interested in how we structured the network for our CTS platform. I explained the CTS network by drawing a schematic. He liked the concept but said he'd have to upgrade the security requirements.

Afghanistan

In April 2005, Jon had yet another surprise for me. Headquarters requested ST's support for a special operation team set to deploy to Afghanistan. The group was known as FAST, Foreign-Deployed Advisory Team. Their primary mission was to suppress the opium coming out of Afghanistan. The annual opium production had skyrocketed from 4,581 tons in 1999 to 8,200 tons by 2004. By 2005, Afghanistan was producing 90% of the world's opium. Opium is the raw material needed to produce heroin.

The FAST teams were tasked with suppressing that production. Their mission called for destroying the poppy fields, processing labs and opium stashes. This approach was reminiscent of the *Snowcap* operations targeting cocaine production in South America during the 1980s and 90s.

It was a Wednesday when Jon told me about the request. Everything needed to be ready by Friday because the FAST team was deploying Saturday morning at 3:00 AM from Andrews Air Force Base. The request specifically called for the radio unit to establish a communications network in the capital city of Kabul. The second request was for my unit to provide Blue Force (good guys) tracking support for the FAST team. In addition, we would try to integrate our tracking feeds with the military's Joint Special Operations Command, JSOC. We filled a shockproof container with assorted equipment that I would issue to the FAST team.

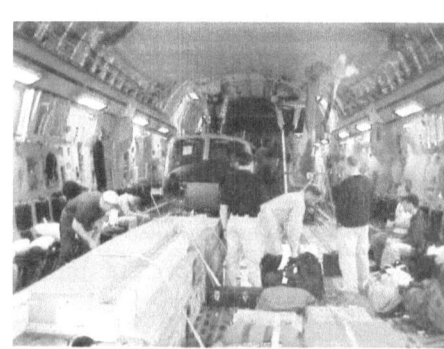

Onboard the C-141

On Saturday morning at 2:00 AM, I met Charlie from the radio unit, and we drove together to Andrews Air Force Base. When we arrived, the guard at the gate told us where to park. A guard walked us into the hangar. I saw Air Force One parked in the middle of the hanger. It was cordoned off with a yellow 'DO NOT CROSS' ribbon. I asked the guard if I could go over and take a picture. He said I could, but if I stepped past the yellow ribbon, he was going to have to shoot me. I think he was joking, but I wasn't entirely sure. I opted to let it go and we continued on. He showed us to a lounge area where we could relax and wait for our plane.

The FAST team was there, having arrived an hour earlier. One of the guys recognized me. I'd been his counselor when he went through the academy. Surprised that I was going to Afghanistan with the FAST team he asked, "How old are you?" At that point I was 50 years old. I laughed and said, "That's what my mom used to say when I was about to do something really stupid." Our logistics specialist, John, was also there. John would have made a great agent except, by the time he finished his army career as a Green Beret, he was past the age limit. As our logistics planner, he was a remarkable problem solver. We called him the 'rain maker.'

At 6 AM, the guard announced our plane's arrival. Nearly everyone had fallen asleep either on the floor or slumped in chairs. We gathered our gear and headed to the tarmac where we boarded an Air Force C141. The inside of the plane looked more like a flying warehouse than an airplane. The plane was set up in a cargo configuration and lacked passenger seats. There were jump seats along the exterior of the fuselage.

The crew chief told us to make ourselves at home. We claimed our territories and laid out sleeping bags and gear. Within 30 minutes, we were airborne en route to Afghanistan via Frankfort, Germany. About an hour into the flight, the crew chief announced the plane was having mechanical issues and we were being diverted to a base in Charleston, South Carolina for repairs. The repair took longer than expected, so we spent the night in a barracks.

The next morning, we took off again en route to Frankfort. In Germany, a new flight crew took us the rest of the way into Bagram Air Base, Afghanistan. Both the crew chief and the assistant crew chief were no nonsense, all business females. The projected flight time from Germany to Afghanistan was a little over 10 hours. Once airborne, we again reclaimed our territories. I laid out my sleeping bag on top of a wooden crate containing rotor blades for the two helicopters on board.

A couple of hours into the flight, the crew chief told us the pilot had extended an invitation to visit the cockpit. A while later the lights were dimmed for the night. I couldn't sleep so I climbed the stairs to a deck area and then crawled to the cockpit. I talked with the pilots for about an hour. They were friendly and wanted to know what DEA was like.

They said they had decided against flying 'nap-of-the-earth,' NOE, in Afghanistan airspace because they didn't want us puking in their plane. I laughed and assured them it was a good decision. Nap-of-the-earth involves flying at extremely low-altitude, following the contours of the ground terrain. This is a military tactic used to avoid enemy radar and reduce the risk of attack by surface-to-air missiles. For us, it would have been a Coney Island roller coaster ride on steroids.

I went back down to catch a few hours of sleep. As I was drifting off, the crew chief announced we were entering Afghan airspace. She set the interior lights to a dim red and told us to take our seats and buckle up. She and her assistant climbed to their observation positions and watched out the windows on each side of the plane.

About an hour later, the plane went into a sudden steep dive, sending my stomach into my throat. The engines went silent. All I could hear was the sound of rushing air. I had a lot of experience flying on commercial planes, but I'd never experienced anything like this. Something had to be wrong. I looked at the other agents on the plane and all I saw were emotionless faces. I sat silent like everyone else but inside my heart was pounding. It was a surreal moment of 'oh shit!'

Suddenly the nose of the plane pulled up and seconds later the wheels hit the ground hard. We had landed. The crew chief opened the side door. We gathered our gear like it was just another day at the office. On my way out, I asked the crew chief, "What the hell was that all about?"

"You've never done a combat landing? That's how we hide from heat seeking surface-to-air missiles. We idle the engines, then go into a steep dive to cool them down. It makes it harder for the missiles to see us."

"Well, damn, I thought the engines died, and we were going to crash." She laughed and said, "Welcome to Afghanistan." Apparently she found scaring the crap out of me to be quite humorous. With a devious personality like that, she would have made a good agent.

It was dark when we landed. As I stepped out of the plane, it looked like we had landed on the moon. Less than 10 feet off the edge of the runway, there was nothing but sand and rocks. We made our way across the tarmac to a reception center in a hanger. By the time we got to the

Charlie and the pilot

hangar, the plane had turned around and was taking off. It was dark inside the hangar except for the glow of a half dozen big screen TVs. The sofas and easy chairs were in line with the TVs. Soldiers in fatigues were either sleeping or watching TV, their rifles nearby. I couldn't tell if they were arriving or leaving.

After a quick check-in process, a soldier led us to a barracks where we picked a bunk and dropped our gear. The door at one end of the barracks led into a reinforced bunker. He told us it was our refuge should the base come under attack. On the second night, there was a rocket attack. From the bunker, we watched a pair of fighter jets circle in unison, firing tracer rounds into the side of a mountain. It was a spectacular sight. The next morning in the mess hall I overheard a female MP, military police officer, talking with one of the pilots. I struck up a conversation with them and they invited us to look at the plane.

In 2005, Afghanistan was an active war zone. The military was in charge and controlled what we could and couldn't do. They permitted the DEA agents to travel unescorted between Bagram and Kabul with restrictions. It was mandatory that our convoy had at least two armored vehicles and four agents armed with long rifles, either M-16s or sub-machine guns.

While the FAST team unpacked their shipping containers, Charlie and I, along with four agents, loaded a pair of armored Toyota Land Cruisers. They looked normal from the outside, but the doors had eight inches of ballistic material built in. Each door felt like it weighed 1,000 pounds or more. The windows were locked shut and made of six-inch-thick ballistic plexiglass. The modification reduced passenger space, resulting in a snug fit. When seated in the vehicle, our ballistic vests pushed up into our chins. We kept our sub-machine guns upright squeezed between our knees. All that made for a less than comfortable ride.

Painted white rocks signaling a cleared area

As we left Bagram, I saw civilian Afghans searching the ground outside the base for Improvised Explosive Devices, IEDs. Several Afghans were lined up in a row on their knees like they were picking strawberries. They were prodding the ground with small poker tools. Like a scene out of a *Mad Max* movie one guy was wearing an old football helmet and shoulder pads. Once an area was 'cleared', they lined it with white painted rocks.

When we left the base, we were told not to stop for any reason until we reached the embassy compound. As we drove, there was nothing but a vast desert with disabled tanks along the road. I did see an unexploded bomb stuck in the ground with its fins sticking up about 40 yards off the road. When we parked in the embassy lot, I noticed a damaged vehicle that had hit a roadside bomb along the road we had just traveled. The embassy building had also been severely damaged. The Marines had a sandbag bunker on the roof.

Roof of the Embassy

The State Department used modified shipping containers for temporary housing at Kabul. Charlie and I shared one. It had a bathroom with a shower and hot water. Each unit contained two bunk beds. We stored our gear on the top bunk and slept on the bottom. I thought it was comfortable but four guys sharing the unit would have made it crowded. Some of the FAST team members were housed in nearby shipping containers. There was a fire pit centrally located in the housing area where we would regularly sit around a fire at night with some of the FAST team guys.

The first week, we attended a meeting with the ambassador and his staff at the embassy. During the meeting, the ambassador stressed the importance of winning the 'hearts and minds' of the people and 'healing the country.' Following the meeting, we had an in-country security briefing including a medical presentation. The doctor gave us a supply of low dose antibiotics and told us to take one each day as a precaution. He explained the air had unacceptable levels of fecal contamination because of the general lack of hygiene. The Afghans made a practice of defecating anywhere and everywhere, leaving it exposed to dry out. It would mix with the desert dust which we could inadvertently breathe.

The city of Kabul held a flea market every Saturday. One Saturday I went with three of the FAST team guys and wandered around the market. There was crazy stuff for sale including lots of Russian military artifacts. I bought several traditional pancake style Afghan hats called pakols. As we left the market, we looked like tourists on holiday.

DEA had an office in the Embassy staffed with two agents and an intelligence analyst. Establishing radio communications between the office and the FAST team was a priority. The local agents had received permission to use the roof of the tallest building in Kabul for the radio antennas.

Early one morning, Charlie, John and I along with two local agents convoyed to the seven-story building. The building was abandoned and in terrible condition. Broken glass littered the ground where explosions had blown out the windows. The elevators were inoperable, so we had to carry equipment up seven flights of stairs to the roof. I made three heavy trips up. This wouldn't have been so bad except I was wearing a 30-pound bulletproof vest and carrying a sub-machine gun.

After our third trip, John and I stayed down to guard our trucks and supplies. Some nearby little kids talked to us in broken English. I had seen a carton of military MREs, Meals Ready to Eat, in the truck's cab and John and I passed them out to the kids. They tore them open and went for the candy and desserts. It was fun watching them gag when they got something they didn't like. When they saw us laughing at them, they exaggerated their gagging to make us laugh more. I think they were playing us to get more candy. We didn't care. We were having fun. It took us a couple of days to get the radio system fully operational. The kids came back every day looking for us, well, looking for more MREs and candy.

Sadly, John Stec passed away on June 9, 2024. He was a terrific man and will be greatly missed by his many friends and family.

Back in my shipping container, I tested the tracking devices. There were numerous technical issues I couldn't resolve. Our equipment wasn't designed for use in a war zone. I recognized our FAST team would join forces with the military's anti-terrorism operators and their missions would overlap. The military's resources were better suited to the environment. In the end, I deferred to their equipment and expertise.

Me leaving my 'home away from home'

One of the embassy agents told us the Blackwater team wanted to have a 'Welcome to Afghanistan' party for the FAST team. Blackwater was a private para-military company known for providing security services in Afghanistan and Iraq. Former Navy SEAL Erik Prince founded the company in 1997.

A few evenings later, we went to their base of operations. It was a large residential house, more like an Afghan mansion. The back of the house had a beautiful courtyard. They had strung multiple rows of white lights across the area, giving a nice ambiance. There was a small Afghan band playing traditional music. The natives were rocking out, with their hands in the air. The song was probably their equivalent to Miley Cyrus's *Party in the USA*. It looked like the Afghan version of the Texas two-step. Apparently this was a men only dance party because I didn't see any females. I'll say this, it is a vastly different culture.

There was a charcoal grill made from a 55-gallon drum cut in half. An Afghan chef was grilling goat meat next to a full-service bar. It was nice in a weird sort of way. The Blackwater guys were great hosts. Some of the guests were drinking and telling funny stories. A couple of Blackwater guys gave me a tour of their house. It had an adult frat house vibe. The basement was fortified with sandbags and had 50 caliber machine gun emplacements.

We returned outside and the smell of the grilling meat was mouth-watering. I watched the Afghan chef working the grill. He turned the goat meat with his bare hands. Looking carefully at his hands, they were not even close to being clean. Remember, fecal dust covers everything in Afghanistan. A thin layer of fecal mud coated his hands after handling the greasy goat meat. I was trying to wrap my head around what I was seeing when one of the in-country agents quietly whispered, "You don't want to eat that." After a few hours of mingling, we headed back to our shipping container village and sat around the fire pit.

With nothing left for me to do, I went to the Embassy to plan my return to the U.S. The only planes flying in and out of Kabul airport were U.S. Air Force or United Nations planes. The next available flight was on a U.N. plane to Dubai, United Arab Emirates. That flight wouldn't leave for a few more days. I reserved a seat and made a hotel reservation at the Emirates Towers Hotel in Dubai.

The embassy agent helping me said there was a 50-50 chance the plane would depart as scheduled. The threat level for planes coming in and out of the airport was extremely high. Basic security 101 is to avoid falling into a pattern or scheduled routine. This created a problem for scheduling air travel. For security reasons, airport controllers randomly canceled or postponed scheduled flights without notice. They would go so far as to call a plane back that had been cleared for take-off. On the day I was leaving, I watched a pair of Blackhawk helicopters circle the perimeter of the airport as we taxied out.

The most lethal weapons the Taliban insurgents had were shoulder mounted Stinger missiles. The missiles were left over weapons the U.S. had given the Afghans to fight the Russians many years ago. They were capable of bringing down a plane up to an altitude of 8,000 feet. Leaving Afghanistan was more nerve-wracking than the combat landing coming in. The city of Kabul is in a valley surrounded by the Hindu Kush Mountain range. As the plane was taking off, it had to clear the mountains. Looking out the window, I could see crevices everywhere providing hiding places for launching a Stinger. Only after I was sure we had exceeded 8,000 feet did I relax.

The flight time from Kabul to Dubai was a little over three hours. It was daylight when we landed. From the air, the city of Dubai looked like a magical sandcastle city with beige monotone buildings. From the airport, I took a cab to the hotel. It was a beautiful building. An international phone call from the hotel was going to cost as much as the room rate. Even though it wasn't my money, I refused to pay $200.00 for a phone call. I found an internet café a few blocks from the hotel on a side street. I sent an e-mail, AOL, telling my wife I was in Dubai and on my way home. I continued to wander the city. It was stunningly pristine, not a scrap of paper on the ground.

My beard had grown too shaggy for my Schick disposable razor. I came across a local barbershop on a side street and got a haircut and shave. All the barbers were Arabic. I thought nothing of it. As the barber lightly pressed my forehead signally me to tilt my head back so he could shave my neck with his straight-edge razor, it hit me. Maybe this wasn't the smartest thing I'd ever done. In the end, he cleaned me up and the haircut turned out fine.

I watched in the mirror as the barber next to me inserted globs of hot wax on long swabs inside a guy's nose. The guy sat for several minutes with two extra-long wooden swabs sticking out of his nose. I'd never seen anything like this. I could hardly wait to see how it would play out. After the wax cooled, the barber put one hand on the client's forehead and with the other hand ripped the swabs out of his nose. I think the guy cursed in Arabic as his feet jerked into the air. I couldn't keep from laughing which triggered an equal amount of laughter from the barbers.

When I got back to the hotel, I sat in the lobby and read the *USA Today* newspaper. The disparity in wealth between the male guests in the hotel flaunting their ultra white Dish Dash robes and the common people like the barber was extreme.

The flight home was long. I had connections in Madrid and London before arriving in Washington 24 hours later. As I was coming into my favorite airport, Washington National, I saw our famous iconic buildings and memorials. Those buildings always reminded me how lucky I was to be an American.

Leaving ST

A standard headquarters assignment was three to five years. After I returned from Afghanistan, Jon called me to his office and informed me I was fast approaching the five-year mark. This meant I could go back out to the field. He told me that with the overwhelming success of the CTS program coupled with our ongoing projects, he could justify extending my tour. I seriously considered it. I wanted to finish the things we had started. I knew we had solidified our flagship project, CTS, making it an essential resource for DEA. The guys in my group were exceptionally talented and I knew they would continue to grow and expand the project, with or without me.

Also weighing on my mind was our one-year-old grandson Brady in Indianapolis. I realized how much I had let the job con-

sume me just as my interviewers had warned me so many years
ago. It hit me how much of my children's childhood I had missed.
I was determined not to make the same mistake again with my
grandchildren. I wanted to move closer to our kids, and the division opening closest to Indianapolis was Chicago.

When I submitted my request, Jon warned me there were a lot
of problems in the Chicago office. He suggested I wait until Detroit
or St. Louis had an opening. However, I was confident that whatever technical problems Chicago had, I could fix them. I think Jon
believed that too, and he gave his approval for my transfer.

For clarification, each of DEA's 21 domestic divisions operate
somewhat autonomously in that they are free to allocate their
workforce and resources as they see fit. In the years preceding
the technology revolution, some old school managers didn't see
much value in the Tech program. Consequently, Tech groups were
used as a dumping ground for what managers perceived as 'problem agents.' This created a self-fulfilling prophecy when their division's technological capabilities fell behind.

The more progressive divisions like Miami recognized early on
that technology was the wave of the future. Those managers found
agents with advanced technical skills and invested in training to
bring their divisions to the forefront of DEA. As a result, the technical support available to street agents varied greatly from division to division. My senior partner and group supervisor Tom in
Indianapolis recognized the value of technology early on. I credit
him for launching me in that direction.

Prior to my departure, the office organized a farewell dinner
in a private room at a nearby restaurant. About fifty people attended. There was a podium and microphone and after dinner
some guys told funny stories about me, a light roast you might call
it. I was then presented with several going away gifts. The Lima
country office sent a country emblem plaque loaded with signa-
tures. Bangkok sent a beautiful wooden wall plaque of a hand-

carved DEA badge. The guys in my group gave me a polo shirt with an embroidered logo of our covert CATS aircraft repair company. That shirt hangs in my closet next to my BA-38 class shirt. There were other mementos sent in from other offices. Most had little humorous hidden meanings. I was sincerely humbled.

~ 10 ~

CHICAGO

What a Change

When I arrived in Chicago, I found some staff members were still rebounding from the catastrophic technical failure in their Title III telephone intercept room. The failure was due to human error in operating the recording equipment. Hundreds of hours of Title III phone conversations were not recorded, posing a serious evidence issue in some ongoing criminal investigations. The event required the intervention by the United States Attorney's office and our ST Telephone unit at headquarters to resolve it.

After the usual blame game was over, the Special Agent in Charge, SAC, divided the overloaded technical group into two groups. The first group's only responsibility was operating the Title III telephone intercepts The second group was responsible for everything else: audio, video, tracking, radio, polygraph, security and inventory.

Looking back, I think there was some residual resentment toward headquarters, ST, by some of the Chicago Field Division Management. I didn't know what I was walking into because the wire room event took place while I was preoccupied in the tracking unit.

The Chicago division encompasses five states: North Dakota, Minnesota, Wisconsin, Illinois and Indiana. The division headquarters is the Chicago office and the person in charge is the

Special Agent-in-Charge, SAC. The second in command is the Associate Special Agent-in-Charge, referred to as the Associate. Next in line are the Assistant Special Agents-in-Charge, ASACs. There were five. There were 8 to 12 various groups, each led by a group supervisor. There were several types of groups: Task force, General Enforcement, Intelligence, Financial and Technical. Most groups were comprise d of 8-12 agents and support personnel.

On my first day, I reported to the Associate's office where the ASACs had gathered for their weekly briefings. My introduction was the last item on their agenda. The Associate introduced me as the new Technical Group Supervisor for the Audio/Video Group. He told them I had transferred in from headquarters, ST, and would report to ASAC Rick.

One of the ASACs sarcastically commented, "Great! That's all we need is somebody from ST." I didn't sense he was joking. The Associate responded by telling him, "I know, but he's on our team now." This was my first clue there might be some misguided resentment toward me because of my association with ST. Jon's caution about Chicago flashed through my mind. I wondered if I had made a mistake.

There were the usual greetings and handshakes after which my new supervisor, ASAC Rick, showed me to my group area. I already knew a few of the guys. My group was comprised of four agents, one of which was the polygraph examiner. The rest were civilian employees: three Telecommunication Specialists, one Inventory Clerk and six Radio Dispatchers.

After the original group was split in two by the SAC, my group was relocated next to the communications center, better known as the radio room. This reshuffling resulted in the remodeling of some of the existing floor space. After Rick finished introducing me to my group, he showed me to my private office and said, "Here you go. It's all yours." I looked at the desk and chair which were in rough shape. My senior backup agent, George, came in and apologized saying it was the best they could find. The loading dock in the basement served as a communal exchange for salvaged furniture.

One of my favorite movies was *Beverly Hills Cop,* starring Eddie Murphy as a Detroit cop working on a case in Hollywood, California. There's a scene where the Hollywood cops arrest Eddie. He's in the backseat of their patrol car amazed at how nice and clean the car was. I looked at my salvaged desk and chair. A week ago, I had a new desk with an ergonomically correct chair at ST. I had to smile at the irony of it, but I didn't care. The less time I spent behind a desk, the better.

The Equipment Needs to Be Secured

The first glaring problem I saw was the technical equipment was stacked in an unsecured hallway outside of our storage room. The inventory clerk was a guy named Gary. I'd known him for years when he worked in personnel. I used to call him from Indianapolis whenever I had a question regarding health insurance or other personnel issues.

I asked him why the equipment was in the hall. He said he was told to move it there while the remodeling project was going on. The project was completed, so I asked why the equipment was still in the hall. He told me the Associate ordered new shelving units, which hadn't arrived. I asked him how long the stuff had been in the hallway. He said at least a couple of months. I told him I wasn't waiting for new shelves. We would use the old ones for now because the equipment needed to be secured. Gary and I began setting up the storage room and moved the equipment inside. I didn't ask for help from the rest of the group, I wanted to see if anyone would volunteer. When that didn't happen, I suspected a lack of motivation and teamwork. *As a side note, we never received the phantom shelves.*

Our group area consisted of two large rooms. One room was dedicated to storage and the other contained desks in a bull pen configuration. I noticed the two rooms had an interior doorway connecting them, but filing cabinets blocked it making it unusable. The blocked doorway puzzled me. It made moving from room to room inconvenient because they could only be entered from an external hallway. I asked Gary why the interior connecting doorway was blocked. He told me some guys in the group didn't like him. It was their way of telling him to stay in the supply room and keep out of their area. Now I knew for sure there was some kind of problem. I wondered if that was why nobody had volunteered to help us.

It seemed to me these grown men were acting childish and it annoyed me. I didn't comprehend what Gary was trying to tell me. Later, it became obvious he was being singled out and ostracized. I walked out of the equipment room, down the hall and into the group room. Looking at the filing cabinets, I asked an open question to the room. "Why is this doorway blocked?"

"We don't have anywhere else to put the filing cabinets."

"Either find a place or get rid of them. I want this doorway opened up today."

Over the next several days, Gary and I continued organizing the room and equipment. We set up a service counter along with his inventory computer and bar-code scanner. The inventory clerk was responsible for issuing equipment and keeping track of the inventory. Technical equipment is expensive and much of it is physically small. Maintaining an accurate inventory was a challenging task.

Gary's dedication to his job was obvious to me. He was knowledgeable about how the devices functioned and I watched him show agents how to operate some of the more complicated devices. He taught himself by reading the manuals and practicing with the equipment. He was clearly functioning above his pay-grade and exceeding his responsibilities as an inventory clerk.

After we finished the equipment room, I asked Gary to start working on the annual inventory reconciliation. This was a massive job having to account for several thousand pieces of equipment spread over five states. Making the task even more challenging, it had to be done while continuing to operate. DEA doesn't shut down for inventory. This was going to take him several months to complete.

The Radios Are a Disaster

In the ensuing months, I grappled with many problems, including serious radio communication deficiencies. During this era, DEA's radios were past their life expectancy and maintaining them was an ongoing challenge. Chicago's radios were so bad that some agents refused to have them installed in their vehicles opting to use their cellphones for communications. I knew DEA was in the process of replacing the entire communications network nationwide with new digital radios. The new system cost millions of dollars, and it would be a year or two before Chicago would be upgraded.

The IRS, Internal Revenue Service, had completed their upgrade to digital radios. The IRS radios were the same make and model as ours except they were in better condition. I was told the Associate scavenged their old radios intending to have them installed in our vehicles. The plan, while well-intentioned, was flawed. Switching out the radios would require a costly contract modification between DEA and Motorola. Plus, diverting funds from the national project to pay for Chicago to replace old radios with more old radios was not a sound investment. At best, it may have provided a marginal improvement. The real problem was convincing the agents that the new 'old' radios would work better. They were done with those radios.

The radios as I found them

Chicago took possession of the old IRS radios and stored them in our off-site warehouse. The division administration officer complained to me that the IRS radios had been piled up in the warehouse for a couple of years.

Greg, my radio technician, and I went to the warehouse to inspect the radios. Indeed, they were in a disheveled pile. Worse yet, mice had taken up residency in the pile. Later, I called Charlie, the Radio Technician at ST, who was overseeing the national upgrade. I explained the situation to him. He told me, "It would be foolish to redirect money to Chicago for that project. Chicago will have to wait their turn like everyone else." He suggested we transfer some of the surplus radios to our local Motorola shop to be used for spare parts. "The remaining radios pose a security risk and must be destroyed." Charlie and I had gone to Afghanistan together and I knew him well. If I pushed the issue, he may have given me the money to do the switch. However, that would have moved us to last place for receiving the new digital radios and I didn't want that to happen.

As our conversation continued, Charlie told me that during his last radio inspection in Chicago, he found several repairable items. He felt that my local technician, with a little effort, could fix many of the problems. When I talked with Greg, he told me he was tired of dealing with the radios and wanted a new assignment. I couldn't do that because he had the knowledge and skill to do the job. The radios were a never-ending cycle of problems and the only feedback he got was negative. It was obvious Greg was burned out. As much as I understood his defeated attitude, the job still needed to be done. I briefed ASAC Rick on the situation and he authorized me to destroy the radios.

Within a few days, I came out of my office to find an agent asking Greg for a replacement battery for his walkie talkie. Greg told him he needed to fill out a requisition form. As the agent was filling out the form, I interrupted and asked if I could see it. The agent handed me the paper. I crumpled it and threw it in the wastebasket. I told Greg, "Nobody needs to fill out a form to get a battery. Give him one." There were fifteen batteries on a shelf behind him. After the agent left, I explained to Greg our mission was to help the agents not hinder them. He had lost his purpose, and I was losing patience. I needed to change his trajectory.

Fifteen minutes later, one of the enforcement group supervisors called me. He introduced himself and said his agent requesting a new battery told the group what had happened. He added, "Welcome to Chicago. You are exactly the guy we've been waiting for. If you need anything, call me." The hardest part of the job was cracking down on my guys because I liked them all.

After a week without any progress on the radios, I set up a card table and chair in the corner of the radio room. I told Greg this was his new desk assignment, and he could return to the group area once progress was made on the radios. He thought it was a joke until it wasn't. What happened next was remarkable. Greg began making repairs. None of it was easy. I believe my card table stunt jump-started his motivation. He got satisfaction from fixing things and doing his job rather than avoiding it. I was quick to show my appreciation and within a few days, he moved back to his desk.

Making the Magic Happen

A group supervisor called to say he was organizing an undercover operation. They had a large cocaine shipment anticipated to be offloaded inside an industrial warehouse in south Chicago. He needed a covert camera installed inside the warehouse to record the delivery. He also wanted a live-stream video delivered a block away where a raid team would be staged. I told him, "No problem. I'll send a couple guys to set it up."

Later that afternoon, the GS called. The video worked great until the overhead door was closed. Closing the door caused the live stream to cut out. The traffickers wouldn't unload with an open door. I said we'd meet him at the warehouse. Upon arriving, I determined the problem was the microwave antenna had been installed inside the warehouse. The warehouse was a steel building, and a microwave antenna couldn't transmit through metal. I told my guys the antenna needed to be moved to the roof. They hadn't found an access point to feed the cable through to the outside of the building. I got a hammer and a metal punch from my tool bag and punched an inconspicuous hole through the wall. Now we had an access point.

As I watched them climb the ladder to the roof, I thought of Elton. He was a Telecom Specialist who had been a friend and former student of mine. He was a good guy and a member of this very group when he lost his life in a tragic accident. He was installing an antenna like this one when he lost his grip and fell from a grain silo. That day must have been awful for his family. I cringed at the thought of telling someone's spouse their loved one died carrying out my instructions. I had just sent two of my guys up a steep metal roof to install the same antenna Elton was installing the day he died. I wanted to call them down and do it myself. But I knew that would be perceived as a lack of confidence on my part, and I didn't want that either. Looking back, I wonder if they too were thinking about their friend and colleague as they climbed the roof without hesitation. The camera feed worked perfectly, and we handed it off to the case agent and his team.

I continually reminded my guys that we were a support group. Our job was to help agents turn good cases into great cases. A few months later, I received a letter from the federal prosecutor assigned to that case. He wrote, "The video was excellent and was instrumental in convincing the defendants to plead guilty." I made copies of the letter and placed it in their personnel files.

One of my veteran agents who understood Chicago office politics explained that I was failing to get the recognition our group deserved. He told me I should be boasting about our accomplishments to the Associate like everyone else did. I reported to ASAC Rick, not the Associate. I respected Rick. He was a good supervisor. Circumventing Rick just to try and schmooze the Associate. I wasn't interested in playing that game.

All Other Duties as Assigned

My group was the catchall for oddball assignments. To be fair, I had a wide spectrum of responsibilities. An example was to provide transportation and support for the Retired Agents Association's convention. DEA has a Retired Agents conference in different cities around the country annually. That year the Association's conference was scheduled to take place in Chicago. When Rick told me about the upcoming conference, it was just a few weeks away. He said the Associate was committed to showing the attendees Chicago-style hospitality. The task reminded me of the WITS Symposium in Washington a few years back.

Rick said attendees would arrive at both O'Hare and Midway airports. Our first job was getting them from the airport to their hotel. He would have his secretary pass on the transportation requests to me as he received them. There were more requests than I'd expected, and I realized we didn't have enough people or cars to shuttle everyone. Rick authorized the rental of a 15-passenger van. We coordinated the transfers, and it went smoothly.

The weekend before the event, my wife and I took a Chicago Mob bus tour. I memorized several stories about the city and its famous gangsters. I used those stories to entertain the passengers as we drove from the airport to the hotel. We transported some of

234 ~ HOWARD OBERST

them to their golf outing and shuttled them to restaurants around the city. Everything went according to plan, and we returned them to the airport on time.

The Inventory Is Done

After two months, Gary told me he had completed the inventory. It was a complicated process because ST had recently implemented a new computerized inventory system. All our equipment had to be cross-referenced with the old paper system and barcoded.

After Gary had transitioned the equipment into the new system, there were about a dozen items he couldn't account for. I told him to fill out a Lost Equipment form for those items. I forwarded the report to ASAC Rick. Rick asked if reporting the items as lost would create a problem for us with ST. I assured him it would not. I had just gone through this process at ST with the tracking unit. This was the process to rectify and remove items from the computer inventory. He said he would send the forms to the Associate for his signature.

Days later, Rick told me the Associate refused to sign the forms. Rick said, "The Associate told me to tell you to either find the items, or he wants to know who lost them." I replied, "I don't want him turning this routine inventory into an internal affairs investigation." We had seven satellite offices in five states each housing a portion of our inventory. All I wanted was an accurate accounting of what equipment we had and where it was.

I could have satisfied the Associate by reporting everything had miraculously reappeared and simply kicked the can down the road for someone else to deal with. But that also meant I'd be held accountable for items I knew we were probably missing. I would have been foolish to put myself in that position.

I met with Rick again and gave him the forms telling him we couldn't account for these items. I explained the purpose was not to blame someone but to simply reconcile the inventory and start anew. Rick stated he would make another attempt with the Associate but couldn't guarantee a signature.

The next day he told me the Associate was not happy with me. He demanded to know who lost the items. I understood the importance of making sure our equipment was not being abused or carelessly lost. In this case it wasn't that simple. According to Gary, Chicago's inventory hadn't been accurately reconciled in years. Further complicating the issue was discrepancies between multiple inventory records. I was frustrated that a simple inventory was getting all blown out of proportion.

I explained to Rick, "In the normal course of business, we have to expect that items will get lost or broken. It's not always a matter of negligence." I told him about installing a tracking beacon inside a cartel airplane in Bogota, Colombia, knowing it would never be recovered. I wrote it off on one of the lost equipment forms and removed it from inventory.

Rick said, "I understand, but I'm just the messenger. The boss says he wants Gary to produce the items or give him the names of the people who lost the items. It's Gary's responsibility." Rick handed me the unsigned forms. I went from frustrated to annoyed. Did the Associate want me to 'blame' Gary? Or was I supposed to falsely report all the equipment was accounted for and run the risk of being blamed later for what was missing? I wasn't going to do either one. I thought about Texas Mike that night at the academy when he removed the handcuffs from our classmate. He did it because it was the right thing to do. Now, do I do the right thing or not?

I handed the forms to Rick, explaining the equipment was lost. "Nobody knows when or where it happened. If the Associate still refuses to sign the forms, ask him who allowed the inventoried equipment to be stored in an unsecured hallway." Rick and I both knew it was the Associate who did it. Rick looked at me and said, "Whoa! Are you sure you want to go down that road?"

"As I see it, he hasn't given me any other option."

Within a couple of days, Rick told me the Associate had signed the forms and sent them to headquarters officially closing the inventory.

Technology Alone Cannot Replace Psychology

One day I walked into the equipment room while Gary was on the phone and I heard him say, "I don't know what to tell you, but my boss is here. You can ask him." There was an agent on the line from one of our satellite offices in another state. He asked if we had an electronic device that could disable a car alarm. Gary had sent him a vehicle tracking kit a few days earlier but when he tried to install it, the suspect's car alarm went off. I told him there wasn't a device that could do that, but he could have the guy turn the alarm off for him. He laughed and said, "You're joking, right?"

"No, I'm serious. Go over at 2:30 AM, bump the car, set off the alarm, hide and wait. After he comes out and finds his car is fine, he'll reset the alarm. Keep doing it until he quits resetting the alarm. Then install the tracker." He skeptically said, "Do you think that'll work?"

"Sure, I'll go with you if you want."

"No, I've got this."

The next morning, he called. "It played out just like you said it would. The second time I set off the alarm he came out but didn't reset it. I waited a bit then slipped the tracker into the bumper." Technology can be an incredible tool, but it can never replace the need to understand human behavior.

Apple released the first iPhone in 2007 and added a tracking feature in 2013. In today's world, tracking someone is simple using a phone app. DEA was doing this over 25 years ago.

Another example of combining technology with human behavior occurred while I was at ST. I received a call from an agent who was trying to locate a suspect. He knew the kind of car he drove but didn't have its license plate. He knew his cell number, but it was a burner phone. I suggested the agent subpoena the suspect's phone records, including cell tower connections.

Whenever a cellphone makes or receives a call, the first connection is to the nearest cell tower. I told him to study the cell tower connections and look for patterns. Humans are creatures of habit. I told him to find the tower that the phone first connected to in the morning and compare it to the last call in the evening. "This will be where your suspect is likely living or at least sleeping." The rest could be accomplished using old-fashioned surveillance work. He called me later to tell me he found his suspect.

He's Not Late for Work

Rick informed me Gary was seen entering the building at 10:00 AM, an hour late for work. He assured me it wasn't coming from him, and he didn't have an issue with it. However, he'd been 'ordered' to look into it. There are only two people in the Chicago division who could 'order' Rick to do anything, the SAC or the Associate.

As far as I was concerned, this was a 'somebody' taking a cheap shot at Gary. I explained that Gary worked at least nine hours a day and ate lunch at his desk, but I'd ask Gary about it.

Gary stated that a former supervisor changed his start time from 9 AM to 10 AM. This was done to accommodate agents coming in later in the day requesting equipment which often happened. I was puzzled because Gary normally came in at 9 AM. I asked him why he came to work at 9 AM instead of 10 AM. He said that since my arrival in Chicago, he enjoyed coming to work again and didn't mind starting at 9 AM, but he still stayed until 6 PM.

Gary gave me a copy of the memo amending his schedule. I passed it on to Rick. I asked him who made the complaint, but he said it wasn't important. It seemed to me 'someone' was trying to cause problems for either Gary or me and they had a direct line to the Associate. The old timers used to say, 'Smells like you've got a skunk in your woodpile,' meaning you may not be able to see him, but you know damn well he's in there.

There's a Storm on the Horizon

With the inventory completed, I thanked Gary for a job well done. I also told him I wanted to upgrade his position from Inventory Clerk to a Telecom Specialist. If successful, it would provide him with a pay increase. My justification was based on his performance and ability to operate the devices and equipment. Gary told me he appreciated the idea, but he would never get a promotion. It was then he told me he had sued the DEA for discrimination and won. Gary is an Asian American. He added that after winning his lawsuit, he was moved from personnel to tech where he felt shunned.

"Remember the day you told the guys to open the doorway between the two rooms? That was the first time I felt like someone had stood up for me. I was afraid to tell you about the lawsuit, fearing it might affect your attitude toward me."

Me: "I am sorry that happened to you."

Now it all made sense, the blocked doorway, the hassle over the inventory, being reported late for work. I told him that, as his supervisor, it was my responsibility to provide him with a safe work environment. I assured him I would not tolerate any kind of harassment or intimidation by anyone and didn't care who it was. If he had any problems again, I wanted to know. "Give me a chance to correct it. If I can't, then go ahead and do whatever you need to do. If that means filing another lawsuit, so be it."

I discussed the idea of upgrading Gary with Rick. He agreed and told me to write the proposal. I was leaving the next day to go to Washington for some unfinished business. While I was in D.C., Rick called. He was distressed, which was unusual for him. "Please tell me you didn't offer to help Gary write another lawsuit against DEA! That's what 'somebody' told the Associate you said. He's outraged, absolutely furious with you. I've never seen him this pissed off."

Me: "Rick, I never said I would help him write a lawsuit. I wouldn't even know how to do that. But I did tell him that as his supervisor, I would not tolerate any discrimination, harassment or intimidation from anyone, and I didn't care who it was."

Rick: "Why would you say that? You've already pissed the Associate off at least twice. This time it's really serious. I just left his office, and he is in an absolute rage. I can't even reason with him."

Me: "Now I'm confused. HR mandates that we watch EEOC training videos every year. From those videos, it is my understanding that supervisors are legally responsible to provide subordinates with a safe work environment, free from discrimination, harassment, or intimidation. Did I misunderstand that?"

Rick: "Look, I'm just the messenger here. I'm doing my best to keep the peace, but this thing has spun completely out of control."

Me: "I'm sorry you're caught in the middle. To be clear, is the Associate telling me I should not reassure a subordinate who reports to me that he's feeling singled out? Especially one who's already won a discrimination suit against DEA. From what I've seen, he may have grounds for another complaint. I'm doing the best I can to keep this from spinning completely out of control."

Rick: "I'll deal with the Associate, but this is not a good situation. My advice is to stay away from him until he cools off. Believe me, you don't want to go to war with him over this. You will loose. It will be like trying to box Casper the Ghost. You can't do it and will look silly trying." I watched Casper the Ghost growing up so I knew the episode he was referring to. Maybe that's why I related so well to Rick. We had the same taste in cartoons.

After I returned, I submitted the paperwork to upgrade Gary's position. Just as Gary predicted, it didn't happen.

A Security Violation

One of my subordinates and I were entering the back door of the DEA office from a public hallway when an ASAC behind us grabbed the door before it closed. I heard him say, "Hey! Hold up. You're supposed to make sure that door closes before walking away. I just caught it and walked right in. That's a security violation." Looking directly at me, he said, "And you, of all people, should know that. You're supposed to be the Security Officer, aren't you?"

I knew he was several yards behind us. He must have done a fast walk to catch the door. I thought he was angry because I hadn't waited and held the door for him. "I knew you were behind us. Sorry, I should have held the door for you."

ASAC: "Not good enough. I want a memo on my desk by the end of the day explaining this violation."

In a flash of anger, I responded without thinking, "That's bullshit. If you want to bring me up on charges, go ahead. But don't hold your breath waiting on a memo from me."

Actually, he was right. It was a technical violation. It was also a technical violation to enter a secure area without scanning your key card, one he had just committed. My response could have been considered insubordination, but I wasn't concerned. However, I shouldn't have responded as I had in front of my subordinate.

It didn't take long for word to spread through the group and beyond. I knew it had become a point of gossip when a group supervisor told me that particular ASAC had been playing that game for years adding, "It's about time someone told him to piss off."

I Think It's Time

I finished my first year in Chicago and was pleased with the progress I had made with my group. Together we had accomplished measurable improvements in the radios, achieved 100% accountability in the inventory along with many other significant accomplishments. But I was becoming increasingly annoyed with the petty politics. I'd butted heads with the Associate more times than I should have and was on his radar. Making matters worse, I was sure he had a couple snitches spying on me. My world had shrunk. It felt like I'd been relegated to working in a fishbowl. Looking back, it's clear I was not adjusting well.

DEA is a world class organization. But denying the existence of internal politics and personal conflicts within the agency would render this book little more than a fairy tale. The strong personality traits agents naturally possess or develop can sometimes send them on a collision course with each other. Most of the time, cooler heads prevail, but not always. Even though I worked for a great ASAC, there was a limit to how much he could cover for me. While I was at ST, Claud, a good friend of mine retired early. I asked him why he was retiring. He simply said, "It's time."

"What do you mean, 'It's time?' How do you know when it's time?"

"Trust me, you'll know."

I thought back on my career and accepted the fact that maybe it was time, time for me to move on. By mid-October, I started the paperwork to retire, estimating it would take a couple of months to process. I notified Rick and declared my retirement date as January 1, 2007.

The Chicago Crime Commission

My last significant assignment was to help provide security for the DEA Administrator's visit to Chicago. The Administrator heads the entire agency and is appointed by the president. She was the keynote speaker for the Chicago Crime Commission's Stars of Distinction 2006 Awards Dinner. The event was to take place on October 18-19, 2006, at the Palmer House Hilton Hotel in downtown Chicago.

The Chicago Crime Commission describes itself as 'an independent, non-partisan, civil watchdog founded in 1919.' The founders were Chicago business people concerned about runaway crime in the city. They used their resources to focus attention on organized crime. They created the first *Public Enemy* list in 1930 declaring Al Capone the first *Public Enemy Number One*. The FBI co-opted the idea and created the FBI's *Ten Most Wanted Fugitives* list.

Before serving as President of the United States, Herbert Hoover served as President of the Chicago Crime Commission and played a role in hiring Eliot Ness and the Untouchables to bring down Al Capone. Today the commission's primary goal is to foster cooperation between business, government, and law enforcement. The annual Stars of Distinction dinner commemorates Chicago's fallen heroes and recognizes individuals whose actions have resulted in improving and protecting the greater Chicago community.

When Rick informed me the Administrator was coming to Chicago, he assigned me to assist her security detail because I was the Division Security Officer. Rick asked if I had done any security details like this. I told him that I had. In 1980 when I was a cop, Ted Kennedy came to Delavan to do a presidential campaign speech. I assisted the Secret Service agents for two days. Rick said, "Perfect, that makes you more than qualified." No matter what I told him, he would have declared me perfect for the assignment.

In truth I was very involved with the Secret Service agents from the arrival of the advance team until Kennedy went 'wheels up,' their code for the assignment was over. The Secret Service team leader taught me a valuable lesson that stuck with me throughout my career. He said, "I know what you're thinking. You think you're just a small-town cop and I'm a big-time federal agent. The truth is, you have more arrest authority than I do."

He explained, "If we get some guy who's being a pain in the ass but not actually a threat, you arrest him and haul him away. If we get some guy with a weapon who poses a threat, I'll arrest him." From that, I understood the concept of a multi-agency task force 'yield to your strength.' I also gained a new appreciation for the power of local police. Once I became a federal agent, I never considered myself better than the local police. Some federal agents never learned that valuable lesson.

For clarification, the term 'Special Agent' is derived from the fact that we are 'agents' of the government with specific or limited 'special' enforcement authority. Our jurisdiction encompasses the entire United States, but our enforcement authority is specific to drug-related violations. State

Kennedy Visit On Schedule

Presidential candidate Sen. Edward Kennedy

Newspaper article

and local police cover smaller jurisdictions but have many more laws to enforce. I often referred to them as the 'real police.'

When the DEA advance team arrived, I chauffeured them around so they could prepare their surveys. I remembered doing the same with the Secret Service agents 25 years prior. We previewed the airport including the arrival gate and the passenger pickup arrangement. We drove a dry run from the airport to the hotel. We identified the Level 1 trauma hospitals and mapped the most direct routes and drive times for each.

I took them to the hotel where a security assessment was done. Their plan was to escort the Administrator into the hotel through the rear loading dock. Their diligence was impressive. They noted a floor drain grate running the length of the loading dock. The agent driving the administrator was instructed to straddle the drain so she wouldn't have to step over it. We walked the route from the loading dock to the meeting room, including a ride in the service elevator. The team leader said she would be OK with riding in the service elevator, but we needed to have the door open and waiting for her. The lists and details went on and on.

When the Administrator arrived, we escorted her to the meeting room. Outside the room was a large plush foyer. I was one of five agents covering the foyer. I had been standing in the foyer for about an hour when the doors opened and the Administrator and the Special Agent in Charge, SAC, walked out. I assumed she had finished her speech. I noticed as they were talking they kept looking in my direction. It felt like they were talking about me, but that was absurd. They walked in my direction. The SAC introduced me to the Administrator, "This is the agent I was telling you about."

Administrator: "I'm glad to meet you. The SAC just told me you're retiring, but you're not mandatory."

Me: "Yes, ma'am."

Administrator: "He tells me you ran the Tracking Unit at ST. I've been hearing good things about that."

Me: "Thank you."

Administrator: "Is there any chance I could convince you to reconsider your retirement? Replacing agents like you is not easy."

Me: "I appreciate that, but it's time for me to start a new chapter in my life."

Administrator: "Well then, I hope it's a good one for you."

We shook hands and they walked away. I knew it was the SAC who had initiated the impromptu introduction. He was a class-act and that's why he was well-liked.

For the next month, things went smoothly, no personnel issues, and no complaints. I wondered if I had made the right decision to retire.

The Showdown

An agent in my group was retiring in early December, a month before my retirement. In the first week of December, I took my group out for a retirement lunch. We walked to a popular food court. We had just gotten our food and sat down when I noticed the SAC, the Associate and an Assistant US Attorney were leaving.

The SAC stopped at our table to congratulate the agent on his retirement and the three of them left. We talked briefly about what a great guy the SAC was, finished our lunch and returned to the office.

Soon after I sat down at my desk, my phone rang. It was GS, group supervisor, Vic, who was standing in for Rick while he was out of town. Vic asked me to meet him in the Associate's office. The job of a DEA Associate is much like that of a school principal in that they both deal with problem children. Now I had been summoned to the principal's office, agent style.

When I walked in, I saw the Associate at his desk and Vic in a nearby chair. Directly in front of his desk was an empty chair. He motioned for me to close the door and sit. It was reminiscent of my childhood visits to the principal's office. I knew the drill. As soon as I sat down, he started, "What in the fuck is wrong with you?"

"I don't know. Could you be more specific?"

"Apparently you have no control over any your subordinates."

His face was red, the veins in his neck were bulging and he was shouting. I suspected he was angry. Admittedly, I had given him reasons to be angry, but I wasn't aware of anything that I had done recently. I looked over at Vic. His gaze swept to the floor. I tried to appear calm as I sorted through my inventory of things he might be mad about. I was trying to predict which issue he was going to bring up so I could prepare my defense. "I'm sorry sir, but I don't know what you're referring to."

"Your agent just called the SAC by his first name in the food court, and you sat there like a dumb ass and did nothing about it."

That's it! For a fleeting moment I relaxed thinking, this must be a prank. Before I could come up with a wisecrack, I sensed he was actually serious, I mean serious as a heart attack. Wow, of all the things he could be mad about, I never saw this coming. "I apologize. I would never disrespect the SAC, nor would I permit anyone to. I'll go get him and we'll both apologize."

"Leave the SAC out of it! He doesn't know anything about this. This is between you and me. I'm fucking fed up with you and all of your bullshit. You've been nothing but a fucking pain in my ass since you got here." OK, I got it. My subordinate using the SAC's first name was just an excuse to bring me to his office. This was going to be payback for everything I had ever done to piss him off.

I really wasn't interested in anything he had to say but I did my best to pretend. After 10 minutes of non-stop berating, most of which I don't even remember, he finished his rant with a great line. "Maybe I should assign you to my secretary and let her keep an eye on you. How's that? You can spend the rest of your career making photocopies and fetching her coffee." I knew he was just blowing off steam because the SAC would never have allowed that. But I have to admit it was a great line.

It's true, I had bruised his ego more than once and he probably considered me something less than a team player with an attitude. Looking back he wouldn't have been entirely wrong. But this was more than just a reprimand, it had become personal. I sensed he was actually trying to provoke me. Indeed, he had pissed me off, but I was determined not to show it. Other than offering to apologize to the SAC, surprisingly I managed to keep my mouth shut. Finally, he took a deep breath pretending to calm himself saying, "If you think I'm being an asshole, why don't you just say it."

While that was exactly what I was thinking, it would have been foolish to actually say it. It was a clumsy attempt to lure me into believing it would be OK for me to call him an asshole. Seriously, I was there presumably because one of my subordinates had called the SAC by his first name! I'm quite sure hadn't actually offended the SAC. Now I was experiencing the rage Rick warned me about when he said, "I couldn't even reason with the man." The whole scene was surreal and had spun out of control.

Vic looked concerned, caught between two old gladiators unsure which one was going to lunge first. All the Associate's blustering didn't intimidate me. But, I didn't want this to end in a messy quagmire either which meant dragging him across the desk by his necktie was not an option. Sarcasm however, had always served me well. "No, of course not. Why? Do you feel like you're being an asshole?"

That really set him off. He was beyond furious. I watched in silent amusement as his tongue slid back and forth behind his lower lip as he pondered his next move. "Alright, FINE! I'm ordering you to reprimand that agent. Now get the fuck out of my office. Go crawl back into your hole where you belong."

I deliberately took my time getting up and leaving, making the point I wasn't scurrying away. As I reached the door he said, "One more thing. When I tell you to do something, I won't be holding my breath waiting for you to do it." Obviously, my previous act of insubordination had also been brought to his attention. I was on a roll.

By the time I left his office, I was pretty sure he didn't like me. But then, I wasn't all that fond of him either. By the way, I never reprimanded the agent. I figured the Associate could just add that to his growing list of my misdeeds. When Rick got back, I told him what had happened but he had already heard about it. Probably everyone in the building had heard about it. I'm quite sure the secretaries had heard it through the door.

I was conflicted about including this somewhat ugly scene. Even though it is an integral part of the story, I didn't want to be unfairly critical of the Associate. It is his job to maintain discipline within the ranks and I probably deserved some measure of discipline. Remember agents live by a different set of rules when dealing with each other so harsh language is just part of that life style thing. So as not to be a hypocrite, I've uttered more than my fair share of harsh words too. Agents need thick skin to survive inside DEA. But this scene provided a great teaching opportunity. First, when reprimanding a subordinate, don't do it when you're still seriously pissed off. That's not a good starting point. Second, when being reprimanded, don't be a smart-ass. It's only going to make matters worse.

Redemption

The last month on the job passed quietly. The Tech secretary organized a midday pizza party for my retirement at a local pizza joint. The day before the party, she told me the SAC wanted to attend but wanted to make sure I was OK with it. I told her, "Of course, why would he even need to ask?" That made me wonder what the hell the Associate had been telling him about me.

There were about a dozen people that came, including the SAC. The Associate was notably absent. After they presented me with a plaque, I gave a short thank you speech. It worked out well because I used it as an opportunity to direct my comments to the SAC. I recounted the group's many accomplishments from the past year. I emphasized Gary's efforts to reach a 100% reconciliation of our inventory. I also singled out other individuals and their achievements. I owed them that.

My Last Day

After lunch, Rick reminded me that I needed to see the SAC for my exit interview. To be respectful of his time, I went directly to the SAC's office. As I was approaching his office, the Associate walked out of his office, which was next door. A coincidence? I don't think so. I'm sure he had his secretary watching for me with a prearranged signal. He asked me, "What are you doing here?" He knew why I was there. I was not a regular visitor in the administration section. The last time I was there was when he called me to his office. "I'm seeing the SAC for my exit interview."

"I'll go with you."

It was obvious he was concerned about what I might tell the SAC. But I'd already told the SAC everything I wanted him to know during my pizza party speech. I had no intention of whining to him about the problems between the Associate and me. As far as I was concerned, that was over. I didn't care if he was in the room or not. The meeting was short. The SAC asked what I had planned for my retirement and asked about my family and grandchildren.

What was amusing to me was the Associate's demeanor in front of the SAC. He sat in his chair hunched forward in a submissive posture unlike the bravado he flaunted on the day of our showdown. As you know, I like matching people with movie characters. He reminded me of John Larroquette's character, Captain Stillman, in the movie *Stripes*. ChatGPT described Captain as, "Captain Stillman's buffoonery reaches legendary levels of absurdity in his exaggerated adherence to military protocol, the type of guy who would reprimand someone for not folding their socks correctly." I nailed that one.

As I left the SAC's office, I realized the conference room next to his office was where I interviewed for this job 22 years prior. My career with DEA had taken me to 15 states and seven countries, and now I was back at the very spot where it began.

Throughout the afternoon, there were a few guys who stopped by to offer congratulations and say goodbye. One of them said he hated to see me leave because it was sort of fun waiting and wondering what I was going to do next to piss off the boss. Honestly, I never intended to piss him off just for the fun of it. Well, until the day of our showdown. At that point, it didn't matter and I didn't care.

As the time ticked by, I remembered Milwaukee Bob telling me before I left for Glynco, "They can do a lot of things to harass you, but they can't stop the clock," and now I couldn't stop it either. About 5:30 PM, Rick came in and told me the Associate ordered him to present me with my Annual Performance Review. Rick told me, "I know you won't be happy with it and I'm not happy with it either." He paused, then continued, "Hell with it, I'm not even going to show it to you. I'm just going to tell him you refused to sign it." At that point, I could only surmise the Associate had ordered him to rate me as 'Unsatisfactory.'

For 19 out of 21 years I'd been rated by six different supervisors as 'Outstanding,' the highest rating possible. Only twice had I received a second place 'Excellent.' Besides my annual performance reviews, I'd received several accommodations and special achievement awards.

DEA Exceptional Performance award in 2002 and again in 2004
DEA Excellence of Performances in 1995 and again in 2000
U.S. Department of Justice Award in 2000
United States Attorney's Award in 1996
U.S. Customs Appreciation Award 1993
Bureau of Alcohol, Tobacco, and Firearms Award 1991

Rick was right. I wouldn't have accepted or signed an 'Unsatisfactory' review, a cheap parting shot ordered by the Associate. I suspect he waited until the SAC was out of the office before sending Rick to give it to me.

It was nearly 6:00 PM when Rick came back and said, "I'm sorry, but I'll need to take your gun and badge." I drew my gun, pulled the magazine, ejected the chambered round, locked the slide back and handed him the weapon. I pulled my badge off my belt, took one last look at it and handed it to him. He knew surrendering the badge would be difficult, and it was. I got a gut punch the moment I handed it to him. He said, "You know you'll get this back, right?"

"Yeah, I know."

"DEA is going to have it reconditioned and add a ribbon that reads 'Retired.' I've seen them and they're nicely done."

DEA agents have a special connection to their badge. It starts on the day they graduate and the badge is awarded to them. DEA badges are minted with sequential serial numbers. Mine was 3335 and it belongs to me. It's a tradition in DEA that an agent's badge retires with the agent. DEA badges are never reissued. The photo on the cover of this book is my badge.

Agents are responsible for safeguarding their badges. Throughout an agent's career, OPR, Office of Professional Responsibility, spot-checks the badge to verify the serial number. Losing a badge triggers an automatic investigation by OPR. A DEA badge can open a lot of doors and that's not a good thing if it falls into the wrong hands.

After Rick left my office, I placed the key to my government vehicle on the desk and left the building. It was a typical winter night
in Chicago, cold and dark. As I walked home on Michigan Avenue,
it was the first time in nearly 30 years I was unarmed. My wife met
me on a bridge over the Chicago River. She looked at me and asked,
"Are you going to be OK?" I replied, "Yeah, it was time."

Honestly though, I was disappointed in myself. It didn't feel like
I retired, it felt like I quit, and I've never been OK with quitting. I
knew there was so much more I could have accomplished with the
knowledge and experience DEA had given me. Thankfully, I was
old enough to know one missing monkey doesn't stop a circus.

Looking back, the Administrator was right when she told me,
"Agents like you are not easily replaced." She was keenly aware
that DEA was losing far too many of their most experienced agents
to early retirement. I'm sure every one of them had their reasons
just as I had mine.

My Badge Is Missing

Despite Rick's assurances, time passed, and I never received my
badge. After I retired, I kept busy with several new adventures and
had forgotten about it. A year later, one of my old bosses from
ST was in town for the Indianapolis 500 race. We met for dinner
with our wives. We had a good time telling stories and laughing. At
some point, I remembered my badge and mentioned to him that
I never got it back. He looked puzzled and asked, "Are you sure?
Something's wrong. That never happens."

"All I can tell you is I never got it back."

I could tell he was troubled. We finished, said our goodbyes and
headed home. My wife noticed his mood changed after we talked
about my badge.

Within days, an agent from my old group in Chicago called me.
He said that 'someone' had just given him my badge with instructions to deliver it to me immediately. He didn't say who gave it

to him and I didn't ask. I asked him to mail it. It was obvious my old boss from ST had contacted someone to resolve the mystery. I called to thank him. He told me that within two weeks after I retired, the badge was reconditioned and sent to Chicago. 'Chicago' returned it to headquarters with a note saying they couldn't locate me. The badge had been locked in a safe at OPR until he claimed it on my behalf.

I don't know who sent it back, I can only guess. What I do know is DEA is a world-class investigative agency with world-class investigators. Anyone there could have located me had they been tasked to do so. I was living in Indianapolis with a valid Indiana driver's license and collecting my government pension. Barney Fife could have hunted me down.

To this day, I don't know who my old boss called, but whoever it was had some serious horsepower. This is just another example of how the stand-up guys in DEA look out for each other.

I was also happy to later learn Gary received a well-deserved Special Achievement Award for his work reconciling the inventory. I have no way of knowing, but I suspect the SAC looked into some of the issues I'd mentioned during my pizza party speech.

254 ~ HOWARD OBERST

When an Agent Retires

I had just finished the first draft of my book. I woke up one morning and this poem had started swirling around in my head. Throughout the day more pieces came to me and by the end of the day it was done.

<u>When an Agent Retires</u>

With his debt tendered
And gun surrendered
Hands once steady and true
May tremble a little now
When out of view
For all the times his nerves were frayed
All for the love of the game he played
With glory days long gone
Shadows whisper 'it's time to move on'
Now as he begins to ponder and dwell
Soon he knows all that's left
Are stories to tell
When an agent retires

Howard Oberst
DEA Special Agent, retired

~ 11 ~

RETIREMENT

"Often when you think you're at the end of something, you're really only at the beginning of something else."

Fred Rogers

After spending our last full day in Chicago with our daughter, son-in-law and Brady, our 1 1/2-year-old grandson, we loaded a U-Haul truck with their help. My wife and I plus our dog Benny headed south to our house in Indianapolis. Retirement was a change. Every morning, I had to go somewhere just to leave the house, even if I only got coffee at McDonald's.

Sports Photography

With the photography skills I'd acquired from DEA, I launched a photography business. I purchased a pair of digital cameras and started a youth sports photography business. I made a deal with a local Pop Warner youth football league to shoot action photos. It was a family effort. My adult children and their spouses pitched in along with my wife. It provided a wonderful opportunity to re-connect with our family. The first year was fun, but by the second year, it became far too time consuming. Our second grandson was born, and we ended the business.

Private Detective

My lifelong friend Bill of the ghost train fame talked me into getting a private detective's license. Bill, retired from the Indiana State Police, had a thriving private detective agency. I worked part-time with him for a couple of years doing everything from spying on cheating spouses to conducting investigations for defense attorneys.

The last case I did was to help a defense attorney defend a contract murderer who had orchestrated the killing of two people. The defense attorney was a former prosecutor and friend. I had a lot of angst about defending a murder suspect. The defense attorney told me the police had a solid case against our client. The defendant had little chance of winning, but the attorney was obligated to give his client the best possible defense. This was a murder charge. A guilty verdict would prompt an appeal. Statistically those appeals are based on ineffective counsel, so he wanted to be sure we covered everything.

I reviewed boxes of evidence, police reports, and documents. From those documents, I created a timeline of every detail in the investigation. I probed for any kind of misstep or discrepancy. I spent hours interviewing the client, dissecting every detail he gave me leading up to, during and after the murder. I compared his story to my timeline and what the detectives believed happened. My conclusion was the prosecution had an airtight case while we had little chance of convincing a jury he was innocent.

I suggested to the client that he cut a deal with the prosecutor and testify against the other two co-defendants. He refused. Not surprisingly, one of his associates took a deal and testified against him, which sealed his fate. During one of many interviews, he told me after leaving the crime scene, a police patrol car stopped them. Our client was in the front passenger seat and the trigger man was in the seat behind the driver. Against all odds, our client knew the officer and liked him. While the officer was writing a traffic ticket, our client successfully convinced the trigger man not to kill the officer. He said that this was the only cop who had ever helped him. If it had been any other cop, he wouldn't have cared.

I had no reason to doubt his story. Minutes earlier the trigger man had shot and killed two innocent people. He was more than capable of killing a police officer. By the grace of God, our client talked him out of it. The story he told sent shivers down my spine. That officer nearly lost his life and never knew it.

The jury found our client guilty of murder. His case was the first and last time I worked for the defense in a criminal case.

Consulting

Another friend introduced me to an optical research scientist named John. John owned a technology development company in Iowa. I consulted with him on a part-time basis for a couple of years. It was John who first introduced me to the power of artificial intelligence. He had several patented inventions including a camera that could detect skin anomalies not visible to the naked eye which may have held some potential for detecting skin cancers. He also had a camera that could see through window glare. To accomplish these feats, he integrated a video camera with computer driven AI software. We presented his inventions at law enforcement and military trade shows across the country.

A 2006 science fiction movie titled *Déjà Vu* starring Denzel Washington featured a scene where a camera removed the sun glare from a window. Few people knew it at the time, but that wasn't science fiction.

John and I met with the owner of a major Las Vegas casino. The owner wanted to upgrade his entire video surveillance system from analog to digital. While doing the assessment, I had a rare opportunity to visit the casino's video surveillance room. Very few people ever see the inside of those rooms.

I was awestruck by the scale of their operation. The cameras were so powerful a monitor could zoom in and count the hairs on the back of a player's knuckles. As you can imagine they spared no expense to combat cheaters. Every camera was a PTZ (pan, tilt, zoom) and hard-wired to its own VHS recorder in the control room. There were hundreds of recorders. Someone tagged and replaced each tape as they popped out 24 hours a day. It looked like a giant game of Whack-a-Mole.

We recommended installation of a computer server capable of storing all video recordings. Along with that, software capable of instantaneously retrieving time-specific clips from any camera would be needed. The project required replacing analog cameras with digital cameras, a massive project. In the end John decided not to bid on it.

While I was talking with the casino owner, he laughed as he told me about their 'facial recognition program.' They had a woman with a photographic memory who worked part-time monitoring the cameras spotting banned players in the casino. Who would have thought a billion-dollar casino relied on a Whack-a-Mole operation and a savant? I'm sure that has changed now.

Anti-Terrorism Assistance Program - ATA

While I was juggling sports photography, private investigating and consulting, Claud Davidson, my friend from ST, called. He asked if I was interested in teaching as an independent contractor for the U.S. State Department's Anti-Terrorism Assistance program, ATA. "Howard, are you interested in joining the travel team? I need one more guy. We're leaving for Yemen in a week."

"What are we going to do there?"

"Training, counter-terrorism."

"Are you sure you got the right guy? I don't know anything about terrorism."

"That's not a problem. The course is an adaptation of the tactics we used against drug cartels like surveillance, undercover, informants. You know all that stuff. We're retooling it. You would be a perfect fit. Are all your passports valid?"

"Yeah."

"OK. Someone will call you soon. Fill out the paperwork right away."

"Where's Yemen?"

"Does it matter? The team is meeting in London, and we'll fly the rest of the way together."

"You're not going to get me killed, are you?"

"No. Well, probably not. So, are you in?"

"Yeah, I'm in."

"Great, then I'll see you in next week in London."

Now I had to tell my wife what I'd just agreed to do. For the next 12 years, I traveled to seventeen countries, several of them multiple times, teaching anti-terrorism classes. It was easy to re-purpose my skills, much like a carpenter who uses the same tools to build a house as he does a barn. I dug deep into understanding the idiosyncrasies of terrorism in much the same way I had learned to understand the drug trade. I interacted with dozens of counter-terrorism units from around the world, giving me an extraordinary opportunity to gain priceless insight from their experiences.

Most courses lasted two weeks with a team of three or four instructors. The program selected instructors from diverse backgrounds. I taught with former Army Special Forces, CIA, FBI, ATF, NCIS, NYPD, and the list goes on. Most of the instructors were retired and had no hesitation in sharing their knowledge and experiences. I gained a treasure trove of knowledge and insight. As the years went by, I expanded my expertise in terrorism and was approved by the State Department to teach five additional terrorism-related courses.

In 2019, I began working as an Independent Contract Instructor and Curriculum Developer for *Professional Law Enforcement Training,* a private company owned by Byron Boston. Byron and I collaborated to develop a two-day course titled Domestic Terrorism. The objective of the class was to present U.S. law enforcement officers with a holistic understanding of domestic terrorism. Developing the course curriculum and keeping it relevant was far more time-consuming than I had anticipated. Over the next five years, I taught the course fourteen times in seven states and produced two webinars during the Covid-19 lock down.

Tennis

In 2012, I developed an obsession with tennis. It happened while I was in, of all places, Pakistan. January 2012, I accepted an ATA contract in Islamabad, Pakistan with Claud. During our embassy security briefing, the Regional Security Officer, RSO, informed us the threat level was extremely high. The political tension between our government and the Pakistan government was severely strained due to the Osama bin Laden raid that had taken place eight months earlier. Embassy security was still expecting some kind of retaliation from Al-Qaeda. Due to the threat level, we were confined to the embassy compound. We traveled every day to the ATA training facility outside the compound with armed escorts.

Fortunately, the Islamabad embassy was a large community that included a tennis club. With nothing else to do, Claud began teaching me how to play tennis. In the following years, Claud and I always traveled with our rackets. Tennis is a great sport for meeting people and networking. Once while we were Kathmandu, Nepal, Claud and I played a doubles match against the Ambassador from Switzerland and his partner, the U.S. CIA Station Chief.

When I returned from Pakistan, I joined the Indianapolis Racket Club, IRC, and have been playing there since. The tennis community at IRC is comprised of the nicest people. It is a breath of fresh air after a lifetime of drug dealers, terrorists and crazy agents.

An Indiana state trooper said it best after pulling me over doing 100 mph in an undercover Corvette loaded with marijuana. "Sometimes you agents are just not right in the head." For sure we did some crazy things, but those were the best days of my life. Well, that's the wild world of the DEA, at least how I remember it.

Maybe one day I'll write a book about my many adventures with Claud and the rest of my ATA contractor friends. But for now, I'm done.

It's time.

~ 12 ~

EPILOGUE

The DEA is alive and well

In 2015, I joined the DEA Association of Federal Narcotics Agents, DEAFNA. This is a benevolent organization that serves several functions. First, it provides retired agents with information and resources, including employment opportunities and contact information for other members. The organization also provides immediate financial help for any DEA agent or Task Force Officer and their family during a crisis, such as illness, natural disaster, or other unforeseen emergencies. It also provides six, $2,500 college scholarships per year for the children and grandchildren of its members.

AFNA holds a National Conference every year where members can reconnect with old friends and meet fellow members. During the conference, AFNA presents their Agent of the Year award, a golden eagle statue. The award recognizes the most outstanding agent(s) for their dedication and exceptional contributions to DEA's mission.

Every year I paid my dues and supported the association but never attended the conference. Then, in September 2024, I attended my first conference at the Francis Marion Hotel in Charleston, South Carolina. The General Meeting took place in the Carolina Ballroom on the opening day of the conference. Several hundred people filled the room.

When my wife and I arrived, the only open tables were on the far side of the room. We made our way across the room to an empty table. Seated behind me was a guy obviously too young to be retired. He shook my hand and introduced himself. "Hi, I'm Justin." I introduced myself and asked him, "What are you doing here hanging out with all these old timers like me?"

He said he was there to receive some kind of award. Some kind of award, all right. Out of 4,000 agents worldwide, he was one of only three to be designated an 'Agent of the Year!' He told me he had been a state prosecutor in Evansville, Indiana before joining DEA as a Special Agent. His career began in Evansville but he'd been transferred to Indianapolis. I surprised him by telling him I had spent 15 years in Indianapolis.

I asked him what he had done to receive such a prestigious award. He was humble about it but said that he had gotten the first homicide drug overdose conviction in DEA. In 2014, Congress passed a law that states anyone providing drugs which results in a fatal overdose is guilty of homicide.

Armed with this federal statute, Justin began investigating drug overdose deaths as unsolved homicides. With his first conviction in Evansville, DEA brought him to Indianapolis, where there was a nearly endless supply of drug overdose deaths to investigate. When Justin received his award, the presenter announced he was being recognized for his actual cases as well as his innovation and pioneering strategy, further noting that he would soon be training other agents how to pursue these kinds of investigations.

Justin told me that although the award was nice, his real satisfaction came from the closure he has given to the victim's families. With young agents like Justin entering the arena, I'm confident the war on drugs is not over.

~ 13 ~

FURTHER READING

Shooting the Moon
The True Story of An American Manhunt Unlike Any Other, Ever
by David Harris

Inside DEA, Operation Snowcap
by DEA Special Agent Bob Hartman

Tweeker Parade
by DEA Special Agent LeVine Phillippa

The Noble Experiment,
True Stories & Hard Truths from My Time in the DEA
by DEA Special Agent David Gaddis

Dancing with the Devil, Confessions of an Undercover Agent
by DEA Special Agent Louis Diaz

Killing Pablo, The Hunt for the World's Greatest Outlaw
by Mark Bowden

Saltwater Cowboy, The Rise and Fall of a Marijuana Empire
by Tim McBride

GLOSSARY

AFNA	Association of Federal Narcotics Agents
APB	All-Points Bulletin
ASAC	Assistant Agent in Charge (GS-15)
ATA	Antiterrorism Assistance program
ATF	Alcohol, Tobacco and Firearms
AUO	Administratively Uncontrolled Overtime
BA	Basic Agent
BA-38	Basic Agent Class #38
BARB	Basic Agent Review Board
BATs	Basic Agent Trainees
C I	Confidential Informant
CATS	Clandestine Aircraft installation Technician Specialist
CIA	Central Intelligence Agency
CTS	Centralized Tracking System

DEA	Drug Enforcement Administration
DEA-6 ROI	Report of Investigation
DIA	Defense Intelligence Agency
DO	District Office(Headed by a GS-15)
EEOC	Equal Employment Opportunity Commission
EPIC	DEA's El Paso Intelligence Center
FARK	Revolution Armed Forces of Columbia
FAST	Foreign deployed Advisory Team (Afghanistan)
FATS	Firearms Training System-interactive shooting video
FBI	Federal Bureau of Investigation
FLETC	Federal Law Enforcement Training Center
FLIR	Forward Looking Infrared (heat sensing camera)
FO/FD	Field Office or Field Division Office(Headed by an SES SAC)
FTS	Federal Telephone System

FTX	Field Training Exercise
GS	Group Supervisor (GS 14)
GS-XX	GS-Government Schedule (pay grade as in 7,9,11..)
HCL	Hydrochloric acid
HRT	Hostage Rescue Team
HR	Human Resources
IMPD	Indianapolis Metropolitan Police Department
IPD	Indianapolis Police Department
IRS	Internal Revenue Service
ISP	Indiana State Police
JIATF	Joint Interagency Task Force
JSOC	Joint Special Operation Command (Kabul)
MDMA	methylenedioxy-methaamphetamine (ecstasy)
MREs	Meals Ready to Eat
MRTA	Tupac Amaru Movement (terrorist group in Peru)
NIA	National Intelligence Academy

NOAA	National Oceanic and Atmospheric Administration
NOE	Nap-of-the-earth (flying below radar detection)
NRO	National Reconnaissance Office
OGV	Official Government Vehicle
OPBAT	Operation Bahamas
OPR	Office of Professional Responsibility (Internal Affairs)
Pes	Practical Exercises
PNC	Peruvian National Police
PT	Physical Training
RAC	Resident Agent in Charge, GS-14
RDNR	Remote Digital Number Recorder (used in tapping phone)
RO	Resident Office Headed by a GS-14 RAC
RPG	Rocket Propelled Grenade
RRT	Rapid Response Team
RSO	Regional Security Office
SA	Special Agent

SAC	Special Agent in Charge (head of a field division office)
SCI	Sensitive Compartmented Information (security clearance)
SCIF	Sensitive Compartmented Information Facility (building)
SF	Special Forces
SF-171	Standard Form #171, Employment Application
SOCOM	Special Operations Command (Tampa Florida)
ST	Science and Technology, located in Virginia
STU-III	Encrypted phone
SWAT	Special Weapons and Tactics
TDY	Temporary Duty Assignment
TFO	Task Force Officer
TKO	Targeted Kingpin Organization
TTY	Teletype
UC	Undercover
UN	United Nations
VOIP	Voice Over the Internet Protocol

VPN	Virtual Private Network
WITS	Working group on International Technical Support

ABOUT THE AUTHOR

Photo by Yvonne Lyons

Howard currently resides in Noblesville, Indiana with his wife Luanne, near his two adult children and their families. He maintains an active lifestyle playing tennis several times a week and travels frequently with his wife. On a part-time basis Howard continues to instruct law enforcement professionals in domestic terrorism courses. He's in a permanent standby mode just in case his friend Claud calls him for a training adventure in some distant corner of the world.

Family is a central focus of his life, particularly his five grandchildren: Brady, who is attending Ball State University; Chase and Lila, both high school students, Kiley, a junior high cheerleader, and Mason, his youngest grandson, who attends elementary school so long as it doesn't interfere with little league baseball. Just like his granddad, the boy has his priorities.

www.ingramcontent.com/pod-product-compliance
Lightning Source LLC
Chambersburg PA
CBHW021711120626
46545CB00004B/1504